THE STORY OF
GLOUCESTER'S PUBS

THE STORY OF
GLOUCESTER'S PUBS

DARREL KIRBY

This book is dedicated to:
My wife, Sharon.
And also to all the landlords of Gloucester who,
against all the odds, keep the pubs alive.

First published 2010

The History Press
The Mill, Brimscombe Port
Stroud, Gloucestershire, GL5 2QG
www.thehistorypress.co.uk

© Darrel Kirby, 2010

The right of Darrel Kirby to be identified as the Author
of this work has been asserted in accordance with the
Copyrights, Designs and Patents Act 1988.

British Library Cataloguing in Publication Data.
A catalogue record for this book is available from the British Library.

ISBN 978 0 7524 5557 0

Typesetting and origination by The History Press
Printed in Great Britain
Manufacturing managed by Jellyfish Print Solutions Ltd

Contents

Acknowledgements

I extend a huge thank-you to everyone who has helped me in putting together this book and/or have had to put up with me while I've been working on it. My particular thanks go to the staff at the Gloucestershire Archives, who are always extremely helpful, and to Nigel Cox at the Gloucester Folk Museum for his help with information and pictures of exhibits.

Photographs are always a challenge to source, so I am grateful to everyone who has provided pictures or helped me to source them. I have tried my best to identify and contact everyone whose picture I have used, but if I have used any without permission I apologise profusely. See page 191 for picture credits.

In pulling together this book I have used a wide range of valuable sources, listed in the bibliography at the back of the book. I have also built on the work of other pub researchers, two of whom deserve special thanks: Mr A. Done carried out much painstaking research ploughing through the *Gloucester Journal* to identify and date pubs. The list he created is held at the Gloucestershire Archives and provided an invaluable start for my research. Secondly, the Gloucestershire Pubs website maintained by Geoff Sandles has provided a wealth of material which I have shamelessly plundered and plagiarised with his permission. In addition, I have benefitted greatly from the knowledge and regular updates on the city's pubs from Gloucester CAMRA chairman Alan Stephens.

Thanks also go to my friends who selflessly agreed to help with the field research – it's much more fun than drinking alone (see Chapter 6). A special mention here is reserved for enthusiastic stalwart field researchers Geoff Trett and Steve Rowbotham. The pub landlords have also been extremely friendly and helpful (with one notable exception!). In particular my thanks go to Ruth and David at the Cross Keys, Martyn at The Pig Inn the City and Keith at the Old Crown, who all generously gave their time to talk to me, but all of the landlords deserve our thanks for making the pubs as good as they are.

Finally, my biggest thanks are once again reserved for my long-suffering wife, Sharon, who has not only stoically put up with being a book widow (again) while this work was in progress, but also provided support, proof-reading and, most importantly, cake.

Introduction

U ntil recently I gave little more than a passing thought to the history of the hostelries in which I sup my ale. This all came to an end when I set about researching my first book: *The Story of Gloucester*. I was struck by how many potential entries were pubs, or had been at some time in their past, so it seemed appropriate to combine my passion for beer and my interest in local history to write a book on the history of Gloucester's pubs. I cannot deny that the prospect of field research also held a certain attraction.

Little did I know when I set out on this project that I would identify a list of more than 600 pubs, and this is just in the centre of the city – my catchment area roughly equates to the GL1 postcode. In reality these aren't 600 different pubs; if a pub has had many names it will be listed many times, but however you look at it, it's a lot.

So what do I mean by a pub? You may think that's a silly question, but it's not always obvious; there are grey areas. Should I include hotels? What about licensed restaurants? And recently the distinction between pub and nightclub has become increasingly hazy. My definition basically boils down to somewhere with a bar that you go to for the primary purpose of drinking. There are still grey areas, but hopefully most people will find my choices fairly intuitive.

Finally a word on what this book is not: it is not a good beer or good pub guide. What you have here is a history and celebration of pubs, past and present. I seek to give a flavour of what they are (or were) like and a sense of their place in the social and historical climate of the city. Where the pubs still exist I have selflessly taken it upon myself to visit them, so my personal opinion may become apparent – in some cases more than others. I have tried to be unbiased, but inevitably these are the opinions of just one forty-something-year-old beer drinker and should be treated as such.

The pub trade is undergoing a major crisis as I write, so this book feels timely. It is testament to the pub's tenacity that you can still find a decent pub in the city centre, and Gloucester has something for everyone from the crusty real ale bore to the alcopop-fuelled pre-nightclub drinker; all you need to know is where to look. . . .

Key to Pub Entries:
Ref: This refers to the main listing in the pubs list in Chapter 8.
Map: This is the map in Chapter 7 on which the pub is shown. It is indicated on the map by reference number.
Date: Best estimate of dates for which a pub is recorded on the site.

1

The Ancient Inns
of Gloucester

Alcohol has probably been with us since the beginning of human history, when our early Palaeolithic ancestors inadvertently got off their heads eating cereal or fruit which had undergone spontaneous fermentation by wild yeasts in the air. We haven't looked back since.

Beer is traditionally thought to have come to Britain from southern Germany with the Celts in the second half of the fifth century BC, and the great British pub was probably brought to Britain by the Romans.

Following the Roman invasion, shops called *tabernae* appeared, selling wine to help quench the thirst of the legionary troops. These quickly adapted to also sell ale and over time *tabernae* became corrupted to tavern. The origins of Gloucester as a town dates from the Romans, who first occupied the Kingsholm area from the late AD 40s, moving to what is now the centre of Gloucester in about AD 68, so it is likely that Gloucester's first pubs appeared about that time.

The first recorded reference to brewing in the city of Gloucester dates from 1200 when Geoffrey de Brachin (of the brewhouse) is mentioned in connection with a land transfer. Gloucester had more than its fair share of monasteries by the thirteenth century, and so because the monks were the great medieval brewers, Gloucester would have been awash with ale and the monasteries would have supplied many of the pubs. Later the city's affluent inns were also great brewers and by the fifteenth century brewing was the fifth largest trade in Gloucester.

It is about this time that we find the first definite mention of pubs in Gloucester. One of the oldest reference documents that we have is a register compiled by Robert Cole, Canon of Llanthony, in 1455. He was a rent collector employed by the bailiffs, and the register made collection of landgavel (the rent payable on land) easier. This register was translated from the original Latin and published by W.H. Stevenson in 1890 *as The Rental of all the Houses in Gloucester A.D.1455*.

The Rental lists all of the owners and occupants of property within the borough of Gloucester, with the descent of the property frequently traced back to previous ownership as far back as the reign of Henry III (1216–72). It mentions eleven inns and hostelries, but only three by name: the New Inn, Savage's Inn (later The Fountain) and St George's in Southgate Street.

At this time there were three distinct categories of drinking establishment: alehouses, taverns and inns. The primary purpose of the inn was to provide accommodation for travellers. In earlier times, when there were fewer travellers, this

The beginning of *The Rental of All The Houses in Gloucester A.D. 1455*. It's looking a bit worn and wrinkled, but so would you if you were over 450 years old!

(Gloucestershire Archives)

An extract from the Cooks & Innholders Composition of 1583 listing twelve 'keepers and holders of ancient inns within the Cittie of Gloucester': John Apperley, alias Reece; John Leeke; John Hill; John Lacey; Robert Ingram; Henry Edwards; Thomas Hale; Thomas Chigley the Younger; George Francomb; Robert Draper; Walter Loveday and William Horseley.

(Gloucestershire Archives)

function was fulfilled by the abbey, and many inns were owned by the church until the dissolution of the monasteries in the sixteenth century.

The city's inns thrived and by 1583 '. . . an inordinate number of tippling houses, new inns and signs have sprung up in Gloucester to the detriment of public order and of freemen lawfully exercising the trade.' This led to the Cooks and Innholders Composition, which decreed that the Corporation may not allow more than fourteen inns in Gloucester. It listed twelve 'keepers and holders of ancient inns within Gloucester', basically giving them a monopoly. Unfortunately no inn names are given, but this magic number of twelve seems to have persisted into the seventeenth century when, during the Siege of Gloucester in 1643, the king threatened to hang the twelve aldermen from the city's twelve inn signs.

The Great Inns of the Abbey

Of the eleven inns listed in *The Rental* of 1455, three are traditionally identified as 'Great Inns of the Abbey'. They were owned by St Peter's Abbey, now Gloucester Cathedral, which has Saxon origins but became a Benedictine abbey in 1022. A major influence on both the abbey's development and the wealth of the city as a whole was the burial of Edward II in 1327, the event which also links the abbey with the inns.

Gloucester Cathedral.

Edward II was not a popular monarch and his wife, Isabella of France, plotted with Roger Mortimer, the 1st Earl of March, to overthrow him. Edward was imprisoned in 1327 and forced to abdicate to his fourteen-year-old son, Edward III.

Edward II was allegedly killed at Berkeley Castle in a manner so gruesome that I will skip over it for fear of putting you off your beer. Only John Thokey, Abbot of Gloucester, was brave enough to risk the anger of Isabella and Mortimer and carry out the funeral. The body was interred near the abbey's high altar just before Christmas, 1327.

Although at the end of his life Edward II was, to say the least, unpopular, suddenly all of this was forgotten. He was called a martyr and pilgrims flocked to the abbey to pray and pay tribute. The sick claimed to be miraculously cured and, of course, the abbey became very rich.

In the Middle Ages, monasteries were obliged to offer hospitality to travellers. Being a Benedictine house, hospitality was especially important to the abbey as central to their philosophy is the obligation to receive guests 'as Christ Himself', but the number of pilgrims to Edward II's tomb was

Edward II's impressive tomb in the cathedral. Dating from about 1330, it is one of the earliest alabaster carvings in England.

too great for them to manage, so they came up with the profitable solution of providing inns for them. These became known as the 'Great Inns' or 'Pilgrims' Inns.'

However, the association of the Great Inns with pilgrims to Edward's tomb seems to be an eighteenth-century invention; possibly a marketing ploy to increase visits to the inns. Certainly the transition from monastic guest houses to inns took place all over the country and was not unique to Gloucester.

Whatever the truth, one thing is certain: the three Great Inns of the abbey are of great historical interest and warrant a closer look.

New Inn, Northgate Street

REF: 333

MAP: A

STATUS: Trading

DATE: 1430 to date

LOCATION: 16 Northgate Street, GL1 1SF

CONTACT: 01452 522177

The first of the Great Inns, and the only one currently open, is the New Inn. This is without a doubt the most historically impressive pub in Gloucester.

The New Inn is situated in Northgate Street, just a few yards from Gloucester Cross. From the street you need to look above the modern shop fronts to see the rather grand, old half-timbered building, but it is only once you walk through the entrance into the courtyard that you really see what all the fuss is about. Stop for a moment and take it in: this has been described as the finest example of a medieval galleried inn to be found in Britain today.

The New Inn was built between 1430 and 1450 on the site of an even earlier inn which had fallen into disrepair, hence the now unlikely and inappropriate name of the New Inn. It is mentioned in *The Rental of all the Houses in Gloucester A.D.1455*, which says, 'The Abbot of Saint Peter of Gloucester holds in fee a great and new inn called "New Inn" lately built from the foundation by the praiseworthy man John Twinning, monk of the same place, for the great emolument and profit of the same and of their successors.'

The earlier inn probably originated in about 1350, which would better fit with the timing of Edward II's burial and the Pilgrims' Inn theory. Further support for the theory comes from the fact that the lane running alongside the

New Inn Courtyard.

New Inn, currently called New Inn Lane, is said to have been called Pilgrims' Lane at some point before 1714. However, I have been unable to make this connection earlier than the eighteenth century and at the time of *The Rental* it was known as Rosse Lane.

The inn stayed in the possession of the abbey until the dissolution of the monasteries in 1539 (St Peter's closing in 1540), after which it was granted to the Dean and Chapter of the cathedral. Evidence of the inn's religious origins can be seen in the now decapitated figure of an angel on the angle post at the corner of New Inn Lane, although you have to look quite hard to make it out. A gilded lion grasping a serpent once stood at the entrance to the inn, representing the triumph of good over evil. This is now in the courtyard above the real ale bar.

The inn consists of oak timber-framed buildings (not chestnut as recorded earlier), enclosing two courtyards with stairs leading up to two tiers of galleries, which originally provided accommodation for up to 200 people: forty sleeping rooms, some in the form of dormitories. At this time it was said to be the largest hostelry in the country and is described as having gardens and a passage

The New Inn, Gloucester. (Circa 1450 A.D)

with houses extending into Eastgate Street. Writing in 1850, John Clarke says, 'Its extent is very great . . . It consisted of two square courts, surrounded by chambers and galleries, but its size has been much reduced by several parts being divided into separate tenements.'

There are rumours of warrens of tunnels criss-crossing below Gloucester's streets. These were allegedly used as escape routes by the monks and one is said to run from the cathedral to the New Inn. Existence of this tunnel was apparently supported when a man fell into it through his cellar. Former landlady Janette Parkin certainly believed the story to be true and told me that there are definite traces of a tunnel opening at the New Inn. Others doubt these claims saying that what the man fell into was nothing more exotic than a bit of Victorian sewer. The main problem facing all of the tunnel theories is the high water table from the Severn, which would cause them to flood.

The New Inn courtyard in busier times, from John Britton's *Picturesque Antiquities of the English Cities*, 1836. *(Gloucestershire Archives)*

The New Inn is also associated with Lady Jane Grey, some reports stating that she was staying at the New Inn when she was reluctantly proclaimed Queen of England in 1553 following the untimely death of Edward VI. This seems unlikely, but the news was broadcast from the New Inn gallery: a proclamation that was only made publicly in two other places in England. Lady Jane Grey was sentenced to death in 1554, aged just seventeen, by her rival Mary who had now been pronounced queen. Ghostly goings-on have been witnessed by guests at the New Inn over the last century (it would be a surprise if there weren't such reports in a building this old) and some claim that it is Lady Jane haunting the place.

On a lighter note, in the sixteenth century the New Inn provided a venue for strolling minstrels and plays by travelling companies. It is claimed that a group later associated with Shakespeare played here, so inevitably there is speculation that the bard himself may have put in an appearance, but I have found no evidence to support this. The New Inn also housed the city's first tennis court by 1649 and in the eighteenth century the inn became an important venue on the London to Gloucester stagecoach route.

In 1858 the New Inn was sold freehold to the Berry family who owned it until 1942. A booklet dating from 1907 entitled *Historical Mementoes of the New Inn Hotel* boasts that visitors can, 'see and enjoy the many nooks and quaint corners of this primitive hostel of our forefathers, and thereby somewhat realise the original scene of Chaucer's Canterbury Pilgrims. . . .'

The front of the inn was restored in 1925 to remove a façade which concealed the original half-timbered structure and in 1954 it was bought by Berni Inns. In a sadly undated leaflet, presumably from the Berni Inn days, thirteen separate bars are listed: Grill Room, Steak Bar, Steak and Duck Bar, Stirrup Bar, Twyning Bar, Coach House Bar, Beaufort Bar, Tudor Bar, Wine Press Bar, Pilgrims Bar, Olde Bar, Scotch Bar and Gallery Bar. You could have a damn good pub crawl without ever going outside the courtyard, then you could sleep it off in a single bedroom for 35*s* or a double for 70*s*.

I remember the Berni Inn from the 1970s, when on rare and special occasions we would be dressed in our smartest clothes and go with our parents for prawn cocktails, scampi and chips and ice-cream sundaes, as was the custom in those days. Later, in my late teens, I rediscovered the New Inn as a hang-out for motorcyclists. By this time it really was in a bad way with only one of the bars still open, and that looking decidedly shabby and uninviting – not least because we were there!

Berni Inns were bought out by Grand Metropolitan in 1970 and the New Inn passed into the ownership of Scottish & Newcastle. In the early 1990s it changed hands again to the Magic Pub Company, who caused much upset by carrying out a series of unauthorised alterations to the Grade I listed building, including knocking out walls and installing electrical trunking to turn the bedrooms into office space.

The Magic Pub Company was bought out by Greene King in 1996, who almost immediately put the New Inn on the market for £450,000. It closed on 18 February 1998 and was bought by the Chapman Group, who spent a lot of money on restoration, reopening it on 27 May 1999. It is now one of three pubs in the city owned by The Chapman Group – the other two being the Dick Whittington (p. 66) and the Station (p. 126).

The New Inn was awarded the CAMRA Gloucester City Pub of the Year award for three years running from 2002 to 2004 and appeared in the *Good Beer Guide* for six consecutive years from 2002 to 2007. The damage to the bedrooms has been rectified and 33 are now in use. Unlike the original rooms, these are all en-suite and well appointed and you don't have to share with a dozen strangers.

The New Inn from
Northgate Street.

Lately all three Chapman pubs have had a high turnover of managers and relations with CAMRA became somewhat strained for a time, although the New Inn was back in the *Good Beer Guide* in 2009.

There are currently four bars open, including a real ale bar and Grey's Coffee House, which sells speciality teas and cakes. There is also a traditional grill and carvery where, according to the website, 'the team of highly trained chefs take great pride in creating classic English fayre.' In the name of my tireless research I visited the New Inn and sampled the grill with friends in spring 2009 and I'm sad to report that we were unimpressed with both the food and the service. However, in February 2010 new managers Mark and Samantha Cooke moved in vowing to bring the New Inn 'back to what it was twenty years ago with the best of British food and ales.' Things look good so far and hopefully the New Inn will once again become a pub worthy of such a magnificent building.

Fleece, Westgate Street

On the south side of Westgate Street, a short way from Gloucester Cross, is a large black and white timber-framed building. Like the New Inn, you have to look up to appreciate it because at street level there are three modern shop fronts, but to the left of them is an archway with 'Circa 1497' inscribed above it. This impressive building was the Fleece Hotel, said to be another of the Great Inns of the abbey, and the archway was the carriageway into its courtyard.

The Rental of 1455 states that the site now occupied by the Fleece was an extensive tenement reaching to Bull Lane, 'which one Benedict the Cordwainer held undivided in the time of Henry III,' but which was divided into three parts in the time of Edward I. One of these parts had a cellar and was held by the abbot of St Peter's.

The cellar, a twelfth-century vaulted crypt or undercroft, still exists under the Fleece and much later became a bar called the Monks' Retreat (see p. 69). This gives good provenance associating the building with the abbey, but there is no suggestion

REF: 181
MAP: A
STATUS: Closed
DATE: 1497 to 2002
LOCATION: 19 Westgate Street

The Fleece Inn, 2006.

of it being an inn until between 1525 and 1544 when there's a reference to, 'a great inn owned by the abbey in St Mary de Grace Parish in upper Westgate Street.' This almost certainly refers to the Fleece, although it is not named; St Mary de Grace Church was opposite St John's Lane in what is now the middle of Westgate Street.

The Fleece Inn was built above the cellar in 1497, presumably replacing the existing tenement and reincorporating at least some of the original extensive tenement held by Benedict the Cordwainer. This seems rather late to house pilgrims to the tomb of a monarch who was buried in 1327.

In 1534 the inn was let by the abbey to Alderman Henry Marmyon, twice mayor of Gloucester. With the dissolution of the abbey in 1540, ownership of the inn passed to the Dean and Chapter of Gloucester Cathedral.

The inn was leased to Gray Cox in 1673, at which time it was known as 'The Golden Ffleece'. The abbey had once been a great producer of wool, but by this time the industry was in decline, so the name was probably older than that. Gray Cox was obviously doing well for himself because after his death his widow, Katherine, he held not only the Fleece and shops fronting Westgate Street, but also the Fountain. The 'Golden' bit of the name was later dropped, leaving it as just as the Fleece – the first mention that I have found of it in licensing records dates from 1681, where it is referred to as 'the Ffleece,' with the licensee shown as what looks like Richard Steight.

By 1770 the inn had fallen into disrepair, the only time in its long history that it was closed until now. The cathedral tried to rent the ailing inn to the mayor and burgess of the city to make a market and shambles on the site – they were prepared to give away the materials in buildings, which they valued at not less than £150. Thankfully the offer was rejected. Subsequently it was leased to the dean, Dr Josiah Tucker, who was recognised as the leading economist of the day. There must have been some concern about how this would look as it was officially shown as being leased in the name of a minor canon.

Considerable alterations and repairs took place between 1772 and 1778, by which time it was once again licensed. These alterations included an extension to the front of the original part of the inn, giving a large semicircular bow window, and the addition of a building near the rear courtyard entrance facing onto Bull Lane. From 1791 it ranked as one of the chief inns in the city.

The Fleece was sold by the church into private ownership in 1799 and further extensive additions were made to the hotel throughout the nineteenth and twentieth centuries. A pamphlet from 1949 boasts that the inn had been 'extended and now consists of thirty-seven fully equipped bedrooms accommodating sixty-eight guests, together with Writing Room and Lounge, Billiards Room, Stock Room and spacious garage.'

All of these additions and alterations make the layout of the Fleece quite complicated. The original part of the building above the cellar is no. 19 Westgate Street and is not actually visible from the street as it sits behind no. 17. To access it you enter through the carriageway from Westgate Street into the courtyard and the building is on your left. This part of the Fleece is Grade I listed.

Courtyard of the Fleece Hotel, showing the bow window added in the eighteenth century and the entrance to the Monks' Retreat on the left.

1 Great Inn

2 Fleece Hotel

3 Westgate St Range

4 Salt Loft

5 Stable Block

6 North Entrance Range

7 Edwardian Block

8 11a Westgate St

9 1930s Linking Block

Plan of the Fleece Hotel. *(South West Regional Development Agency (SWRDA))*

The impressive half-timbered building visible from the street is nos 19a, 21 and 23, and is not all that it appears. It is entirely separate from the main part of the inn, although built at about the same time. Nos 19a and 21 were originally built as part of the inn, but no. 23 was a separate shop and house, which was either rebuilt or converted in the nineteenth century and incorporated into the hotel. The biggest fraud, however, is the half-timbered upper floors. These are timber frame and brick, but in the early twentieth century the whole thing was rendered and boards were applied to imitate timber framing. This part of the Fleece is Grade II listed.

The hotel attracted its fair share of celebrity guests including Gracie Fields, Kim Philby, the spy who defected to Russia, and Margaret Thatcher. It closed in October 2002 and both the Fleece Hotel and the crypt below have lain empty ever since. Owned by the South West of England Regional Development Agency (SWRDA) since 2003, it is in poor repair and listed on the Buildings at Risk register as Category 3. The SWRDA are working with the Gloucester Heritage Urban Regeneration Company (GHURC) to incorporate the Fleece into the heart of the planned Blackfriars creative quarter. What use the hotel will be put to has not yet been decided, it would be nice to see it back in use as a hotel and bar, but it is questionable whether a city centre hotel can thrive in Gloucester today.

The shops fronting Westgate Street are still trading: no. 19a, the smallest of the three, housed Westgate News for a long time, and no. 21 is a jewellers: both are of some interest in their own right as the shop fronts date from the late nineteenth century. The shop front of no. 23 is modern, but for a while this housed Made in Gloucestershire, an interesting shop selling products made by local craftsmen. However, this was recently forced to close due to the high rent.

The Fleece Hotel as it was before the false timber frames were added.

Ram, Northgate Street

The third Great Inn was the Ram. Recorded from 1525, it stood in Northgate Street opposite St John's Church. The Ram is mentioned in Clarke's *Architectural History of Gloucester*, written in 1850, by which time it had already seen better days. He says it was, 'conjectured to have been a Pilgrim's Inn; its original extent was probably to the corner of St Aldate Street.' He goes on to describe the doorway which, 'is still nearly perfect. It consists of a low Tudor arch supported by slender columns, but the spandrels

REF: 424
MAP: A
STATUS: Demolished
DATE: 1525 to 1865
LOCATION: Northgate Street

are ornamented with the oak leaf, and on the scroll above there is an inscription.' This carved oak lintel can now be seen in the Folk Museum, and the inscription can be translated as, 'Behold the once ruinous house which the town monk Osburne, rightly called John, then rebuilt.'

The Rental of 1455 refers to a tenement held by the abbot of St Peter's situated between the North Gate and St Aldate, 'which the parishioners of the Church of Saint Mary in the Market . . . [held] in the time of King Henry III . . . where there is now an inn.' Although the inn is not named, it is suggested that this may be the 'ruinous house' that John Osburne rebuilt as the Ram. This gives it a long connection with the abbey, and means that it may have acted as a Pilgrims' Inn at the time of Edward II's burial.

What remained of the Ram was demolished in 1865, fifteen years after Clarke wrote of it.

The Ram.
(Gloucestershire Archives)

The lintel from the Ram, now on display at the Gloucester Folk Museum. *(Darrel Kirby, used with permission of Gloucester City Museums)*

Other Ancient Inns

Boatman, The Quay

REF: 56

MAP: Location unknown

STATUS: Demolished

DATE: Before 1455 to unknown

LOCATION: The Quay

The Boatman on The Quay is first mentioned by name in 1503, but it is probably the same inn mentioned in *The Rental of the Houses in Gloucester A.D. 1455*: 'Beyond the bridge and Hospital of St Bartholomew, on south side Robert Warmwell, of Salisbury, holds . . . a tenement . . . wherein William Boatman dwells and keeps an inn.'

It doesn't seem too much of a reach to infer that the Boatman and the inn held by William Boatman are one and the same. *The Rental* also states that the abbey owned the premises at the time of Henry III, there is no indication that it was an inn at that time. Robert Warmwell is also mentioned in *The Rental* in connection with what is probably the Crown (p. 30)

I have not seen the Boatman mentioned in any licensing records, so it may have closed before the first records I have found in 1680. The inn would have been located just before Westgate Bridge, on the site now occupied by the garage. A number of pubs are later recorded in this area, but it is not clear which, if any, were on the site of the Boatman.

Boothall Inn, Westgate Street

REF: 62

MAP: A

STATUS: Demolished

DATE: Early fourteenth century to 1957

LOCATION: 71 Westgate Street

The Boothall Inn was located between Berkeley Street and Upper Quay Street. It stood directly in front of the Boothall itself, which was reached through an archway at the side of the inn, and was next door to the Old Bear Inn. In the original numbering it was no. 41, changing to 71 following renumbering in the 1920s.

Westgate Street before the building of the new Shire Hall in the 1960s. The Boothall is the second building on the left; next door is the Old Bear and a couple of doors beyond is the Brewers Arms.

The Rental of 1455 states that, 'The community of Gloucester, by their Stewards, hold a tenement with appurtenances called "the Bothall" or "the Gild Hall" . . . and there is there an inn . . .' It goes on to date the Boothall ('le Bothalle' in the original Latin) to at least the time of Henry III (1216–72), and the inn from the time of Edward II (1307–27).

The Boothall was the merchants guild hall; the merchants guild being the most powerful of Gloucester's guilds, claiming to represent all of the important men in the town. A building on or near the site was recorded as the guildhall in 1192.

The Calendar of the Records of the Corporation of Gloucester, 1528, reports that the Hospital of St Bartholomew released to the mayor and Burgesses of Gloucester, 'their right in a parcel of land in the street called "Westyatestrete" near the inn of the Bere, upon which land one part of the messuage called "the Bothall" is newly built.' This seems to indicate that the Boothall was newly extended at this time. 'The Bere' later became the Old Bear (p. 29).

By 1558 the 'Lease of inn or "great tent" called the Boothall' is recorded, with Robert Ingram as innholder. A number of conditions are made reserving to the Corporation the 'election chamber', and the tenant was to 'provide at own cost a cake made with ½ bushel of wheat flour to be distributed with wine and ale to mayor etc. on day of election of officers of the city.'

The name Robert Ingram is interesting as it is also mentioned in connection with the death of Bishop Hooper, who was burnt at the stake in St Mary's Square in 1555. According to *Foxe's Book of Martyrs*, on the night before his death Hooper came to Gloucester and 'lodged at one Ingram's house.' Fosbrooke elaborates on this, saying, 'he was brought to this city, and lodged in the house of one Robert Ingram, opposite St Nicholas's Church.'

Traditionally, Bishop Hooper's last lodging house is said to be the building now occupied by the Folk Museum, although to the best of my knowledge no evidence has been found connecting anyone called Ingram with this building. It seems to make more sense that he would have been put up in an inn along with his guard – it was normal practice for the military to be billeted at inns. The Boothall was a bit far east to be described as 'opposite St Nicholas's Church', but maybe, and this is pure speculation on my part, Robert Ingram was previously inn holder at the Crown Inn, which was opposite the church.

In any event, a chilling look into the practicalities of that barbaric act of martyrdom is captured in a sixteenth-century expenses claim for 'Giftes gevyn with other necessarie expences' from 1554–5: '. . . also in money by them paid for a dyner made and gevyn to the Lord Chandos and other gentilmen at Maister Maires howse that day that Maister Hooper was brant . . . and more in money paid to Agnes Ingram for wyne . . .'

The Old Boothall from *Illustrated London News*, January 1847. By this time it was in use as stables for the inn. *(Gloucestershire Archives)*

Robert Ingram was deceased by 1568 and the lease of the Boothall passed to his son, also imaginatively called Robert Ingram, who is presumably the same Robert Ingram listed as one of the twelve keepers of ancient inns in the Cooks and Innholders composition of 1583 (see p. 12).

From the mid-sixteenth century the Boothall was used for concerts, plays, and performances by travelling showmen. The Boothall Inn also became an important meeting place and during the eighteenth century it was one of the top five or six inns that became important social centres. In 1742–3 the timber-framed building was refaced with a new pedimented street front which incorporated the city arms, carved by Thomas Ricketts in 1745.

By the 1770s the Boothall was proving inadequate as courtrooms and the city quarter sessions moved to the Tolsey until the new Shire Hall was built next to the Boothall in 1816. The Boothall Inn continued to thrive as a coaching inn and by 1791 the Worcester and Birmingham and Bristol and Birmingham stagecoaches ran from there three times a week.

The Boothall itself became a coach house and stables which became the Boothall hotel. It was largely rebuilt in about 1850 and sold by the corporation in 1868. It became the Alhambra Music Hall in 1869, but fire closed it in 1874. Rebuilt again, from 1876 the building was used as a circus and skating rink, known as the Royal Albert Hall. Later it was a variety theatre and in 1907 it became the city's first cinema, the King's Hall Picture House.

The Boothall shortly before demolition.
(*Gloucestershire Archives*)

The Boothall Hotel closed on 28 March 1956 and, along with the old hall, it was demolished in 1957. The site was later incorporated into the extended Shire Hall. The city arms were removed and re-erected in Three Cocks Lane in 1961.

Fountain, Westgate Street

Although the address of the Fountain is given as 53 Westgate Street, it is not very visible from the main street. Its entrance is via a discreet passageway into a cobbled courtyard garden, which in the summer is festooned with brightly coloured hanging baskets. It can also be accessed from around the corner in Berkeley Street, where the entrance is much more obvious through large wrought iron gates.

REF: 188
MAP: A
STATUS: Trading
DATE: Thirteenth century to date
LOCATION: 53 Westgate Street, GL1 2NW
CONTACT: 01452 522562

Courtyard of the Fountain, entering from Westgate Street.

Plaque commemorating William III's visit to Jacobite rebels at the Fountain in the late seventeenth century.

It has been known as the Fountain since the seventeenth century, but it is much older than that; in fact it is probably one of the oldest known sites connected with the brewing trade in Gloucester. This means that it is, of course, mentioned in *The Rental* of 1455, when it was owned by Sybilla Savage and was called Savage's Inn: '. . . the tenement lately owned by Sibilla Savage, where there is an inn: which Peter Poictevin [held] . . . in the time of King Henry III.'

A link with the abbey is also indicated, as around the corner in Berkeley Street, then known as Broadsmith Street: 'The abbot of Saint Peter has there a piece of vacant land enclosed with palings pertaining to the inn called "Savage's Inn."' The mention of 'Peter Poictevin' in 'the time of King Henry III' (1216–72) and the connection with the abbey provide an interesting link to the king himself.

Henry III had close associations with Gloucester as, on 28 October 1216, following the premature death of his father, King John, allegedly from a 'surfeit of peaches and new beer', the nine-year-old Henry was crowned king in St Peter's Abbey. Gloucester remains the only place outside Westminster to see the coronation of a monarch since the conquest. Henry was crowned by Peter des Roches, the Bishop of Winchester, who originally came from Poitou in France and was often referred to as Peter Poitevin. With allowances for erratic medieval spelling, this is probably the very same Peter Poictevin mentioned in *The Rental*. It seems likely that Henry III gave him this land, which may even have already been an alehouse.

The subsequent holders of the premises listed in *The Rental* include, by the reign of Edward II (1307–27), John Taverner, whose name suggests that it was certainly an inn by this time. *The Rental* also links John the Taverner with the Bear in Westgate Street (p. 29).

By 1502 the name of the inn had changed to the Catherine Wheel (or Katherine Wheele) Inn, which in 1538 was in the tenure of Thomas Bell, the son of Sir Thomas Bell, local businessman and benefactor. By 1694 Broadsmith Street had been renamed Catherine Wheel Lane for the inn.

As well as Henry III, the inn has other connections with the monarchy, as evidenced by a plaque overlooking the courtyard with the motto, 'Dieu defend le droit. GVLIELMVS III'. This is said to commemorate an incident in the late seventeenth century, in the early reign of William III (1689–1702). At this time, Jacobite rebels supporting the cause of the Stuarts held clandestine meetings in an upstairs room at the inn. Allegedly, William heard of this during a visit to Gloucester and to show his contempt he rode his horse up the external stairs to the room.

The current name probably dates from 1672 when the inn was converted as a coffee house and tavern. It was probably named for the nearby Trinity Well. It is certainly listed as 'the ffountaine' in alehouse records by 1680, when the landlord is given as Edward Vaughan. In 1686 'the ffountaine' is listed in the name of Margarett Vaughan, widow, but the 'Katherine Wheele' is also listed, held by David Simond. The Katherine Wheele Inn is also mentioned in deeds from 1686 and 1694, so the name may have reverted for a time.

The Fountain became a coaching inn in the eighteenth century and underwent further remodelling in about 1900. It claims to have been the last of the city pubs to brew beer on the premises.

Today, the Fountain is owned by Enterprise Inns and is a superb Grade II listed pub. The main bar has a panelled ceiling and an impressive fireplace with a seventeenth-century carved and moulded stone chimney piece which dominates the main part of the bar. There is also the 'Orange Room' off the courtyard and the 'Long Room' upstairs which are used for events, functions and meetings.

The Fountain is a regular in CAMRA's *Good Beer Guide*, appearing in 1992, 1994 and 2003–8. Over recent years it has had its ups and downs and has been closed for a couple of brief periods, but at the time of writing it is open and thriving having reopened on 29 August 2008 with new lessees Joy and Peter Rust.

Lower George (now Pig Inn the City), Westgate Street

The Lower George was situated in Lower Westgate Street opposite Archdeacon Street. In the original street numbering it was no. 60, renumbered to 121 in the 1920s. The inn still exists, but it is now called the Pig Inn the City. An odd name, true, but not the worst that it has suffered in recent years, and it is rather a good pub – as I write in early 2010, it is Gloucester CAMRA's favourite. It earned a place in the *Good Beer Guide* from 2008 to 2010 and has just been announced as Gloucester City Pub of the Year for the second year running.

The Grade II listed building dates back to the early sixteenth century, when it was built as a merchant's house before becoming an inn. It was originally simply called the George, and is mentioned in a rent-roll from 1535. This lists the streets in Gloucester and includes the entry, 'Key Lane, or Walkers Lane, is beneath S. Nicholas Church on the South side of the street, by the sign of the George.' It was still known as the George in 1680, the date of the earliest legible licensing records that I have found, when the

REF: 296/387

MAP: B

STATUS: Trading as Pig Inn the City

DATE: By 1535 to date

LOCATION: 121 Westgate Street, GL1 2PG

CONTACT: 01452 421960

Pig Inn the City, 2009.

publican was named as William Cooke. The name was changed to the Lower George when another 'the George' appeared further up Westgate Street, which later became known as the Upper George (see p. 60). The first mention of the name Lower George in licensing records is in 1686.

The building underwent alterations in the eighteenth and early nineteenth centuries, including, as with many buildings in Westgate Street, the addition of a stuccoed brick façade. By 1791 the Lower George had joined the ranks of the chief inns in the city and by 1822 it was one of five establishments in the city operating stagecoaches. The stabling must have been quite substantial because, apparently, when the circus came to town it was here that the elephants were housed.

At some point, probably in the early twentieth century, the inn was extended into the next door property. The façade was also extended and the framed panel above the first-floor windows were inscribed 'Lower George Hotel'.

The Lower George was a Stroud Brewery pub, later becoming part of the Whitbread empire. In the early 1990s it was acquired by the Wolverhampton brewers, Banks', who tastefully restored it. The good taste didn't last long, however, as in 1997 Banks' sold it to the Little Pub Company, who turned it into that scourge of the 1990s, the Irish theme pub, renaming it Mad O'Rourkes. Not content with messing with genuine English heritage and replacing it with a fake Irish one, they also vandalised the exterior, changing the inscription on the façade from 'Lower George Hotel' to 'Low Or Hot'. They were made to put this right, but unfortunately were not prevented from painting the building bright orange and green.

The Lower George under Whitbread Ownership, probably in the 1960s.
(Reg Woolford)

Ownership of the pub then moved to Inn Spired, who changed the name to Pig Inn the City. It is not clear why the pub was so named; a former landlady maintains that it was because pigs were kept in the area during the civil war. Alternatively, it could be a reference to the Gloucester Old Spot pig, or it could simply be inspired by the PG at the end of the postcode – we may never know. Thankfully, whatever the reason for the name, the theme madness subsided. Apart from the pigs that is: they feature in all forms, shapes and sizes throughout the bar.

The Pig Inn the City bar – note the extensive list of real ales on the blackboard.

The Pig is now owned by a company called Property Investments and the current landlord, Martyn Penn, took over with his wife Kay at the end of 2006. Despite its history, the Pig doesn't give off an ambience of 'ye olde worlde charm'. The furniture is basic and where there is carpet it has seen better days. There is a well-used dartboard hanging on one wall and at the back of the pub, beyond the bar, is a separate room with a pool table and projection TV. Paintings by local artist Tony Houlden hang on the walls depicting . . . you guessed it: pigs.

Martyn's philosophy is that anyone is welcome at the Pig 'as long as they are friendly' and he has built a great community pub. As well as the friendly bar staff, the pub offers great food at a very reasonable price and regular live music. This latter tends toward rock, but there are also a wide variety of other styles to suit just about all tastes and the Pig is a staunch supporter of the annual Gloucester Blues Festival. The main appeal, however, is the Pig's well-deserved reputation for the quality and choice of its real ale. The wall behind the bar is festooned with numerous pump clips proclaiming the wide range of ales that have been on offer in the past, and three or four superbly kept ales, including many from local breweries, are available at any time.

The philosophy seems to work: even in mid week the Pig is fairly busy with regulars, and the clientele frequently range from old ladies to formidable looking rockers, all happily co-existing. Martyn told me that it was his mission from day one to steal away the honour of Gloucester CAMRA City Pub of Year, held by the Dick Whittington when he arrived, so when Gloucester CAMRA Chairman Alan Stephens handed over the certificate in January 2009, I thought he was going to burst with pride.

Old Bear, Westgate Street

The Bear was situated next door to the Boothall in Westgate Street, between Berkeley Street and Upper Quay Street. Originally at no. 40 it became numbered 73 Westgate Street on renumbering in the 1920s.

Although not mentioned by name, *The Rental* of 1455, confirms that there was an inn next to the Boothall, 'Thomas French and . . . his wife hold a tenement . . . near there [the Boothall], in which there is likewise an inn.' It goes on to give it a longer pedigree in the brewing world, 'In the time of King Edward II it was the workshop of John the Taverner and his heirs,' a name which clearly suggests a link to the beer trade,

REF: 353
MAP: A
STATUS: Demolished
DATE: Before 1455 to 1927
LOCATION: 73 Westgate Street

Old Bear photographed
by Sidney Pitcher.
(Gloucestershire Archives)

and one we have already seen associated with the site of the Fountain at that time (p. 26).

The first mention that I have found of the Bear by name is the Calendar of the Records of the Corporation of Gloucester, 1528, where it is mentioned in relation to a parcel of land released by the Hospital of St Bartholomew to the mayor and Burgesses of Gloucester for the building of a new part of the Boothall (see p. 23).

The Bear was renamed the Old Bear by 1722 when it is found in licensing records by that name. This may have been to differentiate it from the New Bear built in Quay Street in 1647 (see p. 49). This would suggest that the name change should have happened much sooner, but for some reason there is no mention of the pub in licensing records by either name prior to this.

By 1870 the landlady of the Old Bear was Eliza Bennett, who was charged with keeping a disorderly house. Over a number of months she was found with several other women in the pub too drunk to look after the place and using bad language. She was also charged for allowing notoriously bad characters to assemble in the house when four prostitutes were found in the bar with militia men, all were worse for drink. It was described by the constable as one of the worst conducted houses in the city.

The Old Bear was once tied to Gardner & Branch Crown Brewery of St Mary's Street, later becoming an Arnold, Perrett & Co. tied house before coming under the ownership of Cheltenham Original Brewery. It was referred to the Compensation Authority in March 1925 and closed in 1927. The Old Bear has now been demolished and the Shire Hall is on the site.

Old Crown, Westgate Street

REF: 355/356
MAP: B
STATUS: Trading
DATE: Before 1455 to 1760;
re-established 1990 to date
LOCATION: 81-83 Westgate
Street, GL1 2PG
CONTACT: 01452 310517

The Old Crown sits on the corner of Upper Quay Street and Westgate Street. It is owned by Samuel Smiths Brewery having been 're-established' as a pub in 1990. The original inn on this site, the Crown, was an ancient inn and as such is mentioned in *The Rental of the Houses in Gloucester A.D. 1455*: 'The same [Robert Warmwell, or Stockley, of Salisbury] holds another tenement with appertenances near there: which David Dunning [held] in the time of King Henry III; Alice Taverner in the time of King Edward I; Edmund at the Cellar and his heirs in the time of King Edward II: where there is an inn and other things with a bakehouse, which William Pirie, William Bridge, saddler, and Walter Rude, baker, occupy between them.'

Robert Warmwell is also associated with the Boatman (see p. 22). The names Alice Taverner and Edmund at the Cellar strongly suggest that its use as a hostelry dates back to at least the time of Edward I (1272–1307). This original inn was much more extensive than today's Old Crown: from the fifteenth century it occupied land fronting onto part of Upper Quay Street and Westgate Street as far down as what is now

The Old Crown: originally it extended to include the tall brick building, later the White Lamp Inn, and the building next to it, now Hyett House.

no. 91, opposite St Nicholas' Church, and it clearly shared the site with other trades. Its location has caused me to speculate that it may have been the real last lodging place of Bishop Hooper (see p. 23).

The inn was briefly renamed the Tabard in the early part of the seventeenth century, but reverted to the Crown under the tenure of Thomas Hale, Sergeant-at-arms of James I (1603–25). Although this royal connection can't have been too popular in Roundhead Gloucester during the civil war, it is alleged that the building was used as the lodging house and centre of operations for Lieutenant-Colonel Edward Massie during the Siege of Gloucester in 1643. This claim is also made for the building known as Colonel Massie's House further up Westgate Street, but the Gloucester Civic Trust favour the Old Crown as the correct location.

By 1680 the inn became the Old Crown following the establishment of another Crown Inn in the south of the city, probably in Cross Keys Lane. This curse of unimaginative pub names proves a constant source of confusion for the dedicated pub researcher, but perhaps it's not surprising in this case as the Crown is cited by some as the most popular pub name in Britain. Most, including the *Wordsworth Dictionary of Pub Names*, give this honour to the Red Lion, but they still state that more than 500 pubs named the Crown have been listed in recent directories.

The building was refurbished and given a new façade in 1730. It was described as being, 'a very commodious house and having very good stabling and a large yard.' Nonetheless, it ceased trading in October 1760 and was converted to workshops and stores by local wine merchant Alderman Benjamin Saunders. Saunders' son Thomas later occupied the workshops as a tallow chandler and soap boiler. These workshops and stores were later divided and went their separate ways.

All that remains of the former Crown Inn building is no. 91 Westgate Street. Now known as Hyett House, this timber building dates from the sixteenth century with an eighteenth-century façade. It was the town house of the Hyett family, probably erected by Nicholas Hyett, local lawyer and JP. It is this building that I presume John Clarke, writing in 1850, refers to when he says, 'Another hostelry somewhat similar to [the New Inn] . . . was erected about the same time in Westgate Street, nearly opposite

Lower Westgate Street in 1966, showing the Old Crown building in use as Woods Army & Navy Stores. (*Gloucester Citizen*)

The Victorian interior of the Old Crown.

St Nicholas' Church. Part of it still exists, and forms a very picturesque object.' Having deteriorated to a poor condition, the building was restored in 1988 with the help of Gloucester Historic Buildings Ltd.

The building at no. 87 (no. 45 before renumbering) also spent some time as a pub: the White Lamp Inn. The existing building only dates from 1900 according to the recently refurbished frontage, but the pub pre-dates this as Gloucestershire Archives have inventory and valuation papers for it dating from 1894. The White Lamp closed in 1972 and was left to slowly deteriorate. It was held up by scaffolding for many years until renovation work finally began in July 2002. The façade was retained, but it is now student accommodation.

The current Old Crown clearly consists of two buildings of different origins. No. 81 is a plain, square, painted brick building built in the early nineteenth century as a shop and dwelling. No. 83 is older with a more ornate brick façade, built as a town house in the early to mid-eighteenth century. The buildings were used as a Woods Army & Navy Stores for a long time, but after being empty for some years they were renovated by Samuel Smiths Brewery, who were able to claim that they had 're-established' it as a pub some 230 years after the closure of the original inn.

Inside, the Old Crown looks every inch an authentic Victorian pub, with high ceilings, lots of dark wood, brass and green leather and beautifully etched windows. When it was first reopened it provided a rare opportunity to drink Samuel Smiths ale in this part of the country – both Old Brewery Bitter and Museum Ale were stocked. It was good enough to earn a place in the CAMRA *Good Beer Guide* in 1992–3 and 1995, but sadly Samuel Smiths no longer deliver real ale this far south.

The current landlord, Keith, has been running the pub with his wife Gel since the end of 2008 and is trying to build up a strong clientele. However, his efforts are hampered by restrictions from the brewery, which prevent him from capitalising on the traditional charm of the place by selling real ale, but on the other hand also forbid him from competing with other nearby hostelries by having live music or showing televised events. I wish him well, but in the current climate such handicaps are not helpful.

St George, Southgate Street

The St George is another of the pubs mentioned in *The Rental of the Houses in Gloucester A.D. 1455*. It is listed on the east side of Southgate Street: 'Robert Jackman, mercer, holds in right of his wife Ellen, an hostelry there with the sign of Saint George.' It was situated between 'divers tenements' held by the Prior of Llanthony to the north and the porter's tenement adjoining the city wall to the south. The St George had closed by 1509.

REF: 494
MAP: G
STATUS: Demolished
DATE: Before 1455 to 1509
LOCATION: Southgate Street

Swan, Northgate Street

The Swan is mentioned in *The Rental* of 1509, and the first mention I have found for it in alehouse licensing is from 1686, when it was held by Thomas Aran. I have found little mention of this ancient inn, but it remained licensed into the eighteenth century as there is mention of a flower show being held there in 1746 and the Friendly and Charitable Society of Gloucester met there in 1753.

It is possible that the Swan later became the White Swan which, despite being described in the *History of the County of Gloucester* as one of the most important social centres of the seventeenth and eighteenth centuries, also keeps a very low profile in the records. I have seen reference to it in Gloucester City deeds between 1756 and 1801, although I have found no mention of it in licensing records.

The White Swan had closed by 1811 when city deeds refer to a 'messuage called Old Bank (formerly White Swan Inn) Upper Northgate Street.'

REF: 513
MAP: A
STATUS: Demolished
DATE: By 1509 to unknown
LOCATION: Northgate Street

2

Inns, Taverns & Alehouses of the Seventeenth & Eighteenth Century

The early seventeenth century was dominated by the Civil War, with Gloucester successfully standing against the king in the Siege of Gloucester in 1643. Much of Gloucester's suburbs beyond the city walls were destroyed at this time.

Alehouses, inns and taverns collectively became known as public (or 'publick') houses in the late seventeenth century, probably simply as a contraction of 'public alehouse'. The first registers of alehouse licenses are available at the Gloucestershire Archives about this time, the earliest being 1674. Unfortunately alehouse locations are only given by which 'ward' they are in: North, South, East or West. The frustrating and unimaginative tendency to keep using and reusing the same pub names, even within the same ward, often makes it difficult to be certain which pub is being referred to.

Political pressure continued to be applied to limit the number of licensed premises: Gloucestershire Quarter Sessions in 1706 and 1713 recommended to local justices that they limit the number of alehouses and suppress those deemed to be superfluous. Despite this, numbers of licensed alehouses increased, reaching 129 by 1746, equating to 1 for every 44 inhabitants. Numbers reduced soon afterwards, stabilising at about 70.

For most of the eighteenth century, before Cheltenham muscled in on the scene, Gloucester was an important social centre for the county gentry. The leading city inns staged a variety of events throughout the year including balls, lectures and theatre performances and, on a less genteel note, cockfights. The main event was an annual race meeting held in September and during that week the principal inns made a special effort with social events. For the culturally inclined, every third year this coincided with the music meeting of the three choirs of Gloucester, Hereford and Worcester.

The main development in the eighteenth century was the advent of the coaching inn, with a coach running from Gloucester to London as early as 1722. Coaches carried both passengers and mail and the horses needed changing regularly, which was always done at an inn. The innkeepers owned the horses and rented them to the coach company, and while the horses were changed the inns provided refreshments for passengers. Any mail was also collected and dropped off at the inns, making them a combination of stations, post offices and pubs. And of course, on longer journeys, passengers would stay at the inns overnight.

The Primary Inns

Bell Inn, Southgate Street

The Bell Inn was an impressive building and possibly Gloucester's most prestigious hotel. Situated in Southgate Street next door to what is now the Old Bell, it extended almost down as far as Bell Lane, now Bell Walk. The Old Bell is named for the fact that from about 1912 its upper floors were leased to the Bell as meeting and function rooms (see p. 70). The Bell Inn itself closed its doors for the last time on the afternoon of Friday 29 September 1967 and was demolished to make way for the construction of the sadly unimpressive Eastgate Shopping Centre in 1973.

The Bell Inn existed from at least 1544, but it may have had much earlier origins. *The Rental* of 1455 lists two pubs on the east side of Southgate Street which were probably on the site later occupied by the Bell. The first of these was between the Cross and Bell Lane: 'The prior of Llanthony and the Sacristan of the same place hold . . . the next tenement there toward the south . . . where there is an inn.' The origins of the building are dated back to Henry III, but with no indication of whether it was an inn at this time.

The second inn mentioned is a short way to the south on the north corner of Travel Lane, an early name for Bell Lane: 'William [Rigby] holds in fee a corner tenement with appurtenances [at the corner] of Travel Lane, wherein — Grove, cutler, dwells and keeps an inn.'

Whether either of these formed the origins of the Bell is unclear, but by the sixteenth century it was quite extensive, comprising the main inn, outhouses, stables, several shops, and land and a garden worth £130 a year in rent.

One of The Bell's most significant claims to fame was the birth of George Whitefield, one of the eighteenth century's foremost evangelists, on 16 December 1714. His

REF: 31
MAP: A
STATUS: Demolished
DATE: By 1544 to 1967
LOCATION: 11 Southgate Street

The Bell Hotel looking south. The Bell Hotel Annex in the foreground still exists as the Old Bell.

The Bell Hotel, Gloucester.

George Whitefield.
(Gloucestershire Archives)

father, Thomas, was landlord of the Bell, a role later taken on by his brother Richard.

It was during the eighteenth century that the Bell came to pre-eminence as one of the city's most important social centres. Both the local gentry and travellers frequented the Bell, which offered a range of entertainments. One of these was horse racing, which took place on the meadows by the Severn. Inns contributed money by subscription for one of the prizes – the Innkeepers Plate. In exchange they were allowed to keep booths on the course, and it was only at inns that had paid their subscription that the race horses were permitted to be kept. In 1739 it was stated that, 'All horses to be kept at the Bell, Mr Whitfield being the only Innkeeper that subscribes to the plates.'

The Bell tended toward high-brow entertainment, advertising such things as a ball for the assizes and a course of lectures on philosophy. Regular assemblies for the gentry and leading citizens, which were originally held at the Tolsey, the local government building, were held weekly at the Bell Inn between October and March in 1744. Not everything was high-brow though; by the early 1740s the Bell had jumped on the lucrative bandwagon of cockfighting, already popular in many other inns in Gloucester. It hosted inter-county cockfights, often for large purses.

The Bell's success seems to have made it unpopular with the competition. Richard Whitfield was forced to advertise refuting reports that his inn was full and, on one occasion, premature claims of his death, 'It having been industriously reported that Mr Whitfield, Master of the above Inn is dead, he begs to certify the Publick that the said report is entirely false, and was dispers'd only to prejudice his business.'

The Bell's reputation was such that it was immortalised in Henry Fielding's classic satirical novel of 1749, *The History of Tom Jones, a Foundling*. Jones travels to Gloucester where, 'Being arrived here, they chose for their house of entertainment the sign of the Bell, an excellent house indeed, and which I do most seriously recommend to every reader who shall visit this ancient city. The master of it is brother to the great preacher Whitefield; but is absolutely untainted with the pernicious principles of Methodism, or of any other heretical sect.'

Richard Whitfield left the Bell in about 1758, selling it to Gabriel Barnes of the Crown Inn at Wotton-under-Edge. By 1774 it had changed hands again and was owned by Thomas Pruen, who took the Bell onto its next great venture as an important coaching inn. He set up a rival company to that started by a Gloucester mercer, John Harris, who had a coach running from Gloucester to London as early as 1722. By 1733 this operated from the King's Head in Westgate Street. The enterprise was taken on by John Turner in 1753 and he became the leading Gloucester coach master for the next twenty-five years until the business passed to Paine & Co.

In August 1785, Isaac Thompson, landlord of the King's Head, partnered with Paine & Co. to introduce one of Britain's first London mail coach services, but the contract was soon transferred to the Bell, where John Phillpotts was now landlord, having taken over in 1782. On 22 August 1786, *The Times* reported that a coach left the Angel Inn in the Strand, London, at 5 a.m. and travelling via Abingdon, Faringdon, Lechlade, Fairford and Cirencester reached the Bell Inn, Southgate Street, Gloucester, that evening – a journey that in 1722 took three days. Possibly with the wealth created by the coaching business, the Bell's long pedimented front was built about 1793, by which time it was again under new ownership, Phillpotts having left in 1791.

The business rivalry between the Bell and the King's Head went further than the coaching business and it was heightened at election times, when the Bell was the headquarters of the Tories and the King's Head of the corporation-backed Whig interest. A Pitt Club was established by the Tories in 1814 and a Constitutional Whig Club followed in 1816, and these competing political societies held their annual meetings and dinners at the two inns. On a less serious political front, the Bell was also the annual meeting place of the self-appointed 'court' to elect the mock mayor of Barton. The political allegiances had to be curtailed when in 1883 legislation was passed banning committee rooms in licensed premises in parliamentary elections, extended to municipal elections in 1884.

In October 1831 the owner of the Bell Hotel, Thomas Marsh, died. Ownership passed to his wife, then his daughters, who seemed to die in alarmingly quick succession, finally passing to Martha Marsh in November 1858. Martha sold the hotel to the Gloucester Bell Hotel Co. Ltd on 18 August 1864 for £5,600.

A *Report of the Committee of Management* on 3 September 1864 had, 'Pleasure in stating, that notwithstanding the difficulties arising from the state in which the hotel was taken to, a very fair amount of business has been done.' Shortly thereafter, the inn was rebuilt.

Although the railway arrived in the mid-nineteenth century, coaching seems to have remained an important part of the business into the twentieth century. A 1908 advertisement for the Gloucester Bell Hotel Co. still boasted a posting department with, 'Superior Rubber-tyred Broughams, Brakes, Omnibuses, Landaus, Hansoms, and every description of Carriage on Hire.' It also advertised a Funeral Carriage Department, 'The oldest established, Largest and Best in the City and County.'

Golden Heart, Southgate Street

The Golden Heart appears in alehouse license records from 1680. It was on the east side of Southgate Street, between Bell Lane and Greyfriars. Because buildings were not numbered in the eighteenth and early nineteenth centuries, they were frequently identified in deeds by their position in relation to the buildings around them. It is lucky, therefore, that, although I have found no deeds for the Golden Heart itself, Gloucestershire Archives holds extensive deed information on its neighbour at what later became no. 27. Much of the inn's history can be discerned from this (see plan on p. 42).

The earliest of these deeds are from 1722 and they show that the Golden Heart was to the south of no. 27 and the innholder there was Thomas Howe. He was still at the Golden Heart in 1733, when he took on a stagecoach service between Bristol and Gloucester, attempting to significantly undercut the price of the service from the King's Head. As well as running a coach service, the Golden Heart also came to importance as a social centre in the 1730s, particularly hosting social events in connection with the races.

By 1744 the deeds show that Howe had left to be replaced by Thomas Atkinson, but he had also moved on by 1763 when John Heath is recorded as operating the coach service from the Golden Heart as one of the proprietors of the Birmingham, Worcester, Gloucester and Bristol Post Chariots. This service ran a two-way postal chariot route between Bristol and Birmingham, taking sixteen hours for the journey, which was pretty good for that time.

When the Golden Heart closed is unclear; the next deeds are from 1815 by which time the building was in the possession of Messrs. Saunders, Wine Merchants.

REF: 211
MAP: A
STATUS: Demolished
DATE: By 1680 to after 1763
LOCATION: Southgate Street

King's Head, Westgate Street

REF: 274
MAP: B
STATUS: Demolished
DATE: 1520 to 1865
LOCATION: Westgate Street

The King's Head was on the north side of Westgate Street. It adjoined St Nicholas House, now the Dick Whittington, on the east side and extended to the entrance to Three Cocks Lane. In the early eighteenth century the licensee of the King's Head, James Pitt, was also the tenant at St Nicholas House and may have been responsible for adding the impressive Georgian façade to the otherwise medieval building.

The first licensing reference that I have found for the King's Head is from 1736, although it is clearly older than that, dating to the early sixteenth century, probably about 1520. From the early eighteenth century it was one of the most important social centres in the city and by the start of the nineteenth century it was vying with its arch rival, the Bell in Southgate Street, as the most important.

The King's Head was a coaching inn with stabling for more than eighty horses. Gloucester mercer John Harris started a coaching business with a coach running from Gloucester to London as early as 1722. By 1733 this was kept at the King's Head. He also ran a stage from Gloucester to Bristol with Nathaniel Underwood of Bristol, becoming embroiled in a price war over the route with the Golden Heart in that year.

The enterprise was taken on by John Turner in 1753 who operated a 'Flying Stagecoach' which stopped overnight at the King's Head on its route from Hereford to London. The journey from Gloucester to London took two days. Despite this early success we have already seen how in 1785 Isaac Thompson, landlord of the King's Head, lost to the Bell in the battle to run the London mail coach (see p. 36). We have also seen something of the political rivalry between the two inns. Here, though, the King's Head probably played the more significant role.

In the 1720s and '30s the King's Head was generally chosen by the City Corporation for its nomination dinner and it was the established venue for all corporation dinners when they were revived in 1838. The Duke of Wellington apparently dined with the city council at the King's Head in 1816, just a year after his victory at the Battle of Waterloo.

Politically the corporation backed the Whigs and a Constitutional Whig Club, established in 1816, held their annual meetings and dinners at the King's Head. At election times the inn provided the Whigs' headquarters while the Bell supported the Tories.

Due to the shortcomings of the courtrooms at the Boothhall and the Tolsey, in the early years of the nineteenth century the King's Head was also used by the county magistrates. This was not unprecedented – as early as 1723 the Quarter Sessions were held at the inn.

The landlords of the King's Head were usually men of substance. They included Alderman Benjamin Saunders, a wine merchant, in 1737, who also established his 'Great Room' in 12 College Green for the holding of dances and assemblies. Giles Greenaway kept the inn from 1758 until 1776 or 1777, and obviously wasn't badly off because in 1779 he bought the manor of Little Barrington and later acted as agent to the Duke of Norfolk. In 1789 he became a city alderman. John Dowling, who was landlord in 1838, was elected mayor in 1844 and one of his sons, John, was rector of St Mary de Crypt and master of the Crypt School and another, James, bought Barnwood Court.

The King's Head must have had a good reputation because Queen Victoria stayed there as a princess. By 1854 it was known as a hotel rather than an inn, but like other coaching inns the King's Head lost much of its trade to the railway and by 1865 the hotel had closed. The building became Victoria Chambers, housing an auctioneer's, a solicitor's, county court offices and a veterinary surgeon.

At the end of the King's Head on the corner with Three Cocks Lane was the King's Head Tap, which had a separate address in St Mary's Street. I have seen little reference to this pub – a meeting was held there in 1831, at which time it was the house of Reuben Rickards, and it appears in *Hunt's Directory* of 1847. With the closure of the King's Head this was renamed the County Shades.

The *Gloucester Journal* of 25 September 1869 carried an item from John T. Morris, late of the Booth Hall Hotel, who, 'Begs respectfully to announce that he has taken to the [County Shades, late King's Head Hotel] where he hopes, by strict personal attention to the comforts and requirements of his patrons, to meet and secure a continuance of those favours so liberally bestowed upon the late Proprietor.' He goes on to boast of the quality of his wines and spirits and to recommend the Wine and Smoking Room which is supplied with newspapers and 'adjoining is a convenient lavatory.'

By 1894 the County Shades was a tied house of the Gloucester City Brewery. Its licence was objected to in February 1927 on the grounds of redundancy, although it still appears in *Cope's Directory* of 1935. The pub was closed and the building was occupied by a fruit merchants. The whole of the building previously occupied by the King's Head Hotel was demolished after the Second World War.

Ram Hotel, Southgate Street

The Ram Hotel stood opposite St Mary de Crypt Church in Southgate Street, at no. 21 in the original street numbering, changing to no. 44 in the modern numbering system.

The Ram in South Ward is recorded in licensing records from 1680, when the licensee was George Palmer. By 1791 it joined the ranks of the main city inns of importance as social centres in Gloucester. It was rebuilt in about 1840, which is probably when it became known as a hotel. It is listed as a commercial and posting hotel by 1847.

It became the first commercial premises in Gloucester to have a telephone. In April 1887 the Western Counties & South Wales Telephone Company established an exchange at 9 Berkeley Street. The *Gloucester Journal* wrote, 'During the past

REF: 425/329

MAP: A

STATUS: Trading as Mystiques Hotel & Restaurant

DATE: By 1680 to 2009 (as New County Hotel)

LOCATION: 44 Southgate Street

Southgate Street & Robert Raike's House, Gloucester.

RAM HOTEL RAM HOTEL

ANTIQUES

Looking up Southgate Street toward the Cross in about 1905, showing the canopy for the Ram on the west side.

New County Hotel,
2009.

few days the Ram Hotel and the exchange have been connected by a wire and the success of the telephonic system of communications has been demonstrated completely.'

The hotel was re-fronted in 1890. In an advert of 1924 it describes itself as a 'Family & Commercial Hotel'. It boasts electric light throughout and accommodation for cars, but it is unlicensed. It was later renamed the Ram & County Hotel, then after extensive refurbishment during which it was completely remodelled internally, it reopened as the New County Hotel on 30 January 1937.

In my early drinking days in the 1980s it had a very good bar known as the County Tavern and for a while it was a regular in the CAMRA *Good Beer Guide*, appearing in 1985–6 and 1988–91. However, the New County began looking increasingly worn until 2 June 2008 when the company who owned it went into administration and it ceased trading. The closure came as something of a surprise and resulted in job losses for nineteen staff and several disappointed couples, including my brother, who had booked wedding receptions there.

In the summer of 2009 plans were put forward by Quedgley-based company Mystique to turn the Grade II listed building into a 'lifestyle hotel' with fantasy rooms and an adult-themed restaurant for gay parties and swinging couples. Initially the response to the application seemed surprisingly positive, but this did not last long. The moralistic, NIMBY attitude normally associated with such schemes quickly raised its head and the objections that flooded in caused one councillor to comment 'I have not read anything quite so homophobic in some time.'

The application was rejected, but Mystique carried on anyway having taken legal advice that planning consent for change of use was not required. A much-needed facelift was completed on the building, which opened as Mystiques Hotel & Restaurant on 12 December 2009. Although I am neither gay nor a swinger I feel that a live and let live attitude should be adopted and the venture may inject a little colour into the city. In any event, it is surely better for the building to be used than left empty to slowly deteriorate.

Spread Eagle, Market Parade

REF: 487
MAP: A
STATUS: Demolished
DATE: By 1680 to 1972
LOCATION: Market Parade

The Spread Eagle Hotel was situated in Market Parade, which is now part of Bruton Way, although its yard was accessed from Northgate Street so it was sometimes given this address. It was closed in September 1972 and demolished to make way for a £2 million development which was to include a Tesco store. The development never happened and the old Spread Eagle site remains as a wasteland and a very rough car park.

An alehouse in the North Ward by the name of Spread Eagle is listed in alehouse licensing records as far back as 1680, when the licensee was Edward Charlton. By

The Spread Eagle
Hotel in its heyday.
(Gloucestershire Archives)

1682 it was listed as the Black Spread Eagle with the same licensee. It seems to have remained the Black Spread Eagle until at least 1747, although in 1686 it was listed just as the Black Eagle and in 1722 it seems to be listed as the White Spread Eagle.

The Black Spread Eagle was a substantial coaching inn boasting stabling for over 100 horses. In the 1740s it was an overnight staging post for the very slow Hereford to London stage-wagon. These were similar to the covered wagons well known from westerns and travelled at just two miles per hour, so obviously needed plenty of overnight staging places.

The Spread Eagle in the
1970s after closure.
(Gloucester Citizen)

The more recent Spread Eagle, however, was not built until 1770, although I have found no mention of it in licensing records until 1825. By this time it was benefitting from the opening of the new cattle market, which the City Corporation moved to what is now the bus station in 1823, moving it to the ranks of the city's leading inns.

The *Gloucester City Guide* of 1924 carries an advertisement for the Spread Eagle Hotel, under proprietor Stanley G. Smith, in which it boasts the largest dining room in the city, specialising in 'banquets, agricultural shows, race meetings, wedding receptions, balls, &c.' It was also the headquarters of the Rotary Club and the A.C.U.

The hotel is commemorated by the naming of Spread Eagle Road, which leads to the car park, and Spread Eagle Court. The latter, an impressive gothic red-brick building on the junction of Northgate Street and Bruton Way, was next door to the hotel and was originally called Northgate Mansions. At the time of writing, developers have been appointed to design a replacement building for Spread Eagle Court. Describing it as a 'landmark site' and 'an important "gateway" into the city centre', they are challenged to come up with an 'iconic landmark building' which must 'preserve or enhance the character of the area'. Enhancing the overall character of the area is unlikely to prove difficult, but it is a shame that this magnificent building has to go to make way for it.

White Hart, Southgate Street

REF: 587

MAP: A

STATUS: Demolished

DATE: By 1711 to 1836

LOCATION: Southgate Street

The White Hart is the fifth most popular pub name in the country. This is appropriate as the white hart is the personal emblem of Richard II, who passed the act making the displaying of inn signs compulsory in 1393. However, this is no excuse for having two pubs of that name within a few yards of each other! As well as this White Hart, there was another later inn of that name just around the corner in Bell Lane (see p. 130). This gives plenty of opportunity for confusion.

The White Hart was just to the north of the Golden Heart, close to Bell Lane. Like the Golden Heart, this information comes from the deeds of its neighbour. In this case the neighbour was on the corner of Bell Lane and deeds of 1811 and 1813 describe this 'messuage' as being bounded by Bell Lane to the north, Southgate Street to the west and the White Hart inn on all other sides, so the White Hart faced onto Southgate Street and backed onto Bell Lane.

The first mention I have found to the White Hart in licensing records dates from 1722, but the inn is older than that as deeds of 1711 refer to 'Moiety of a messuage in Southgate Street . . . adjoining the White Hart Inn.' Stables were added to the White Hart by 1735, when the innkeeper, Mr James Dancocks, boasted of two new stables, ideal for the stabling of horses competing in the regular horse races held on the meadows by the Severn, as they were 'very commodius for running horses, as having a way from them to the course, without going upon stones.'

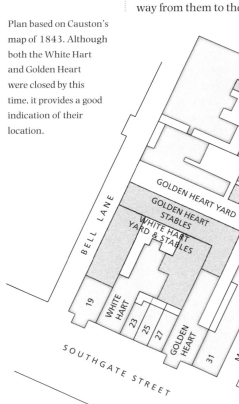

Plan based on Causton's map of 1843. Although both the White Hart and Golden Heart were closed by this time, it provides a good indication of their location.

The deeds for no. 27 Southgate Street, to the south of the White Hart (see the Golden Heart, p. 37), describe the property as being bordered to the east by stables from the White Hart Inn by 1815. This indicates that they must have been of a good size.

By the mid-eighteenth century the White Hart was advertising a variety of entertainments at the inn and by 1791 it ranked among the chief inns of the city. It continued until at least 1836, but the deeds for no. 27 suggest that it was closed by 1838 as by then it states that it was bordered to the east by stables formerly belonging to the White Hart.

By 1861 the White Hart had been divided into two buildings, one of which had been sold as a dwelling house. The other part had remained as an inn for a time, but was now pulled down and a new dwelling was built in its place.

The other White Hart on the south side of Bell Lane was in existence by 1869. This must have been close to the rear of the older White Hart, but I have seen no evidence for a link between the two.

The Lesser Hostelries

Bolt Inn, Longsmith Street

Medieval Gloucester was renowned for iron working, particularly in the south-west quarter of the city as evidenced by the street names – the smith's street became Longsmith Street by 1549, and running from that to Westgate Street was Broadsmith Street, which is now Berkeley Street.

There were plenty of requirements for iron goods, not least by the crown for military and naval purposes. These would have included nails, horseshoes, ironwork for spades, kitchen utensils, anchors and crossbow bolts. And so we come to the point (so to speak) – it is presumably for the latter that the Bolt, located on the south side of Longsmith Street, was named.

The Bolt is found in the alehouse licensing records from at least 1680, when the licensee was a Thomas Chandler, a name that suggests association with candles rather than iron working. By 1714 the east end of the street had been renamed for the inn, becoming Bolt Lane. The last reference I have found for the Bolt is about 1859.

Meanwhile, another Bolt Inn existed at about the same time in Eastgate Street near to the Greyhound (Ref 58, Map A). First found in licensing records in 1682, by 1752 it is advertising to quash rumours of its demise. The last mention I have found for this inn is 1759.

By 1869 a new inn name is found in Longsmith Street – the Ducie Arms. Presumably named for the Earl of Ducie, this was probably on the same site as the Bolt. The Earl of Ducie title originated with Matthew Ducie Moreton, who represented Gloucestershire in the House of Commons and became Lord Ducie, Baron of Moreton, in the County of Stafford in 1720. In 1837 the 4th Baron Ducie, Thomas Reynolds Moreton, was created Baron Moreton of Tortworth in the County of Gloucester, and Earl of Ducie. We are currently on the 7th Earl of Ducie, David Leslie Moreton, who succeeded in 1991. How proud the earls must have been to have this pub named in their honour; the Ducie Arms had a 'colourful' reputation. A newspaper report from about 1906 described it as 'being frequented by women of bad character . . . that drunken persons were seen coming out at closing time, that there was filthy language, fighting, general disorderly behaviour and indecency outside.' This is the last reference that I have found for the Ducie Arms, so may have been the cause of its closure.

REF: 59
MAP: A
STATUS: Demolished
DATE: By 1680 to at least 1906
LOCATION: Longsmith Street

Bull Inn, Bull Lane

The Bull Inn was situated in Bull Lane, a narrow lane off Upper Westgate Street. The lane was probably named for the pub, because in earlier times, from the thirteenth century, it was known as Gore Lane owing to the presence of pig sties and slaughter houses there.

The Bull Inn is first found in licensing records in 1682, when it was owned by Ann Peress, a widow, although it is probably much older. It was a twin-gabled pub, later a tied house of Arnold Perrett & Co. of Wickwar. It was submitted for closure in 1909 as 'not being required to meet the wants of the neighbourhood' and closed in 1910. The building remained and for a time was used as an antiques warehouse until it was demolished in 1952 to make way for the extension to Gloucester telephone exchange.

At the site of the Bull a large stone slab was found, known as the Bullstone. Measuring 2ft 9½ins long by 4ft 4ins wide and 2 ins thick, it is marked out in fifteen squares. These

REF: 78
MAP: A
STATUS: Demolished
DATE: By 1682 to 1910
LOCATION: Bull Lane

Right: Bull Inn 1896, taken by Sidney Pitcher. *(Gloucestershire Archives)*

Far right: The 'Bullstone' found on the site of the Bull Inn, now in the Gloucester Folk Museum. *(Darrel Kirby, used with permission of Gloucester City Museums)*

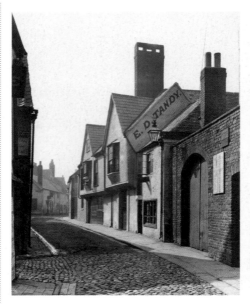

contain numbers in multiples of 10 up to 110 plus 200, one square has a B and the other 2 remain blank. This is thought to be a game where the players stood back and threw discs or pennies onto the slab. Whoever got his penny on to the B square was the winner and took the pool; otherwise it went to the first to reach a set score.

Coach & Horses, St Catherine Street _____

The first thing you see as you enter St Catherine Street from Worcester Street is a wonderful black and white half-timbered building; this is the Coach & Horses. Today St Catherine Street is something of a back street, but the Coach & Horses would have originally been in a prime location as it is directly opposite the end of Hare Lane, which was the main route in and out of the city to the north until Worcester Street was built in the 1820s. It was also close to one of the city's outer gates, Alvin Gate.

REF: 105
MAP: C
STATUS: Trading
DATE: By eighteenth century to date
LOCATION: 2 St Catherine Street

The core of the building dates back to the early sixteenth century. It is not known whether it was initially used as an inn, but it certainly was by the eighteenth century. However, the first definite licensing reference that I have found for it is 1806. The pub's name and location both suggest that it would have been a coaching inn – the name Coach & Horses was used to indicate that the inn had a yard large enough to turn a coach around. The pub does have a good sized garden, but I have found no references to it in connection with the coaching business.

St Catherines Knap taken by Henry Medland at the end of the nineteenth century. The Coach & Horses is on the right and the first girls' Sunday School is in the background. *(Bristol & Gloucestershire Archaeological Society)*

The Coach & Horses in about 1988.

The Coach & Horses has been continually refurbished over the years and was extended in the eighteenth and nineteenth centuries. Although the building is genuinely half-timbered, with the upper storey protruding over the ground floor, the timbers that you see are actually painted onto render.

Lately it has had a very quick turnaround of landlords, with more than twenty in as many years. One of the reasons for this may be that it is said to be haunted; ghostly children have been seen and heard by a number of landlords and even Gloucester's fearless ghost investigator Lyn Cinderey was so uneasy there that she couldn't stay the night to complete a planned investigation.

The Coach & Horses was closed through late 2008 and most of 2009, but at the time of writing it has just reopened. Inside, modern alterations to the bar mean that the building does not reflect its age well and it is decidedly tatty. Steve, the new manager, is full of enthusiasm and good ideas but is reluctant to invest too heavily while the future of the owners, Admiral Taverns, remains uncertain. I hope this will soon be resolved and wish him well.

Cross Keys Inn, Cross Keys Lane

Cross Keys Lane is a very narrow lane running west from Southgate Street to Bull Lane. In medieval times it was known as Scroddelone or Scrudde Lane, scrudde being an Anglo-Saxon word for a shroud or garment, reflecting the fact that clothiers' workshops were here in the tenth century. This was unfortunately occasionally corrupted to Crud Lane and for a time it was also known as Milk Street, but since at least 1780 it has been named for the pub that stands on its south side.

The Cross Keys Inn is in an early to mid-sixteenth-century Grade II listed timber-framed building, which was originally probably three cottages. The first mention that I have found of it in alehouse licensing records is from 1720. Prior to the Reformation, the sign of the cross keys meant that the inn was supplied with beer and wine from a nearby monastic house. They are also an emblem of St Peter, to whom Gloucester Abbey, now

REF: 135
MAP: A
STATUS: Trading
DATE: By 1720 to date
LOCATION: Cross Keys Lane, GL1 2HQ
CONTACT: 01452 523358

the cathedral, is dedicated. If the name is original, this may well suggest that it does, at least in part, date back to the early sixteenth century as a pub.

A document from 1853 hanging above the fireplace in the bar shows that there was a brew house alongside the inn. However, by 1894 it was a tied house of the City Brewery. In the 1950s it was a popular Stroud Cotswold ales pub, later coming under Whitbread ownership.

It was a popular CAMRA pub with entries in the *Good Beer Guide* in 1975–6, 1981–4 and 1987–9. For a while the pub then became something of a real ale desert, but the current owner, Ruth Bourke-Cross, and manager, David Fuller, have changed all that and they now have two well kept ales and were one of the first pubs in Gloucester to sign up to CAMRA's LocAle scheme, agreeing to stock at least one locally brewed ale at all times. It secured a well-earned place in the 2010 *Good Beer Guide*.

Ruth has been at the Cross Keys since the summer of 2007, taking over at the time of the floods that largely brought Gloucester to a standstill and also held up the opening of the pub. Ruth has extensive experience of running pubs: she is Irish and says this is what the Irish do. Before buying the Cross Keys she managed pubs in Dublin, New York and even Dubai. She is very positive about settling in Gloucester, which she says has a good, friendly atmosphere.

From the outside, the Cross Keys retains its medieval appearance – it is a stuccoed timber-framed building with the first floor hanging out supported by a jetty. The atmosphere is enhanced by the narrow cobbled lane, and only spoiled when you walk past the pub and encounter the jarring incongruity of the 1970s multi-storey car park next door. The pub backs onto Ladybellegate Street, where there is a pleasant deck. Unfortunately, not only is this overshadowed by the car park, but a monstrous concrete carbuncle of a bridge cuts across the back of the pub. This no longer leads anywhere and its removal is long overdue.

The Cross Keys building underwent alterations in the eighteenth century, including increasing the left side of the building from the original two storeys to three, and further alterations took place in the nineteenth and twentieth centuries. Ruth was

kind enough to give me a tour of the building, and the alterations have resulted in an interesting maze of rooms. In the cellar are old archways which have clearly been bricked up and Ruth wonders whether there could once have been tunnels. Given the pub's links to the abbey this is as credible a claim as any, but it is more likely that they were once just more extensive cellars.

The bar is not large despite having been mostly opened up into a single room. It retains the old-world charm that you would expect from the outside, with plain wooden floor boards, dark wooden ceiling beams and supporting posts and stone fire places at both ends of the room.

Further back on the right-hand side is another small room with a separate bar, which at weekends provides a late night lounge for members called VIPs at the Keys.

The Cross Keys is something of a Jekyll and Hyde of the pub world, and seems to manage the two sides of its character well. The aim, Ruth says, is to make it a social place, creating a pub culture rather than a drinking culture. Midweek lunchtimes and some evenings are generally quiet, frequented by regulars. Other nights are livelier, with well-attended live music, generally tending towards blues and jazz. There are also regular karaoke and open-mic nights.

So, this is the Cross Keys as Dr Jekyll, but traces of Mr Hyde can be discerned. On the ceiling above the bar, for example, hangs a glitter ball, and there are disco lights affixed to the ceiling. In front of the bar a steel pole is fixed from floor to ceiling, in stark contrast to the dark wood structural timbers – this is not structural, but purely for entertainment purposes. In short, at the weekend the Cross Keys becomes a full-on party pub, with a resident DJ and loud, drunken revellers.

On my selfless mission to visit all of Gloucester's pubs, the Cross Keys is probably one of the liveliest that I have been to. The clientele tend to be older than you get in the disco pubs and venue bars of Eastgate Street, and as a consequence, despite having to fight your way to the bar, the atmosphere is much more relaxed. David had assured me that on a good night there are plenty of people willing to give the pole a go, but on the night I was there it wouldn't have been possible to swing a cat much less a pole dancer – someone would have lost an eye!

As may be expected from a pub of this age, it is said to be haunted. Although he is slightly sceptical, David says there have been a number of instances where the gas taps in the cellar have mysteriously been switched off and lights get turned on over night. Ruth has also seen what she describes as a shadowy figure.

Inside the Cross Keys: note the pole on the right of the picture (not for structural purposes).

Green Dragon, Southgate Street

REF: 219
MAP: G
STATUS: Demolished
DATE: By 1683 to 1868
LOCATION: Southgate Street

Until 1860 Parliament Street was known as Green Dragon Lane, after the pub located on its north corner with Southgate Street. Situated just outside the South Gate, the Green Dragon is recorded from about 1683.

The Green Dragon was demolished in 1868 to make way for the enlargement of the Gloucester Infirmary. Parliament Street was subsequently redirected to the north of where the Green Dragon had stood. The infirmary itself was demolished in 1984 and a modern office building known as Southgate House is now on the site.

Imperial, Northgate Street

REF: 253
MAP: A
STATUS: Trading
DATE: By 1722 to date
LOCATION: 59, Northgate Street, GL1 2AG
CONTACT: 01452 529918

Right: The Imperial in about 1900. *(Gloucestershire Archives)*

The Imperial is on Northgate Street, below Hare Lane. It is only a small two-storey building, but what it lacks in size it makes up for in ornamentation. A former Mitchells & Butlers pub, the ground floor is faced with elaborately moulded and coloured glazed tiles. According to the Schedule of Listed Buildings, the current Grade II listed building dates from about 1890, but its origins as a pub go back much further.

The original building on the site was owned by a Mr John Wyman, who in 1556 left provision in his will that the property should be left to his wife and after her death it should pass 'to the Proctors and Parishioners of the Church of St John the Baptist.' Whether it was a beerhouse at this time is not clear; it first appeared in alehouse licensing records in 1722, when it was called the Plough.

In 1877 'the Plough Beerhouse' was leased to a Mr George Cummings and it was probably at this time that the name was changed to the Imperial; it is listed by this name in the *Gloucester Directory* for 1879. The pub was still owned by the charity of John Wyman, who rather uncharitably gave Mr Cummings notice to quit at Christmas 1897. On 20 May 1898 it was sold by auction at the New Inn and was purchased by Mitchells & Butlers for £2,050. It was described as a 'freehold beerhouse . . . containing on the ground floor, front bar with two entrances, back bar, small sitting room, lean-to scullery fitted with furnace [and] courtyard.' Shortly afterwards the pub was rebuilt.

Now owned by Bass, the frontage has thankfully remained unspoiled, but the interior has been refurbished over the years and the original three rooms were knocked into one in 1985, so there are no original interior features. It still retains a wonderful Victorian feel, however, and has a pleasant local atmosphere despite its town centre location. It also sells real ale and earned a place in the CAMRA *Good Beer Guide* in 1995.

King's Arms, Hare Lane

The King's Arms was at no. 3 Hare Lane, referred to in some places as Tewkesbury Street. It was just off Northgate Street on the west side of the road. The first reference that I have found for the pub is in city deeds from 1786, which refer to a 'messuage, court, backside, brewhouse and garden with the appurtenances in Hair [sic] Lane, in the parish of St John the Baptist, Gloucester and known as the King's Arms.' The building next door to the King's Arms, on the corner of Northgate Street and Hare Lane, later became the Tabard and the two pubs were amalgamated, probably in the late 1970s or early 1980s (see p. 127).

REF: 271
MAP: A
STATUS: Trading as part of Varsity (see p. 127)
DATE: By 1786 to late 1970s
LOCATION: 3 Hare Lane

New Bear, Quay Street

The New Bear was built in 1647 by John Singleton, an innkeeper, on the corner of Quay Street and Castle Lane. Castle Lane no longer exists, but it used to be a continuation of Upper Quay Street through to the castle, which was roughly on the site now occupied by the prison.

King's Arms Hotel

(OFF NORTHGATE STREET)

᷿ GLOUCESTER.

Visitors, Foresters and Friends Cordially Welcomed.

᷿ THE NOTED HOUSE ᷿

for Heather Dew, John Walker & Son's Scotch Whiskey,
Dunville's Irish Whiskey,
OAKHILL STOUT, Bottled and Draught.
Guinness's Bottled Stout.   -   -   Bass's Bottled Ales.
Special Line in Cigars (Warranted Seasoned).

UP-TO-DATE BILLIARD SALOON

Proprietor - WM. H. RASBACH.

Advertisement from
the *Ancient Order of
the Foresters Guide
to Gloucester* 1901.
(Gloucestershire Archives)

The building of the New Bear was part of a drive by the Corporation to rebuild the suburbs following the destruction of the Siege of Gloucester in 1643. It was the largest of a row of new houses fronting on to the south of Quay Street, built on eleven plots leased by the corporation.

Calling the new pub the New Bear may have been a bit galling for the nearby Bear Inn in Westgate Street, which later changed to the Old Bear (see p. 29). The pub name probably had less to do with the large hairy animal than the fact that it was built in the area known as Bearland. This in turn is also not named for the animal, but is a corruption of 'bare land' referring to the area around the castle, where all buildings were removed leaving it bare to stop the enemy sneaking up unseen.

By 1680 the licensee at 'ye New Beare' was John Rogers, alderman, who by 1682 was mayor. This is the last year that I find mention of the New Bear in licensing records, but there are other mentions of it – at Gloucester City Quarter Sessions of Michaelmas 1724 there was a hearing for 'John Pace Shoemaker for a nuisance in keeping a pigg Stie and throwing the dung in to the street leading from the New Bear to the Key.' Also, in March 1726 the *Gloucester Journal* refers to the Gloucester, Bristol and Bath stagecoaches which set out from 'Thomas Winston's near the New Bear'.

REF: 328
MAP: B
STATUS: Demolished
DATE: 1647 to after 1726
LOCATION: Quay Street

Things are confused by the frustrating eighteenth-century habit of recycling pub names – by 1767 another New Bear appeared further up the road in Longsmith Street. The later references above could be to this new New Bear, but it seems unlikely. This pub was formerly known by the sign of the Black Boy, which appears in licensing records from at least 1680 and was still known by this name by 1731 when the landlord, Joseph Webley (possibly a descendant of Katherine Webley from the Oxbody Inn?), was in trouble for keeping a disorderly house. This pub was demolished in 1868.

Oxbody Inn, Oxbody Lane

REF: 371
MAP: A
STATUS: Demolished
DATE: By 1680 to 1927
LOCATION: Oxbody Lane

The Oxebode runs from Northgate Street to King's Square. It is a broad, tree-lined street flanked by the huge monolith of Debenhams on one side and a row of shops with modern frontages on the other. Originally it was a much narrower street, known from medieval times as Oxbodelome, becoming first Oxbody Lane then Oxebode Lane. The name was shortened to the Oxebode when it was redeveloped as part of the Oxebode/King's Square redevelopment in the late 1920s. The Oxbody Inn was on the north side of Oxbody Lane and is listed as the 'Oxe body' in alehouse licensing records of 1680, the earliest that I have found. At this time it was in the hands of Katherine Webly.

How the lane and inn came by their name is the subject of some speculation; we have the classic question of which was named first, the street or the inn? According to Rudder's *A New History of Gloucestershire* of 1779, Oxbody Lane was 'so called from an alehouse, which is the sign of the ox's body.' However, there is reference to the street name as far back as the thirteenth century, so it seems more likely to be the other way round. Another suggestion of how this narrow lane came by its name is given in a local, and rather macabre, nursery rhyme written by E.P.R. Berryman in the 1950s:

Oxbody Lane. *(Reflections of Clapham Group/ Bernard Polson)*

There's an ox lying dead at the end of the lane,
His head on the pathway, his feet in the drain.
The lane is so narrow, his back was so wide,
He got stuck in the road 'twixt a house on each side.

He couldn't go forward, he couldn't go back,
He was stuck just as tight as a nail in a crack,
And the people all shouted, 'So tightly he fits
We must kill him and carve him and move him in bits.'

So a butcher despatched him and then had a sale
Of his ribs and his sirloin, his rump and his tail;
And the farmer he told me, 'I'll never again
Drive cattle to market down Oxbody Lane.'

There was a second hostelry on the opposite side of Oxbody lane, named the Mitre (Ref 318, Map A). Although there is some confusion in the licensing records with it listed variously in West, North and East Wards, it too seems to date back to at least 1680, when it was owned by Cornelius Platt, gent. Oxbody Lane was renamed Mitre Street after this inn in the nineteenth century.

The Mitre was just to the east of Rudhall's Bell Foundry, which from 1727 to 1848 stood on the site now occupied by the post office. Causton's Map of 1843 shows it as a small building in a broad open yard stretching from Mitre Street back to New Inn Lane. The Mitre had disappeared by 1883 and the street name reverted to Oxbody Lane by 1900.

The Oxbody continued trading into the early twentieth century, when it was tied to Godsell & Sons, but Oxbody Lane was one of the poorest areas of the city and was tackled as one of Gloucester's first slum clearances. By this time the pub was at the rear of the old Bon Marche building and the area was demolished to make way for the large new building erected in 1931, which is now Debenhams. The last reference that I have seen for the Oxbody is 1927.

Pelican, St Mary's Street

Early alehouse licensing records going back to 1679 list a house called the Pelican (or Pellicane), when the tenant was Samuel Jones. These early records locate the Pelican in the North Ward because it just crept into the north Parish of St Catherine. In 1680 there is a second 'Pellicane' listed in the North Ward with Robert Morrall as tenant, and in 1686 they became the 'White Pelican' and the 'Grey Pelican'. There is only one remaining by 1806, by which time it is once again referred to as just the Pelican.

The Pelican is at no. 4 St Mary's Street, on the corner with Pitt Street. This is the north-west boundary of the cathedral precinct, and it would have stood right next to one of the city gates, the Blind Gate, which was located here until it was pulled down in the mid-eighteenth century.

It is claimed that the Pelican uses beams from Sir Francis Drake's ship, the *Golden Hind*, in its construction. This perhaps sounds a little far-fetched, but there may be something in it when you consider the name of the pub. What has a boozer in Gloucester got to do with a large-beaked, tropical water-fowl? Well, when Sir Francis Drake set off on his global circumnavigation in 1577 he did so on an English galleon called *Pelican*. He renamed the ship mid-voyage to the *Golden Hind*. The voyage completed in 1580 and the *Golden Hind* remained rotting away in Deptford Docks for about the next 100 years until it was broken up – that brings it spookily close to the first date that I have found for the pub. There are a number of things reputed to have been made from surviving timbers of the *Golden Hind* and, like supposed remnants of the True Cross or the Berlin Wall, probably amount to many times more than the original artefact, so it could just have been good seventeenth-century marketing, but it would be nice to think that it's true.

REF: 380
MAP: B & C
STATUS: Trading
DATE: By 1679 to date
LOCATION: 4 St Mary's Street

St Mary's Street looking toward Pitt Street, 1959. The Pelican is on the left.
(Gloucester Citizen)

A number of pubs in this area met an untimely end due to the Westgate Comprehensive Redevelopment (see p. 132), and the Pelican was nearly one of them. However, the minutes of a meeting on 18 January 1954 report that 'the "Pelican Inn" is to be retained.'

The Pelican broke with its long history briefly when it was renamed the College Arms in about 1993, but it reverted in 2007, albeit as the Old Pelican Inn & Bistro. At the end of 2007 new landlords arrived with the laudable aim, after restoring the damage caused by the previous year's floods, of converting it back to a 'proper British boozer'. However, in 2008 the pub closed down as it was not getting the necessary trade – a fact which was largely blamed on the smoking ban. Against expectation it reopened at the end of 2009. It is a small, basic pub, but well worth a visit.

Raven Tavern, Hare Lane

REF: 427
MAP: C
STATUS: Building in different use
DATE: By 1641 (uncertain)
LOCATION: Hare Lane (uncertain)

Hare Lane leads off Northgate Street and was once the main approach to the city from the North, running from the North Gate to the Alvin Gate. It was originally called Here Straet, meaning 'military road' and in its heyday it contained the homes of merchants and craftsmen as well as the tanners guild, the remains of which can still be seen alongside Gouda Way. It also housed a number of inns, although records of most of these are sketchy.

The fortunes of Hare Lane began to turn when Worcester Street was built in the 1820s, relegating Hare Lane to a back street. In the nineteenth century Gloucester's population grew dramatically and slum cottages were built in the back yards of older buildings.

The pre-war slum clearances of the 1930s followed by more recent developments have decimated most of Hare Lane, relegating it to a sprawling car park with few buildings, much less any of historic or architectural merit. At the Northgate Street end, however, two excellent Grade II listed buildings survive. The first of these is an excellent fish and chip shop and restaurant, the other, of more interest in the context of this book, is an old peoples' centre popularly called the Old Raven Tavern.

The Raven Centre today, facing onto Hare Lane.

Perched between the modern Sainsbury's supermarket and the car park, opposite the junction with Pitt Street, the Old Raven Tavern is a well preserved black and white building which dates from about 1520, when it was built as a merchant's house. Beyond this its history is unclear.

For a start there is the somewhat fundamental question over whether the Old Raven Tavern is, in fact, the old Raven Tavern. I have found no evidence to support this popularly held belief. The only Raven Tavern that I have found is listed in licensing records as being in the South Ward, and that only from 1682 to 1686, although Dodd & Moss include it in their list of eighteenth century alehouses.

The only contemporary reference I have found for the Raven Tavern is in papers of the Guise family, which includes the will of Leonard Tarne, Alderman of the City of Gloucester, dated 1641, which leaves '. . . My greate Burgage or tenement . . . called the signe of the Raven or the Raven Taverne nowe in occupacion of William Warwick, vintner.' Sadly this does nothing to shed light on the location of the tavern. Alehouse licensing records show William Warwick at the Raven in South Ward by 1682, which seems to support the case for mistaken identity. However, this is not conclusive; it is not unusual for the licensing records to list inns in the wrong ward. Alternatively, as this is forty years after the date of Tarne's will, it is not impossible that Mr Warwick could have moved to a different pub and, having become attached to the name, taken it with him. Again, the unimaginative re-use of pub names is by no means unusual. It is possible that we will never know.

An old picture of the Raven Inn.

One of the recipients of Tarne's will was Thomas Hoare, son of Charles Hoare (deceased), which supports another popular belief that the building is connected to the Hoare family, who sailed to America on the *Mayflower*. It does leave a slight wrinkle though, as the *Mayflower* sailed in 1620, more than twenty years before the date of the will.

Whatever the truth, it is due to this history, real or not, that the building narrowly escaped demolition in the 1930s. There was a lengthy and concerted effort by a number of Gloucester's worthies, including the dean, Hope Costley White, and Alderman Bellows, to preserve the building.

The Old Raven Tavern toward the end of restoration showing the north elevation – the side shown in the above picture. *(Gloucestershire Archives)*

An architect's report from 1935 states that the buildings 'probably once formed part of the Raven Inn, and it is likely that they occupied the southern side of a courtyard, and that a northern wing with central archway on the west side once existed'.

Obviously the bid to save the building was ultimately successful and it was restored in 1949 by H.F. Trew for trustees of the Raven Fund and with support from the Society for the Protection of Ancient Buildings. *Kelly's Directory* of 1955 lists a pub called the Old Raven Tavern in Hare Lane, which presumably established in the building briefly, but it was gone by 1957. The building underwent further alteration in 1964 before opening as an Old People's Centre called the Raven Centre.

Red Lion, Northgate Street

REF: 433
MAP: A
STATUS: Demolished
DATE: By 1722 to 1920
LOCATION: 41 Northgate Street

As pub names go, the Red Lion is pretty common. According to the *Wordsworth Dictionary of Pub Names* it is the most popular of all, with at least 600 pubs bearing the name. So it is perhaps not surprising that there were four in Gloucester in the eighteenth century: one in Barton Street, one in Littleworth (outside the South Gate) and two in the North Ward. It is difficult to separate the two in the north in early licensing records, but one was in Hare Lane and one in Northgate Street. Both were recorded by 1722, one as the Red Lyon Cellar, the other simply as the Red Lyon.

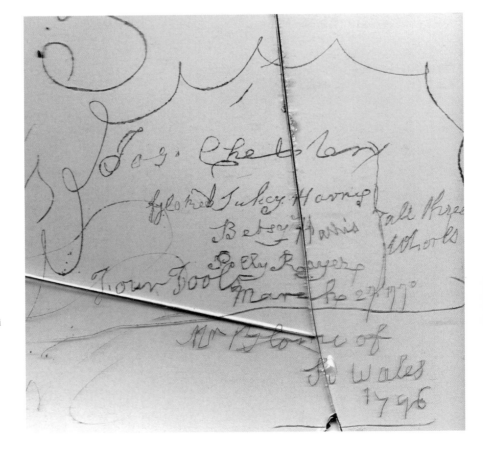

The window from the Red Lion is held at the Gloucester Folk Museum. Unfortunately it is broken, but the graffiti can still be seen, including the section about Jos Chester and the 'three whores', as shown in this scan of the glass. *(Gloucester City Museums)*

The inn in Hare Lane was operating from at least 1703, as in Easter of that year the Chamberlain was presented to the Gloucester City Quarter Session 'for not repairing the high way in Haire Lane from the Red Lion back dore to the Alvin Gate.' I have seen no other mention of this inn after 1722.

The Red Lion in Northgate Street, on the other hand, survived into the twentieth century. It was described as 'an ancient and well accustomed inn' in the *Gloucester Journal* of 1750 and in 1769 Joseph Pitt's Stage Wagon ran three times a week from there to the Sun in Cirencester. The building fell into other use around the end of the eighteenth century until, on 20 October 1811, an application was made for a licence renewal by a H. Wilton, who 'hath purchased the . . . Buildings lately occupied by William Powell Coachmaker . . . heretofore used as an inn called as known by the name or Sign of the Red Lion, and . . . is desirous of converting the same again into an inn or tavern.' The application was obviously successful as the Red Lion is again found in alehouse licensing records from that point.

The Red Lion was a timber-framed building at no. 84 in old street numbering. By 1919 the numbering had changed to 41 and it was owned by Arnold Perrett & Co. It was referred to the competition authority in that year and was closed. It was demolished in the mid-1970s to make way for the hideously boring retail buildings that now blight the area. Prior to its demolition archaeologists found a first-floor window pane with eighteenth-century graffiti scratched into it, the most interesting of which was a list of names: 'Jos Chester, Sukey Harris, Betsy Harris, Polly Rayner.' The latter three are bracketed with the words 'all three whores' and underneath is written 'Four Fools March 27th 1770.' Little is known about the ladies mentioned, but Jos, or Joseph, Chester was curate of Sandhurst Church! The window is in the possession of Gloucester Folk Museum.

Saracen's Head, Eastgate Street _____

Record of the Saracen's Head is found in the earliest alehouse licensing records I have been able to read, dating from 1680. It was located at no. 34, immediately to the east of the Bluecoat Hospital, opened as a school for poor boys just a few years earlier in

REF: 466
MAP: A
STATUS: Demolished
DATE: By 1680 to 1961
LOCATION: 25 Eastgate Street

Eastgate Sreet looking to the Cross in about 1948 showing the Saracen's Head Hotel in the foreground on the right.

1668. The school was a legacy of Sir Thomas Rich and later became Sir Thomas Rich's School.

The Saracen's Head was originally a small, non-descript pub, although Causton's Map of 1843 shows it extending back as far as New Inn Lane. It was entirely rebuilt in 1890, when the whole area was redeveloped and the Bluecoat Hospital was replaced by the Guildhall. The new Saracen's Head, owned by Francis Wintle, Forest Brewery, Mitcheldean, was far more impressive. It was a hotel with public, saloon, snug and lounge bars, bedrooms with hot and cold running water and electric fires and a yard with stabling.

In modern street numbering, post 1920, the Saracen's Head became no. 25. It continued trading until 1961, when the 'extinction of licence' is recorded on 5 April. The building was demolished in 1964 to make way for a new development and Dorothy Perkins is now on the site.

Talbot Inn, Southgate Street

REF: 524

MAP: G

STATUS: Building in different use

DATE: by 1722 to mid-1970s

LOCATION: 67 Southgate Street

The Talbot Inn was a tall three-storey brick-built building with a gabled roof located on the east side of Southgate Street just before Commercial Road, opposite Kimbrose. It was numbered 117, becoming no. 67 under the new street numbering. It is probably the only remaining part of an originally much larger inn, which was recorded in licensing records at least as far back as 1722 and must have stood on or close to the site of the St George (p. 33). By 1724 it was one of a number of Gloucester pubs with a cockpit.

There are few records relating to the Talbot throughout the eighteenth and nineteenth centuries. By 1901 the *Ancient Order of the Foresters Guide to Gloucester* carries an advert for the Talbot boasting 'the Largest and Best fitted Saloon Bar in the City' and the proprietor, E. Kilminster, was band master of (Kilminster's) Military and String Bands. By 1934 it was owned by the Stroud Brewery and in the early 1970s it had a reputation as being a cider pub.

The Talbot Hotel closed in the mid-1970s and in 1978 it became home to Severn Sound, the first local radio station in Gloucestershire, which started transmissions on 23 October 1980. Severn Sound moved out in 1998 to Bridge Studios in the

Far right: Severn Sound logo at launch in October 1980. *(Gloucestershire Archives with permission from Heart FM)*

Eastgate Shopping Centre and in March 2009 it was rebranded Heart 102.4. Owned by Global Radio, most of its output is now networked from London.

The old Talbot building was left empty for several years before being converted into nineteen apartments in 2004.

Three Cocks, Three Cocks Lane

Just at the end of the pedestrianised area in Westgate Street is a narrow street leading to St Mary's Square, which revels under the bizarre name of Three Cocks Lane. The reason for the odd name dates back to the eighteenth century when it was renamed for the Three Cocks Inn, which stood on the western side of the lane near the junction with St Mary's Square. This strikes me as an unsatisfactory explanation – it is a lane with an odd name because it was named after a pub with an odd name. I have been unable to shed any light on why the inn was so called, but presumably it relates to cockfighting which was popular in the city's inns.

In medieval times, the lane was much more sensibly called Abbey Lane (or Abbeylone) as it gave access to the western gateway in the abbey wall. The name changed by 1649 to Portcullis Lane, named after a different inn, although the first mention in licensing records of the Portcullis Inn is from 1686 when it was owned by Thomas Ady; it was still listed in 1720.

The lane became Three Cocks Lane at some time between 1721 and 1743, but Three Cocks Inn is seen in licensing records by at least 1680, when it was owned by William Merrett, so the change in street name was presumably due to the closure of the Portcullis Inn.

The landlord of the Three Cocks in 1705 was William Laurence, who was fined for 'suffering tippling on ye Lord's Day'. He must have moved on or mended his ways because by 1724 the Three Cocks claimed to be the usual lodging place for clergy travelling on the coach service between Oxford and South Wales.

The inn was sold at auction on 25 June 1878, one of 20 lots sold by Messrs. Bruton, Knowles & Bruton at the Corn Exchange. The lot consisted of the inn, a dwelling house, stable and courtyard 'in the occupation of Mr Barber' and a number of other adjoining buildings, including a malthouse at the rear. This is the last mention I've found for the Three Cocks Inn and the street was renamed to St Mary's Street by 1883, reverting back to Three Cocks Lane only in relatively recent times, presumably following the Westgate redevelopment.

REF: 533
MAP: B
STATUS: Demolished
DATE: By 1680 to 1878
LOCATION: Three Cocks Lane

Union, Westgate Street

The Union occupies 43–5 Westgate Street, originally two separate buildings both of which date from the sixteenth century. Originally they both looked the same, but today the left-hand building is gabled, whereas the right is square-fronted. This is because, in common with many other buildings in Gloucester, the right-hand building was re-fronted in the eighteenth century. If you look closely you will notice that there is nothing behind the top left and right windows, they are just there for show.

The left-hand building, no. 22 in the old street numbering, was a pub by 1680, when it was called the Sword and the licensee was John Taylor. The last licence that I've found for a pub of this name is 1736 and I don't find mention of it as the Union until a single reference in *Hunt's Directory* of 1847, when Thomas Maynard is listed as landlord. By

REF: 558
MAP: A
STATUS: Trading
DATE: By 1680 to date
LOCATION: 43–5, Westgate Street, GL1 2NW
CONTACT: 01452 521750

1849 it is listed as John Dobells Wine & Spirit Merchants, which later became Dobell, Mott & Co. wine vaults. The next mention of the Union is in 1920.

It has been suggested to me that the name refers to the Acts of Union with Ireland, which dates from 1800. A resurrection of the name in 1920 may have been inspired by the Government of Ireland Act of that year, which brought to an end the Irish War of Independence and created Northern Ireland.

About this time the Union became 43 Westgate Street following Gloucester's street renumbering. It was tied to the Stroud Brewery in the 1950s, which was subsequently taken over by Whitbread, who in 1990 set about making improvements to the pub. The term 'improvements' when used in relation to pubs can be controversial, especially in the 1990s when it was often synonymous with the word vandalism, but the Union didn't fare too badly, although leaded light windows and oak panelling were removed from the façade. The most significant aspect of the improvement was that the pub was enlarged to incorporate no. 45, the building which was once the workshop of the tailor John Pritchard, the real 'Tailor of Gloucester' made famous by Beatrix Potter.

In 1897 Beatrix Potter heard the story about John Pritchard, who had gone home for the weekend leaving an uncompleted waistcoat and returned on Monday to find it finished. He capitalised on this mystery by displaying the waistcoat in his shop window with a sign saying, 'Come to Pritchard where the waistcoats are made at night by the fairies.' The true story of how the waistcoat got finished did not come to light for some years and is less quaint and totally devoid of cute animals. Apparently the

The Union before expanding into no. 45.
(Reg Woolford)

tailor's workers had been out on a bit of a session on the Saturday night and couldn't get home. One of them had a key to the shop, so they stayed the night in the workroom. The following day, being Sunday, they didn't dare go out in their dishevelled state, so to pass the time until it got dark they finished the waistcoat – all except the last button hole, which was explained by the note they left: 'No more twist.'

A Whitbread exec obviously latched onto the Tailor of Gloucester connection and, not unreasonably, changed the name of the pub to 'The Tailor's House'. The improvements can't have been bad because the pub made its only appearances in CAMRA's *Good Beer Guide* in 1990–1.

The name reverted to the Union in about 2003, but the pub sign now suggests a link with the European Union rather than Ireland. The pub itself retains an old-world charm with low beamed ceilings and traditional pub fittings and it generally has a couple of decent beers on offer. The large bar counter fills most of the original building on the left, with the right-hand building laid out with tables. The fact that they were once two separate buildings is highlighted

by the flag-stoned entrance, which was once an alleyway between them. The building was apparently haunted, but rather than utilise this fact for marketing purposes, the current owners tell me that they had an exorcism and all is now quiet.

Upper George, Westgate Street

REF: 560
MAP: A
STATUS: Building in different use
DATE: By 1680 to 1869
LOCATION: 50 Westgate Street

On the north side of Westgate Street, between College Court and College Street, opposite the entrance to the Fountain, is a narrow but impressively ornate three-storey red-brick building. Originally no. 138, it is no. 50 in modern street numbering and it currently houses KFC. Clearly it is far too good to be just the home of a fast food outlet.

From 1913 to 1927 this building housed the Palladium Picture Theatre, an early silent cinema. It was converted from a shop, but before that it was a pub, the Upper George.

The Upper George started out as just the George, but this was very confusing as there was another, older, pub called the George further down Westgate Street, which later became the Lower George (see p. 27). The Upper George is found in licensing records by 1680, when the publican was John Soule.

In the eighteenth century the Upper George was 'a most notorious house of entertainment and hard drinking . . . attended by gentlemen of the highest position, and by men and prostitutes of the lowest order.' It was renowned for bare knuckle prize-fighting and the landlord was described as 'the prince of good fellows and the generous patron of every game and sport.'

By the later eighteenth century coffee houses became popular and by 1802 the Upper George was Gloucester's the leading coffee house. It is still referred to as a coffee house in papers of 1835, but its alehouse licence was retained throughout the period, so it seems that it continued to sell something stronger than coffee.

It is possible that the Upper George was renamed the Cathedral Tavern by 1867, although it is listed by its original name in *Bretherton's Directory* of 1869. This is the last mention that I have found for the pub.

KFC, formerly the Upper George.

Welsh Harp Inn, London Road

The Welsh Harp was on London Road 'without the Lower North Gate', opposite Oxford Street, at no. 36 in modern street numbering – the Lower (or Outer) North Gate was located roughly on the junction of Bruton Way with London Road/ Northgate Street. The pub dates back to the early eighteenth century, although I have only found a single reference to it in alehouse licensing records of that time, in 1722. As might be expected from its prime location on the London Road, the Welsh Harp was a coaching inn. There was also another Welsh Harp listed from 1722 to 1806, in the West Ward.

At one time the Welsh Harp was tied to the Bristol Brewery Georges & Co. Ltd. and a souvenir book for the brewery shows an old building set back from the road with two large bays added to the front. The building is rendered and etched with a brick pattern with the pub name painted in large letters above the upper windows. Comparing the photographs shown here, the road appears to have been widened, causing the removal of the additions to the front of the building along with the adjacent buildings to the west, leaving the Welsh Harp with a plain façade onto London Road.

The Welsh Harp made CAMRA's *Good Beer Guide* in 1979 and 1982 and when I started drinking shortly after that it was still a good pub. A good, authentic drinkers' pub, the main bar stretched back quite a long way and behind that there was a good sized entertainment bar and skittle alley where they frequently hosted bands. In later years the pub went down hill quite badly and in 2007, by which time it was owned by

REF: 576
MAP: E
STATUS: Closed
DATE: By 1722 to 2007
LOCATION: 36 London Road

London Road in about 1963, showing the Welsh Harp on the right. *(Reg Woolford)*

No. 36, formerly the
Welsh Harp 2009.

Admiral Taverns, its name was changed to No. 36 and it was given a dreadful, messy
white paint job.

If things had been looking bleak for the pub before, they now got increasingly
worse. In January 2008 it was raided by the police following complaints of drug abuse,
disorderly conduct and noise. It transpired that, although the premises were licensed,
the licensee was not eligible to hold a licence, so No. 36 had the dubious honour of
being the first pub in the city to be closed by police under section 19 of the Criminal
Justice and Police Act of 2001.

Admiral Taverns expressed the hope to have the pub reopened as soon as possible,
but at the time of writing, two years later, the pub remains empty, boarded up and for
sale.

3

Pubs in Historic or Interesting Buildings

Sometimes buildings are purpose built as pubs, but quite often they are not. Especially in recent times, pubs have increasingly been opened in buildings which already have long and interesting histories behind them. This chapter looks at some of the more remarkable buildings behind Gloucester's pubs.

Café René, Marylone

Although Café René's address is Southgate Street, the entrance is actually tucked away on the left-hand side of St Mary's Lane or Marylone. The lane is probably of Saxon origin, but is first mentioned in 1316. It originally ran from Southgate Street, past St Mary de Crypt Churchyard and the precinct wall of Greyfriars, to the east wall of the town.

Café René is a great pub situated in a medieval building opposite the churchyard. Entering from Marylone you pass through a large outer foyer area into the dimly lit, atmospheric bar with wine bottles lining the walls. The bar is divided into two areas – the main bar is to the left, with the bar counter running along the back. Beer casks sit directly behind the bar, from which the beer is dispensed directly. Straight ahead is an area laid out for use as a dining room, at the back of which is a superb old, manually operated dumb waiter in which food is delivered from the kitchens upstairs.

The buildings which house the Café René have a lot of history and legend surrounding them. Just inside the bar is a circular brick structure which surrounds an authentic well of Roman origin. Franciscan friars, known as grey friars from the colour

REF: 88
MAP: A
STATUS: Trading
DATE: 1979 to date
LOCATION: 31 Southgate Street, GL1 1TP
CONTACT: 01452 309340

A Roman well once in the courtyard but now inside the bar of the Café René.

of their robes, arrived in Gloucester in 1231 and established their monastery nearby at Greyfrairs and it is claimed that they used the site for making beer and wine. Given the presence of the well this is quite possible. The grey friars were also instrumental in bringing piped water into the city from springs on Robinswood Hill, which would undoubtedly have been used in brewing. Following the dissolution, the monastery was immediately turned into a brewery to utilise the fresh water supply, but whether that included the Café René buildings is not clear.

Ancient origins are also attributed to the cellars beneath the pub. Some of these cellars are still in use as a cellar bar, but they extend far beyond this. As with many other cellars in Gloucester these are said to be part of an extensive system of tunnels, in this case extending as far as Barnwood. This seems unlikely, but the cellars may well have extended into the crypt of St Mary de Crypt Church next door, and possibly as far as Greyfriars.

The Café René claims that their tunnels were used not only by monks as escape routes during the reformation, but also by Oliver Cromwell to escape cavaliers during the Civil War. Neither of these claims are likely to be accurate, although if the building was used by the friars they may well have hidden in the cellars and perhaps died in the building. The latter claim especially sounds suspect as Gloucester famously held out against the crown in the Civil War, so no such escape should have been necessary.

To make sense of the history of the Café René buildings you have to realise that, prior to remodelling in the 1980s, the area that now forms the main part of the bar, the part with the well in it, was an outside courtyard. This courtyard has a long association with pubs as, going back to the eighteenth century, it was the yard of the Golden Heart Inn (see p. 42).

The pub's cellars once housed Washbourn's Wine Vaults, but it did not actually become a pub until the late 1970s when it was refurbished to become a wine bar called the Inner Court. This name reflects the fact that the courtyard in the middle was still open. During the refurbishment it is said that a series of sealed rooms were discovered containing what appeared to be top-secret documents. The Home Office apparently quickly swooped in to take everything away, but it is rumoured that the building was a secret MI6 emergency headquarters from the Second World War.

In 1987 an application was made to alter and extend the pub, including covering over the courtyard. It reopened as Greyfriars, which is how I first remember it. At this time the well was covered over by glass at floor level with a fake skeleton at the bottom and an African grey parrot roamed freely around the bar. Upstairs was a pool room. I also remember that at some point around this time the cellar was turned into a separate bar called the Underground.

Unsurprisingly for a building of this age, there are numerous ghost stories attached to it, including the ghosts of the grey friars mentioned above. The renovation work is said to have stirred up the spirits and staunch workmen were driven from the building by unexplained instances of electrical equipment turning on and off by itself and furniture flying around. Gloucester's ghost lady, Lyn Cinderey, carries out regular overnight investigations here and I have attended one of these myself. Although on this occasion no ghosts presented themselves, it did provide the opportunity for a snoop around the cellars.

The cellars known as Deep Six: keepers of MI6 secrets?

Sadly, whereas the cellar bar and the tunnel leading from it are brick vaulted, as you move back you go beneath the Eastgate Shopping Centre and the cellar there now consists of a concrete roof and supporting pillars dating from about 1973. The place is also piled high with junk and rubble. Beyond that you get to the deepest cellars still accessible which, for reasons I've been unable to ascertain, are known as Deep Six. These still have brick vaulted ceilings, plus more modern brick partitions – is this where MI6's secrets were stored?

Anyway, back to the history. By March 1998 the pub was owned by the Little Pub Company, who converted it to a French style restaurant, café and bar and changed the name to the Café René. In September 2002, following another make-over, it was renamed again to the Courtyard Tapas Bar & Restaurant, selling, as the name suggests, tapas. It also boasted a selection of fifty quality wines. This name change was short lived and it reverted back to the Café René.

In 2005 the Café René was the first pub in Gloucestershire granted permission for 24 hour opening. There was much outcry in the national press about the effect that 24-hour drinking would have on the populace – 'People will run amok in the street on week-long drinking binges!' they wailed in horror. The jury is still out on whether 24-hour opening is a good thing, but I haven't noticed blood flowing in the streets and it means that at the weekend, for a small entry charge after 11 p.m., you can carry on drinking in the Café René until late in a welcome alternative to a nightclub.

Dick Whittington, Westgate Street

REF: 150
MAP: B
STATUS: Trading
DATE: 1982 to date
LOCATION: 100, Westgate Street, GL1 2PE
CONTACT: 01452 502039

The Dick Whittington is located at the lower end of Westgate Street, next door to St Nicholas Church. It occupies a magnificent fifteenth-century building called St Nicholas House, which had a long and interesting history before becoming a pub. Originally built as a merchant's house, the area is mentioned in *The Rental* of 1455; 'The Prior of Llanthony hold all those houses and buildings . . . from . . . Abbey Lane to the common and processional way there near the chancel of the Church of Saint Nicholas and the tenements of Richard Whittington, lord of Staunton, which are called "Raton Row" and "Ashwell's Place".'

These tenements must have been removed to make way for St Nicholas House, which was built in the late fifteenth century. Richard Whittington, Lord of Staunton, was not *the* Dick Whittington of pantomime fame, but was probably the son of Robert of Pauntley, Dick Whittington's brother.

The story of Dick Whittington being a poor boy going off to London with a spotted hanky on a stick does have a basis in fact. He was a real person who lived from about 1350 to 1423. Born at Pauntley in the Forest of Dean, he did go off to find his fortune in London. At the age of thirteen he was apprenticed to a London merchant banker, John Fitzwaryn. He turned out to be quite the whiz as a businessman,

A view from the side of the Dick Whittington, showing the original fifteenth-century building beyond the eighteenth-century façade.

becoming the greatest merchant in medieval England. Oh yes, and he did become Mayor of London four times, in 1397, 1398, 1407 and 1420.

Dick Whittington is not the only interesting history associated with St Nicholas House. Elizabeth I is alleged to have stayed here when she visited Gloucester in 1574. There used to be a fine wooden-panelled room with a carved fireplace bearing her royal coat of arms, but the whole thing was sold off to a Chicago collector for £750 in 1907. Columnist for the *Gloucester Citizen*, Martin Kirby (no relation), tried to track this down but fears that it ended up in a brothel which has since been demolished.

In the early seventeenth century the house was leased by John Taylor, a council member, who got into a lot of trouble for having the mayor and alderman round while he had servants dead and dying from the plague in the house. One poor servant girl was apparently left in the cellar to die of the plague, untreated, in 1604, and it is speculated that she is one of several ghosts said to haunt the building. Despite this and the fact that he was imprisoned several times, John Taylor became mayor of Gloucester in 1613, but was removed from office for embezzlement, receiving bribes, extortion and drunkenness. It almost makes our politicians seem dull by comparison!

The merchant's house underwent alterations in the sixteenth century and the magnificent brick façade onto Westgate Street was added in the early eighteenth century, possibly by James Pitt, licensee of the King's Head Inn which adjoined St Nicholas House on the east side. In 1822 the house was used for public worship by Protestant dissenters, and it became known as Church Court until 1846. It was converted into a shop and dwelling in the late nineteenth century and was home to Merrylees, Pugh & Co., who manufactured leather belting for machinery.

In the early 1980s St Nicholas House was one of the first restoration projects of Gloucester Historic Buildings Ltd, a building preservation trust, a joint charity of the Civic Trust and City Council. Renovations revealed part of a decayed fifteenth- or sixteenth-century wall painting, probably a townscape, and a late sixteenth-century

painted dado of fruit, flowers and foliage, both on plaster, which is described as 'a rare and significant survival'. The building is Grade I listed, described as 'of high architectural quality' and is one of only forty-two Scheduled Ancient Monuments in Gloucester. It subsequently opened as the Dick Whittington public house in about 1982, which roughly coincided with my early drinking days. My friends and I frequented it quite often, drawn especially by the availability of Theakston's Old Peculiar. However, in those less tolerant days the Dick Whittington was one of a number of pubs that would forcibly evict you for no other crime than wearing a leather jacket, and since this was our regular attire we didn't always get to stay long enough to drink a pint!

Inside the Dick Whittington is very atmospheric – large and airy for such an old building it has tall ceilings with authentic wooden beams and the wonderful medieval building is blended with a large Victorian style bar. It is now one of three pubs in Gloucester belonging to the Chapman Group; the other two being the New Inn (p. 14) and the Station (p. 126). A favourite of CAMRA for some time, it was awarded CAMRA Gloucester City Pub of the Year for four consecutive years in 2005–8 and earned a place in the *Good Beer Guide* in 1994 and 2006–8. Unfortunately, a series of management changes resulted in it losing the honour and being removed from the 2009 *Good Beer Guide*.

At the end of 2009 yet another new manager was brought in and things looked very positive, but after just a few weeks they decided they'd had enough and walked out just before Christmas. This is extremely disappointing; the Dick Whittington is potentially a superb pub and if only the Chapman Group could stop meddling and allow a decent landlord to stay for more than a few weeks I am sure that it could once again grace the hallowed pages of the *Good Beer Guide*.

Linden Tree, Bristol Road

REF: 290
MAP: H
STATUS: Trading
DATE: 1836 to date
LOCATION: 73–5, Bristol Road, GL1 5SN
CONTACT: 01452 527869

The Linden Tree at is at the end of a Grade II listed Georgian terrace of ten houses built by Thomas Fulljames in the Greek Revival style starting in 1836. The terrace runs from 73 to 91 Bristol Road (odd numbers) between Theresa Street and Alma Place and was originally called Theresa Place. All the buildings are two storeys with basements and attics and are set back from the street behind front gardens.

Previously no. 73 was the Norfolk House Hotel, which once housed a micro-brewery known as the Hawthorn Brewery. The name was changed to the Linden Tree in 1984 and it was acquired by Wadworth of Devizes in 1988.

Although a bit of a walk out of town, the Linden Tree is well worth the effort. Inside, the pub is very rustic and traditional looking, albeit that many of the features are not authentic. It has beamed ceilings, exposed stone walls, an open log fire with an unusual canopy, carriage lamps and even a carriage wheel as a seating area boundary. When it made its debut appearance as the Linden Tree in the 1985 supplement of CAMRA's

Real Ale in Gloucestershire it was described as a 'well-kept "country pub" in town.' More importantly, it continued its reputation for good real ale; it is in the 2010 CAMRA *Good Beer Guide* – its twenty-fifth appearance since 1975, by far the most entries of any pub in Gloucester.

Monks' Retreat, Westgate Street

Underneath the Fleece Hotel in Westgate Street was an unusual bar called the Monks' Retreat; in fact it was frequently referred to as 'The Most Curious Bar in England'. What I didn't realise when I used to occasionally drink here in the early 1980s was that this 'cellar' is in fact a twelfth-century tunnel-vaulted undercroft. I paid scant regard to the arches supported on round Norman pillars, and had no idea that it had been described as the finest example of its type to be found in Northern Europe.

A number of theories have been put forward as to its original purpose. Some say it was built as a charnel house (somewhere to store bones and corpses – nice!) for St Mary de Grace Church, which used to stand in the middle of Westgate Street. Others claim that it was a chapel in its own right, and a holy water stoup is said to have been found there. However, the most likely explanation is that it was just a cellar. Although this sounds obvious, this theory was not put forward until it was examined by an expert in medieval buildings in 1860.

Gloucester prospered in the twelfth century and some merchants got very rich. With that wealth they were able to build stone houses and stone cellars or 'undercrofts', which allowed foodstuffs and valuables to be kept both cool and protected from fire – a major problem in towns densely packed with wooden houses. I discussed the Fleece Hotel in Chapter 1 (p. 17), where we saw that *The Rental* of 1455 records that the cellar was part of a tenement held by Benedict the Cordwainer in the time of Henry III, so it is possible that he had it built.

Inevitably this cellar comes with its own tunnel rumours. There is a tradition that there is an underground passage starting in the cellar which joined the Fleece Inn to the abbey. In fact, some say that it is part of a tunnel which ran from Llanthony Priory to the Llanthony Bridge Inn before reaching the Fleece and continuing on

REF: 321

MAP: A

STATUS: Closed

DATE: By 1927 to 2002

LOCATION: 19 Westgate Street

The Monks' Retreat, Gloucester.

to the abbey. Part of the tunnel was said to remain until relatively recently, but this was more likely to have simply been part of the larger original cellar which extended under Westgate Street and was blocked up when the weight of modern traffic threatened its collapse.

The Monks' Retreat has been licensed several times, the latest venture being established on 17 October 1998. Now, like the Fleece above it, it is closed and its fate awaits the outcome of the GHURC Blackfriars redevelopment.

Old Bell, Southgate Street

REF: 354
MAP: A
STATUS: Trading
DATE: 1912 (as part of the Bell) to date
LOCATION: 9a, Southgate Street, GL1 1TG
CONTACT: 01452 332993

Just a short way from Gloucester Cross, in Southgate Street, is one of the most ornate buildings in the city. Like most buildings in any city you need to look above the street level to appreciate it, because on the ground floor it has a fairly unremarkable twentieth-century shop front which is, at the time of writing, home to a Costa Coffee shop. However, if you cast your eyes upwards, you find a particularly impressive Jacobean timber façade which dates from about 1664–5 and was designed by one Gilbert à Becket. The upper floors of this fine Grade I listed building are home to the Old Bell.

The building was originally built for Thomas Yate, apothecary and younger son of the Lords of Arlingham. He was an alderman of Gloucester and mayor in 1665. There is a superb, highly decorative fireplace in the front room on the first floor, which is now the main bar of the Old Bell. Bearing the date 1650, the date of Yates' first marriage, it may be several years older than the construction of the house and appears to have been designed for somewhere much larger – it dominates the small, square room, which is still decorated with Jacobean style panelled walls, and it appears to be slightly too tall for the ceiling. The fireplace displays the Yate family coat of arms, crossed with those of Berkeley. Four seated cherubs are carved into the mantel, which, it has been suggested, represent Yates' first four sons. One of these has six fingers on one hand, as, apparently, did one of the Yates boys.

It has been suggested that much of the timber in this magnificent old building may have come from the *Mayflower* of Pilgrim Fathers fame. This legendary voyage to America happened in 1620 when the ship was hired from the Virginia Company, owned by the powerful Gloucestershire family, the Berkeleys. By 1624 the ship had fallen into decay and the Virginia Company had folded after a tax dispute with the king. The boat was scrapped and the timber sold to an unnamed buyer who, it is suggested, may have been the Berkeleys – remember the Berkeley's coat of arms on the fireplace. Supporting this theory is the fact that the windows look suspiciously like those found on ships of that period, and during restoration in 2005 a large deposit of salt was found behind some of the beams, suggesting that the timbers may have been used at sea.

In the late eighteenth century James Lee, tobacconist and 'bluemaker' painted the whole façade blue. Because of this the building became commonly known as 'The Old Blue Shop'. Traces of a dark grey-blue substance have been found on the façade, presumably from this time. There are indications that this isn't the only colourful period in its history as fine traces of an orange russet colour have also been found.

The building spent a long period as a tea warehouse. At the turn of the nineteenth century Mr Clark, tea merchant, erected a large fascia board announcing in 2ft high letters, 'THE CITY TEA WAREHOUSE', along with a huge metal tea canister on the parapet. He would surely turn in his grave to see the place become a coffee shop!

From 1912 the upper floors were leased to the Bell Inn next door (see p. 35) for use as function and meeting rooms. The Bell was closed in 1967 and demolished to make way for the new Eastgate Shopping Centre, but these rooms survived and became known as the Old Bell, a ghost of the former inn.

Speaking of ghosts, apparently, not all of the old residents have left – the Old Bell is said to be haunted. Back in 2005 members of the Paranormal Investigation Team carried out extensive research; the landlady believed that it had four or five ghosts, including a cavalier who had stabbed her, and mischievous Martha who pinches men's bottoms. Although the latter sounds more like a cover story than a haunting, the team put the Old Bell above all of the other buildings they'd investigated in terms of paranormal activity.

In May 2006 the building was sold at auction with a guide price of more than £1.55 million and it closed down shortly afterwards. It remained empty for over a year until it was sub-let in October 2008 to Paul Soden, owner of Café René, who planned to convert it to Gloucester's only Japanese themed bar and restaurant. Unfortunately the sushi venture didn't work out, but the restaurant reopened in March 2009 as the Tiger's Eye Restaurant, a 'black rock grill dining experience' which I can highly recommend. The bar itself, which used to tend to overly loud music, flashing lights and, worst of all, karaoke, is now a vodka bar, but if you need a chaser for all that vodka it also sells a real ale. The bar retains all of its period features and has an excellent laid back, mellow feel to it.

Regal, King's Square

REF: 437
MAP: A
STATUS: Trading
DATE: 1996 to date
LOCATION: 33, St Aldate St, King's Square, GL1 1RP
CONTACT: 01452 332344

Situated on the north end of King's Square, the Regal was Gloucester's first J.D. Wetherspoon pub, opening on 3 April 1996. It has an impressive, if slightly austere looking, Bath Stone frontage and before becoming a pub, as the name suggests, the Regal was a cinema.

Designed by the architect William Glenn, it was built on St Aldate Church's graveyard. Construction started in 1939 but was delayed due to the war and it didn't actually open until 19 March 1956. Opened as the Regal, this was the last ABC cinema to be given a 'proper' name, but in March 1963 it was renamed the ABC in line with company policy.

During the sixteen-year hiatus in building, plans were updated, including alterations to allow its use as a theatre, and on 18 March 1963 the Beatles played there on tour with Chris Montez and Tommy Roe (who?).

I have fond memories of the ABC as I was lucky enough to be born just in time to enjoy the phenomenon of Saturday morning cinema, before Saturday morning TV took over. We were the 'ABC Minors', and not only did you get to see your weekly helping of cartoons, a regular serial and a film all on the big screen, but it was also a great social occasion. And it was a big screen, because this was before the move to multi-screen cinemas. A really good Saturday morning concluded with a visit to the adjacent Wimpy bar for burgers and ice-cream floats. This was opened in 1961, taking over part of the cinema's large waiting area.

By 1974 the cinema was owned by EMI, who altered it to a three-screen multiplex, reopening it on 22 July 1974 as the ABC 123. In February 1987 the ABC became the Cannon, but not for long because on 12 December 1990 it was closed and a new multiplex cinema opened at the Peel Centre on the southern outskirts of town two days later.

And so the old cinema remained empty for several years. Great plans were debated about turning it back into a theatre or concert venue, but ultimately, as

Below: Souvenir brochure marking the opening of the Regal Cinema. *(Gloucestershire Archives)*

we know, it became a pub. It was bought by J.D.Wetherspoon, who resurrected the name the Regal and refitted it to be reminiscent of the old cinema.

Inside, the Regal is so vast that you expect it to house aircraft. There is a small entrance area with seating, from which you go down a flight of steps into the huge single bar area. At the far end, another flight of steps takes you up onto the old stage, where there is another seating area in front of a vast glass wall where the cinema screen used to be. A large stuffed King Kong looms from the balcony.

Originally the Regal followed the Wetherspoon philosophy of no music or games machines, but it is now a Lloyds No 1 Bar, with loud music and a dance floor. It stays open until 2 a.m. at the weekend, making it a popular and welcome alternative to a nightclub, and despite its size it is invariably packed. If the more traditional Wetherspoon philosophy is more to your taste, try the Water Poet (see p. 128).

ASSOCIATED
BRITISH
CINEMAS
LIMITED

REGAL

GLOUCESTER

✱ *19th MARCH, 1956*

MANAGING DIRECTOR   D. J. GOODLATTE

Head Office   10-31 Golden Square   London   W 1

Page One

Robert Raikes's House, Southgate Street

REF: 443/207

MAP: A

STATUS: Trading

DATE: 1975 to date

LOCATION: 36-38,
Southgate Street, GL1 2DR

CONTACT: 01452 526685

Opposite St Mary de Crypt Church in Southgate Street is a marvellous timber-framed building with three gabled bays which jetty out at each storey in an impressively Tudor manner. It is a very ornate building described as a good example of West Country decorative timber-framing. Lately most of this impressive building has been home to a less than impressive pub, the Golden Cross. However, the current owners, Samuel Smiths, have recently carried out considerable restoration to bring the building back to its former glory. In November 2008 they reopened the pub under a new name: Robert Raikes's House.

The building dates from 1560, when it was built as a merchant's house. It was divided into two units in the eighteenth century. The left-hand unit, now no. 38, was two gables wide and the right-hand unit, now no. 36, was just one gable wide. The reason for the renaming of the pub is that Robert Raikes, founder of the Sunday School movement and editor of the *Gloucester Journal*, published the paper from this building from 1758 and later lived here.

Robert Raikes's House in 2009, shortly after restoration.

The *Gloucester Journal* was founded by Robert Raikes's father and the first edition was published on Monday 9 April 1722 from an office in Northgate Street opposite the New Inn. It quickly established itself as a leading provincial newspaper of the eighteenth century. Raikes the elder died in 1757 and his son Robert Raikes the younger took over editorship of the paper and moved it into what is now 38 Southgate Street in 1758.

At this time the Raikes family lived at Ladybellegate House in Longsmith Street. Following Robert Raikes's marriage to Anne Trigge in 1767 his mother, Mary, moved into what is now 36 Southgate Street, where she lived for the rest of her life. In 1772 the rest of the Raikes family moved next door into no. 38. By the time Raikes retired in 1802 he had moved to Bell Lane. He sold the paper to David Walker, publisher of the *Hereford Journal*, who moved the offices to Westgate Street. The *Journal* partnered with the *Citizen* in 1879 making it the second oldest continuously published newspaper in the world – a pity that its operation has now almost entirely moved out of its home city to Cheltenham.

(Gloucester Citizen)

The old Raikes building continued as a merchant's house and shop. By 1901, The *Ancient Order of the Foresters Guide to Gloucester* carries an advert for The Southgate Vaults with offices in the old Raikes Building at 17 Southgate Street (the old street number for the smaller part) as well as in Longsmith Street. The larger building became the Dirty Duck restaurant in 1973, becoming the Golden Cross a few years later.

You would think that being in such a magnificent old building with important historical connections that it would have been a corker of a pub, but alas not so. It did manage a single appearance in the CAMRA *Good Beer Guide* in 1977, but by the time I first started drinking in the early 1980s it was lively, loud and full of young people, but not, in hindsight, necessarily a good pub. It was most notable to me for the fact that it stood in front of, and had a connecting alleyway to, my favourite pub, the Malt & Hops (p. 119). Since then it seemed to go into a terminal slump and several times has appeared on the verge of closing.

The recent restoration is therefore not before time and it has been very well done. Taking two years and an estimated £4.5 million, it has stripped the building back to its original state, but reflecting the extensions and alterations of the eighteenth and nineteenth centuries. The twentieth-century shop fronts have been removed and replaced with traditional looking wood framed walls and small leaded windows. Inside there are seven separate rooms, each individually furnished. The original large walled courtyard has also been resurrected behind the pub. This unfortunately necessitated the demolition of the Malt & Hops that previously occupied it, but given that this had long since closed and had no architectural merit whatsoever, it's only real loss is its nostalgia value. The only downside is that there is no real ale, as Samuel Smiths will not deliver it as far south as Gloucester.

Sloanes, Brunswick Road

Sloanes is located in Brunswick Road opposite the Gloucester City Museum. It is a good pub – open and spacious with a long wooden bar down the left-hand side boasting a good number of real ale bar pumps, which earned it a place in CAMRA's *Good Beer Guide* in 2001. The interior is modern, but the furniture consists of fairly typical pub tables and chairs, nothing too contemporary or wine-bar-ish. At quiet periods Sloanes is a good place to go to have a coffee or a meal and there are big screen TVs where they show major sporting events. At the weekend, however, it comes alive, joining in the party atmosphere of lower Eastgate Street and is packed with the pre-nightclub drinkers on which the area thrives.

The building in which Sloanes is located is an impressive Victorian three-storey red-brick structure which contrasts with the nasty modern brick building alongside. It is only recently that this building has been put to use as a pub. An inlaid plaque at the top of

REF: 480
MAP: F
STATUS: Trading
DATE: 1999 to date
LOCATION: 3, Brunswick Road, GL1 1HN
CONTACT: 01452 382080

the building's façade contains the name Caxton House, and it was built by the printer John Jennings, for whom the alleyway that runs to the right of the pub is named.

John Jennings was born in 1840 and after a seven-year apprenticeship he started his own printing business in Bell Lane in 1876. Caxton House was his family home, in front of the new printing works that he had built. Jennings died in 1923, but the business continued in his name with Caxton House becoming Jennings Printers and Stationers for many years before being converted to a pub.

Whitbread opened it first as the Hogshead on 3 January 1999 after a £953,000 conversion. It had become Sloanes by 2003.

Theatre Vaults, Westgate Street _____

REF: 529
MAP: A
STATUS: Building in different use
DATE: 1799 to 1958
LOCATION: 30 Westgate Street

Westgate Street in the 1890s. The Theatre Royal is in the foreground with the Theatre Vaults next door. *(Gloucestershire Archives)*

One of the most prominent buildings in Westgate Street is no. 30, on the north side of the street just a couple of doors down from 'Colonel Massey's House'. Once home to the Theatre Vaults, it stands out from the other buildings as the upper floors project out into the street, jettied from the ground floor in the medieval style. Unlike its neighbours, the building did not succumb to the craze for a new façade in the eighteenth and nineteenth century, but retains its gabled roof and stuccoed timber frame.

The building did not begin life as a pub, but was built in the early seventeenth century as a merchant's house. It was first occupied in 1622 by John Whithorne, a tailor, but by 1640 James Commeline the apothecary had the lease. The man was obviously jinxed: he came here hoping for a quiet life, having fled the religious turmoil of the Netherlands, and ended up slap bang in the middle of the Siege of Gloucester, just two doors away from Massey's HQ! On the evening of Friday 25 August 1643 he ended up sharing his chamber with a red hot cannon ball fired by the Royalist battery at Llanthony.

The building stayed in the hands of Commeline's descendants until 1746 when George Worrall, a partner in one of the city's many pin-making firms, took the lease. It finally fulfilled its higher purpose as a pub when it became the Theatre Vaults in 1799. Situated next door to the Theatre Royal, it provided access to the pit entrance of the theatre.

The theatre had been opened some years previously on 6 June 1791 by John Boles Watson and it was the most successful theatre built in Gloucester in the later eighteenth century. It was called the Theatre Royal from the late 1830s and was enlarged in 1859 by John Blinkhorn. It changed hands a number of times over the years, finally being acquired by Poole's in 1903, who in 1907 renamed it the Palace of Varieties, which became the Palace Theatre. On 6 March 1911 the Palace became a cinema. A Gloucester guide described it as 'one of the prettiest theatres in the provinces' and the elegant auditorium was described in an advert as 'one of the brightest, smartest and cosiest in the Empire.' It was closed by 1922 when Poole's acquired the Hippodrome in Eastgate Street (formerly the Rising Sun, see p. 123). The theatre was dismantled and the site was occupied by Woolworths stores until it moved to Eastgate Street in the 1970s. The site is now occupied by Poundstretcher, which is said to be haunted by actors of the past.

The Theatre Vaults was owned by Godsell & Sons and outlived the theatre for which it was named, continuing as a pub until its licence lapsed on 26 April 1958. The building currently houses 'Reflections', a salon.

4

The Docks

The Gloucester Docks, situated to the south of the city, encompass a water area of more than 14 acres. They opened for business in 1827 at the terminus of the new Gloucester to Sharpness Canal, allowing large sea-going ships to reach Gloucester. Before this The Quay on the River Severn was used and had been granted port status by Queen Elizabeth I in 1580.

Heavy industry sprang up along the canal, and heavy industry is thirsty work; consequently a lot of pubs also sprang up in the area. The early quay probably accounted for the popularity of Lower Westgate Street and The Quay as a location for pubs, but now it was the turn of the south of the city.

The docks trade started to fall off by the late nineteenth century. Gloucester continued as a commercial port, but traffic declined in the twentieth century and

The Dock main basin in its heyday.
(Gloucestershire Archives)

had virtually ended in the 1980s. The docks were allowed to fall into a sad state of dereliction and the associated industry closed or moved away. Luckily many of the warehouses still stand, giving a marvellous feel of history and attracting TV and film cameras.

Over recent years the docks have been subjected to a lot of regeneration, undergoing a shift to retail, office and accommodation use. In May 2009 the area was given a huge boost with the opening of the £250 million Gloucester Quays complex. As I write, Phase 2 has started to open, bringing restaurants and bars. This is a welcome addition to the city, but I hope that it will complement rather than compete with the existing, more traditional pubs in the area.

The Docks now: Tall Ships Festival, May 2009.

Baker Street, Southgate Street

Baker Street is right at the end of Southgate Street, just before it becomes Bristol Road, on the corner of Baker Street for which the pub is now named. Prior to the 1980s it was called the Hauliers Arms and the first mention that I have found for it is 1852, when it was in a row of buildings known as Raglan Terrace.

This was the height of the dock industry, and the name suggests an association with the haulage business carried out at the docks. It is the furthest south of the pubs that I have defined as docks pubs and therefore seems a bit far out, but this date roughly coincides with the arrival of the High Orchard Iron Works and the Hauliers didn't have to wait long before it found itself in the midst of the docks-based industrial area as the Atlas Ironworks (which were taken over by Fielding and Platt in 1866) soon followed.

By later in the nineteenth century the docks branch of the railway serving High Orchard Wharf and Bakers Quay was immediately to the south of the pub and beyond that was the huge Railway Carriage and Wagon Works. This would have been a real, hard, working man's boozer, and it was once one of seven pubs crammed into this

REF: 13/239
MAP: G
STATUS: Trading
DATE: By 1852 to date
LOCATION: 230, Southgate Street, GL1 2EZ
CONTACT: 01452 383457

Hauliers Arms, now Baker Street. *(Gloucestershire Archives)*

small corner, the others being the Ship & Castle, the Leopard, the New Pilot, the Jack, the Ball and the Old Pilot. But this heyday has long since passed, and Baker Street is the only one of these pubs that still remains.

Today Baker Street stands right outside the new Gloucester Quays development. From outside it is not much to look at: it is a three-storey Victorian brick building with bay windows at the ground floor. Inside it has a very welcoming, traditional feel, despite the wide screen TVs dotted about showing sports and the fruit machines and juke box lined against one wall. At the front of the pub the walls are wood-panelled and at the back the wall is painted white with black wooden beams giving a presumably fake half-timbered effect. Although Sherlock Holmes appears on the pub sign, they have resisted the temptation to go overboard with the theme inside, and instead the walls are covered with old advertising prints.

Baker Street, 2009.

The landlord, Mark, is obviously keen to develop a community spirit around the pub. As well as a skittles team, which plays on an alley around the corner at the end of the long wooden bar, a rare feature inside a city centre pub, it also has a football team called Baker Street FC.

City Barge, Merchant's Road

If I was to nominate my favourite pub in Gloucester, ever, it would have to be either the City Barge or the Malt & Hops (see p. 119). Despite the fact that it was very short-lived, I think this one might just get the edge.

The City Barge opened in about 1985 in the Pillar Warehouse, situated on the east bank of the canal just beyond Llanthony Bridge. Onedin's Restaurant was upstairs, named after the TV series filmed at the docks in the 1970s, but I never ventured in there, I was more interested in the cellar downstairs which housed the City Barge.

The Pillar and Lucy Warehouses are two identical semi-detached bonded warehouses. They were built in 1838, the north one for Samuel Baker and the south for J.M. Shipton. They were constructed with the front of the upper storey supported on pillars, providing a covered wharf and allowing goods to be hoisted directly out of a ship's hold while still retaining a passageway along the quayside.

The warehouse cellars provided an excellent environment for storing ale, which was served directly from the casks stacked behind the bar. The furniture in the City Barge was basic, frequently constructed from old barrels, and the walls were plain, slightly musty brick. It always sold a good range of beers and ran several beer festivals. One that I remember most fondly had a vast array of beers around the whole cellar and a tall ship moored outside with a band playing on it. With the bravado and folly of youth, my

REF: 101/570
MAP: G
STATUS: Closed
DATE: 1985 to 1998
LOCATION: Pillar Warehouse, Merchant's Road

Pillar & Lucy Warehouse, former home of the City Barge.

friends and I sought out and drank the most inadvisably strong beers and far too much of it for our own good, but it was a great evening!

It was renamed the Waterfront at some time before 1993 and took over the former Onedin's restaurant upstairs. It remained good for a while, earning a place in CAMRA's *Good Beer Guide* in 1993–4. The *Real Ale in Gloucester Guide* for 1993 lists it as having a 'permanent festival of 11 real ales (all gravity dispense) with the 9 guest ales constantly changing. With free peanuts by the sackful . . . it's gimmicky but popular, a pub for all ages.' The peanuts were a nice touch as you were encouraged to discard the shells on the floor, giving a real rustic sawdust floor appearance.

Sadly it went badly down hill and closed in July 1998. Now most of the Grade II listed building is used as offices, but the front facing the canal remains vacant and looks in a sorry state of disrepair. It is included in Phase 2 of the Gloucester Quays development, which will bring bars and restaurants to the area. I live in hope, but doubt that it will ever be able to regain its former brilliance.

Coots, the Docks

REF: 120

MAP: G

STATUS: Trading

DATE: Early 1990s to date

LOCATION: Llanthony Warehouse, the Docks, GL1 2LG

CONTACT: 01452 318200

Coots did not start out life as a pub; it started out as the Waterways Museum café. Actually, strictly speaking, that's not true: it is in Llanthony Warehouse, so obviously it started out life as a warehouse. Built in 1873, Llanthony Warehouse was the largest and the last of the warehouses built at the docks and is situated between the barge basin and Llanthony Road. It was saved from demolition in 1972 and became the National Waterways Museum on 5 August 1988, opened by the Prince of Wales.

As is the way with museums, a café was installed. It became a pub in February 2008 following a £30,000 refurbishment, which expanded it from one to two rooms. A modern new bar and a pool table were installed with the aim of attracting students from Gloucestershire College, which had opened its new campus on the docks just the previous year, while retaining the museum customers.

The museum has been struggling lately, not least because it is hidden away from the main docks behind some of the less attractive new flats. Coots, however, continues to thrive, helped now by its proximity to the new Quays development. It is a strange kind of bar, still having a café feel to it, but it sells a real ale, has had a couple of beer festivals and provides a good venue for bands as part of the Gloucester Blues Festival.

Coots is the single-storey building in the foreground, with Llanthony Warehouse behind.

Fosters on the Docks, the Docks

Fosters on the Docks really is 'on the docks', situated in a converted warehouse on the east side of the main docks basin. Kimberley Warehouse is one of three warehouses built in 1846 for the corn trade and is flanked by Herbert Warehouse to the north and Phillpotts to the south. These were the first of the Docks' warehouses to be renovated in 1985.

Kimberley Warehouse was converted to a pub in the early 1990s, originally called Doctor Foster's after the well known nursery rhyme:

> Dr Foster went to Gloucester
> In a shower of rain
> He stepped in a puddle
> Right up to his middle
> And never went there again

REF: 187/151
MAP: G
STATUS: Trading
DATE: Early 1990s to date
LOCATION: Kimberley Warehouse, the Docks, GL1 2ES
CONTACT: 01452 300990

It is popularly held that this rhyme refers to a visit to the city by Edward I. It is said that he travelled to Gloucester in the middle of a rainstorm and as he entered the city his horse fell. Both king and horse ended up in the middle of a huge puddle and the townspeople had to use planks of wood to remove them from the mud. King Edward was enraged by this misfortune and refused to return to Gloucester. This is entirely believable as in those days the dirt roads were churned by the hooves of horses and rutted by cartwheels: they were treacherous indeed. Even 200 years later, in 1472, Gloucester citizens petitioned King Edward IV to the effect that the town was 'fully feebly paved, and full perilous and jepardous . . . to ryde or goo within.' However, I have found no good explanation of why Edward I, popularly known as 'Longshanks', should be referred to as Doctor Foster.

The building has been converted to a single large open-plan bar with the counter running the length of one side. The ceilings are quite low and have impressively large wooden beams supported on sturdy black metal poles. A wooden staircase winds from the centre of the bar to the upstairs restaurant, originally called Steamboat Willies, but now just the Fosters on the Docks Brasserie. Between Kimberley and Phillpotts Warehouse and along the quayside overlooking the main basin is a conservatory, ideal for sunny summer days.

The pub and restaurant were refurbished in 2004, becoming Fosters on the Docks, a brasserie and wine bar with a menu created by award-winning chef and proprietor Jonathon Butler. The furnishings are a mixture of comfy leather sofas and contemporary style chairs and tables, and the long granite-topped bar is dominated by modern shiny keg fonts, but there are also proper hand-pulls, usually with a couple of decent beers on offer. Early on, in 1992, the pub warranted an entry in the *Good Beer Guide*, but today, although they continue to sell good beer, the emphasis is much more on food. I can't speak for the brasserie, not having tried it, but the bar food is good and excellent value.

Kimberley Warehouse, home of Fosters on the Docks.

Goat Inn, Llanthony Road

REF: 204

MAP: G

STATUS: Building in different use

DATE: By 1851 to late 1950s

LOCATION: Llanthony Road

The Goat Inn was located on Llanthony Road between Church Street and High Orchard Street. It was opened by 1851 as it is shown on the Board of Health map of that year as a beerhouse. It was therefore around at the peak of Gloucester's docks activity and conveniently situated for the heavy industry in High Orchard Street.

As a young man in the early 1940s my step-father, Ken, worked for Charlesworth Bodies in Hempstead Lane making undercarriage doors for Lancaster bombers. He remembers that one of his older colleagues always turned up late for his shift due to drinking in the Goat, where, despite the restrictions imposed by the war, regulars could always get beer and cigarettes.

The Goat Inn was once tied to Francis Wintle's Forest Brewery in Mitcheldean and then, by 1954, to Cheltenham & Hereford Breweries. It closed as a pub in the late 1950s or early 1960s; the last reference that I have found for it is in *Kelly's Directory* 1955.

In March 1969, a planning application was made by Colwell's Garage to either demolish the building to provide parking or change its use for storage purposes. Both options were approved, but the building was not demolished and it still survives alongside the new Gloucester Quays retail centre. On the side of the three-storey rendered building is a large square with 'The Goat Inn' in stone lettering.

Inn on the Docks, Llanthony Road

REF: 255/478

MAP: G

STATUS: Trading

DATE: By 1861 to date

LOCATION: 28 Llanthony Road, GL2 5HQ

CONTACT: 01452 520631

The Inn on the Docks is located at 28 Llanthony Road, on the corner with Severn Road which, as the name suggests, is near Gloucester Docks. Prior to being taken over by new owners in October 2008 it was known as the Sir Colin Campbell. The first record that I have found for the Sir Colin Campbell is from 1861, when it had a beerhouse licence. This wasn't upgraded to a publican's licence until 1 March 1955. The original pub was a substantial building to the east of the present day pub, but this was demolished in 1968 and West Country Breweries replaced it with the current structure. To say that it is not a pretty building is something of an understatement: it is a plain square brick structure all too typical of the period. It is said that it was built in just two days, and they certainly didn't waste any time on architectural niceties.

Arkell's of Swindon acquired the pub in the early 1990s and it was refurbished in 1997. It underwent another refurbishment when the new owners took over in 2008, and when I visited in early 2009 it still looked very new. The single open-plan bar has clean, bright, light coloured carpet on the floor, contemporary light wooden furniture, and a small, light coloured wooden bar. The pub is nice enough, but somehow lacks

Above: Sir Colin Campbell, Lord Clyde (1792–1863).

character and atmosphere, although that might be because when I visited it was mid-afternoon and very quiet.

Although the Severn runs just a few yards from the back of the pub it does little to capitalise on this: you'd think that putting the newly laid wooden decking to the rear of the pub overlooking the river would surely provide a much more attractive view to enjoy over your beer in the summer than the Llanthony Road.

It is always a shame to see pubs renamed and the historic names lost; however, in this case it is hard to see the relevance of the original name. Colin Campbell was born in Glasgow in 1792 and had a distinguished military career. Amid much else he led the Highland Brigade at the Battle of Balaclava during the Crimean War and later became commander-in-chief during the Indian Mutiny of 1857–8. He was made a Knight Grand Cross of the Bath (GCB) and Knight of the Order of the Star of India (KSI) and in 1858 he was elevated to the peerage as Lord Clyde of Clydesdale. In 1860 he was presented with the freedom of the city of London, and in 1862 he rose to the rank of Field Marshal. He died in 1863 and was buried in Westminster Abbey. He was credited as one of the bravest soldiers of Britain, but as far as I can see, none of this had anything whatsoever to do with Gloucester.

The Inn on the Docks was leased by Arkells to the same company that manages Coots Bar (p. 82). They were keen to push real ale, but in early 2010 the pub closed due to lack of trade. This had just happened at the time of writing, so I live in hope that it will be open again by the time you read this.

Llanthony Bridge Inn, Llanthony Road

As the name suggests, the Llanthony Bridge Inn was located next to Llanthony Bridge on Llanthony Road. It was on the east side of the canal and licensing records and directories variously refer to it as Llanthony Bridge Inn, Llanthony Inn, or just Bridge Inn. The first reference that I have found for the inn is from 1847, when the docks were in their heyday. It was in this year that, due to the huge amount of traffic at the docks following the repeal of the Corn Laws in 1846, the second basin, known as Victoria Dock, was opened.

REF: 291

MAP: G

STATUS: Demolished

DATE: By 1847 to 1974

LOCATION: Llanthony Road

Rear of the Llanthony Bridge Inn in 2007, shortly before demolition.

Given its location, it is perhaps not surprising that the inn had a notorious reputation for smuggling. It is alleged that there were a network of tunnels under the inn, which could be used both as an escape route and a store for contraband. There were apparently twenty-two doors in the inn, most of which were kept locked; in the event of a visit by the customs and excise men, the landlord was able to go through a lengthy, elaborate charade of locking and unlocking these doors to give the smugglers plenty of time to escape. This deceit did not always go to plan and at least two murders are said to have taken place at the inn, which was said to be haunted. In their book *Haunted Gloucester*, Eileen Fry and Rosemary Harvey report that the banging and crashing of slamming doors had been heard even after it ceased to be an inn.

The rumours of tunnels are obviously older than the date that I have for the inn as the canal is said to cut through the tunnel that gave smugglers direct access to the ships just above the waterline, which presumably must have been on the Severn at or near The Quay. In fact, some rumours give these tunnels even greater length and prominence, claiming that a tunnel goes from Llanthony Priory to St Peter's Abbey, calling at Llanthony Bridge Inn and the Fleece on the way (see also Monks' Retreat, p. 69).

The last reference that I have for the inn is *Kelly's Directory* of 1974. It closed about that time and was later used as premises of a tool-hire firm. It was demolished in 2008 to make way for the Gloucester Quays development.

Nelson Inn, Southgate Street

REF: 324
MAP: G
STATUS: Trading
DATE: By 1815 to date
LOCATION: 166, Southgate Street, GL1 2EX
CONTACT: 01452 313606

The Nelson Inn stands on the west side of Southgate Street just before the junction with Llanthony Road in the area originally known as Littleworth. It was originally numbered 88, becoming 166 Southgate Street on renumbering.

The Nelson has probably been around since about 1815, although in the early years its name was a variation on the theme, first being known as Nelson's Head Inn, then by 1830 as the Lord Nelson Inn, finally become simply the Nelson Inn by 1847. The pub is in a plain three-storey brick building, but the front of the ground floor is covered in green ceramic tiles with the name 'The Nelson Inn' in bold gold letters above the ground-floor windows.

The Nelson was once owned by the Brimscombe Brewery before passing to Georges Bristol Brewery, later taken over by Courage. A souvenir book from Georges & Co. shows that the exterior of the pub has changed little since then; the windows bearing the brewery name have gone, the brickwork has been painted white and the whole building has become somewhat shabbier, but otherwise it looks much the same. It is now an Ushers pub.

For some years the Nelson had a reputation as something of a 'problem' pub and anything approaching decent beer was noticeably absent. There were signs of hope a few years ago when a new landlord started to turn it around and introduced real ale, but sadly, as is too often the case, he was thwarted in his attempts by an over-demanding pub company and he left in early 2007.

The pub was closed for about four months before being taken over by the current landlord, John, who has continued to provide a real ale. Inside the pub is basic and quite old-fashioned looking, painted white throughout. The bar, also painted white, runs down the right-hand side of the single room, beyond which is a dartboard

and pool table. When I visited in February 2009 the pub was swathed in scaffolding as the flats above were being refurbished, with the pub interior scheduled to follow in the summer. However, at the time of writing this does not seem to have taken place.

New Pilot, Southgate Street

It is perhaps not surprising that Pilot was a popular name for pubs near the docks: in the nineteenth century the automatic association would not have been with flying aircraft, but navigating ships in and out of port. I have seen mention of a Pilot Inn in the late 1850s, whose location is given as Bristol Road or High Orchard. It seems likely that this became the Old Pilot (Ref 362, Map G), which was located on the corner of Southgate Street and St Luke's Street by 1864, when it was recorded as being owned by the City Brewery in Quay Street. *Smart's Directory* of 1883 gives the address as Raglan Terrace.

REF: 337
MAP: G
STATUS: Building in different use
DATE: By 1869 to 2001
LOCATION: 159 Southgate Street

Lower Southgate Street looking north toward Llanthony Road with the New Pilot in the foreground.

The Old Pilot was referred to the compensation authority on 8 March 1909 as 'not required to meet the wants of the neighbourhood' and the licence was not renewed.

Further down Southgate Street, on the opposite side of the road at what is now 159 Southgate Street, almost opposite the Hauliers Arms (now Baker Street) and the Leopard, was the New Pilot. This is recorded from at least 1869 and was probably built by Godsell & Sons of Salmon Springs, Stroud, as their trade mark 'malt shovel in hand' emblem is displayed above the front door in ornamental plasterwork (see p. 93). Godsells were taken over by West Country Ales, whose plaques adorn both sides of the front door.

The New Pilot had three bars, two on the ground floor and a third upstairs which hosted Gloucester's first nightclub in the 1950s. CAMRA's *Real Ale in Gloucester Guide* of 1996 describes it as Gloucester's only gay pub. Shortly afterwards the name was changed to Professor Moriarty's, presumably continuing the Sherlock Holmes theme from Baker Street opposite. It closed on 3 April 2001.

In January 2003 writer Joanna Trollope opened the Vaughan Centre at the old pub – a day centre for homeless people run by Gloucester Emergency Accommodation Resource (GEAR), but the ornamental plaster work, the name 'New Pilot Inn' and the West Country Ales plaques are all still there.

Squirrel, Southgate Street

REF: 491/3 & 492

MAP: G

STATUS: Building in different use

DATE: By 1830 to 1927

LOCATION: 77 Southgate Street

I have mentioned before how difficult it is trying to identify and keep track of pubs, but sometimes they seem to deliberately go out of their way to make life difficult, the Squirrel being a case in point. The Squirrel was originally located on the east side of Southgate Street at no. 111, opposite the entrance to the docks in the area known as Littleworth. The first mention that I have found for the pub is 1830, but presumably it pre-dated that by some time because in 1831 it was demolished and rebuilt to the design of Thomas Fulljames, a well-known Gloucester architect, and renamed the Albion Hotel. This must have been pretty big, because in September 1840 Ryan's circus-royal came to the Albion with features included acrobatics, a trampoline exhibition and weight-lifting.

Located at no. 77 in the new street numbering, the Albion is built of Bath Stone in a style known as Severe Greek Revival. The hotel closed probably in the 1930s, the last reference that I have for it is from *Cope's Directory* of 1935.

Albion House.

The Grade II listed building now known as Albion House remained as offices for a time but for the past ten years it has stood empty and unmaintained. It is badly deteriorating and is on the Risk Register as Category 3. Most evenings the doorway is used as a convenient shelter by derelicts, the homeless and street drinkers, so has a somewhat grungy, unwholesome appearance that does not show it off to best effect. It was hoped that this was set to change in May 2009 when planning permission was granted to convert the building into flats, but at the time of writing no progress appears to have been made.

The complication arises because no sooner is the Squirrel Inn demolished than a new one springs up on the opposite side of the road. This was further south, opposite Norfolk Street at no. 79 in the old street numbering, no. 150 in modern numbering. This one appeared by 1847 and plans of 1888 show it to be a long, narrow plot with bar, kitchen, parlour, cellar and scullery, with stables and a skittle alley at the rear. It lasted until probably 1907.

Tall Ship, Southgate Street

The Tall Ship is a white-painted two-storey building located on the south-west corner of the entrance into the docks on Southgate Street. Previously called the British Flag it dates back to at least 1870, but as it was originally just a beerhouse it probably dates back further than that. The name changed to the Tall Ship probably in the mid- to late 1980s.

Although fairly modest to look at, the building is Grade II listed. Dating from the mid- to late nineteenth century it is described in the Schedule of Listed Buildings as 'Stuccoed brick with stone details . . . Italianate style. An externally complete public house of this date historically linked with and prominently sited close to the docks.'

There are two different faces to the Tall Ship: on the one hand it has a reputation for food, being well regarded for seafood and hosting monthly 'Urban Nights' where a special menu, including local produce, is provided. On the other hand, it caters for the student crowd with cheaper student menus.

A sturdy, traditional wooden bar counter runs along the back of the bar, which is divided in two with a pool table dominating one side and more formal restaurant-style seating on the other. The pub has a very spacious feel, with high ceilings and lots of wood.

REF: 525

MAP: G

STATUS: Trading

DATE: By 1870 to date

LOCATION: 134, Southgate Street, GL1 2EX

CONTACT: 01452 522793

Above: Ela behind the bar at the Tall Ship.

Whitesmiths Arms, Southgate Street _____

REF: 601

MAP: G

STATUS: Trading

DATE: By 1871 to date

LOCATION: 81, Southgate Street, GL1 1UR

CONTACT: 01452 414454

The Whitesmiths Arms is situated directly opposite the entrance to the docks on Southgate Street, originally no. 109, becoming no. 81 on renumbering in the 1920s. The Whitesmiths is named for the ancient craft of the whitesmith. Responsible for polishing and finishing metal, the whitesmith has long been associated with working on the metal parts of ships. The first mention that I have found of the Whitesmiths Arms as a pub is from 1871. Originally a beerhouse, it upgraded to an alehouse licence probably in the early 1960s.

A Mr Len Parsons contacted me to tell me about his great-great grandfather, John Parsons, who he says managed the pub in about 1919, selling it to emigrate to Canada. It was once tied to Arnold Perrett & Co. Ltd of Wickwar, and brewery mergers and acquisitions brought it under the control of West Country Breweries, as evidenced by the plaque next to the entrance, and then Whitbread. The pub was acquired by Arkell's of Swindon in 1995.

The pub clearly consists of two buildings of different ages. The entrance from Southgate Street brings you into the main bar, which is in a Grade II listed eighteenth-century building which started life as a house. The room is dominated by a central bar and has a vaguely nautical theme to link into the docks location, with pictures of ships on the wall and rope trim around the bar.

To the right of the main bar there's another small room, partitioned off by an old timber-framed structure. This was originally the next door building, which the

Whitesmiths extended into in 1996. The room, much needed when the pub is busy, is fairly unremarkable . . . until you look up. Here you are looking up into the original fifteenth-century roof. Hanging incongruously in the middle of the wall, now that the floor added in the seventeenth century has been removed, is a Victorian range.

When this part of the building was young it was situated outside the city walls beyond the South Gate. Areas outside the walls were not subject to the same rules as those within the walls; they were self-policing and literally lawless places. It was here that 'foreigners' settled. In medieval times the term foreigners applied to anyone from outside the area, and they were not allowed to live inside the city. The area outside the South Gate became known as Littleworth. During the Civil War and the Siege of Gloucester in 1643 most of the buildings outside the city walls were demolished. This is one of the few buildings outside the South Gate to survive.

During the 1996 renovations the remains of an underground cellar were found along with a possible tunnel that is rumoured to be a smugglers' tunnel connecting the pub to the nearby Gloucester Docks. Unfortunately this was not excavated, but frankly it would be unusual for a building of this age and this close to the docks not to have a rumour of smugglers' tunnels.

Interior of the Whitesmiths showing the fifteenth-century roof and Victorian fireplace.

Remarkably, for such an old and unique building, this part of the pub is also only Grade II listed, but the listing was made as renovations were underway and describes it as a building with 'a complicated structural history which requires detailed investigation.'

I like the Whitesmiths Arms a lot; it is a traditional, unpretentious boozer, with a pool table, a thriving darts team and a consistently excellent pint of Arkell's. There is always a friendly welcome behind the bar from Steve and Sharon, the landlord and landlady, and their daughter Laura. It was a CAMRA favourite for quite some time, appearing in the *Good Beer Guide* twelve times in 1981, 1989–90 and 1992–2000.

5

Nineteenth Century to 2009

The nature of the brewing industry changed dramatically in the nineteenth century, becoming increasingly centralised. Gloucester had a number of breweries, including the City Brewery in Quay Street, the Eagle Brewery in Westgate Street and the Northgate Brewery in George Street, but these had all been bought out by the end of the nineteenth century. Gloucestershire was dominated by

Brewery Mergers & Acquisitions

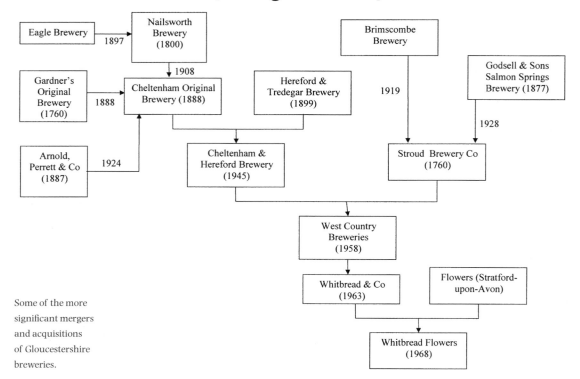

Some of the more significant mergers and acquisitions of Gloucestershire breweries.

The 'malt shovel in hand' trademark of Godsell & Sons of Salmon Springs, Stroud. This example is from the New Pilot in Southgate Street.

breweries from Stroud and Cheltenham and increasingly these breweries also owned the pubs in which the beer was sold, through the tied house system. Throughout the twentieth century the Gloucestershire breweries coalesced through mergers and acquisitions, resulting in the supremacy of Whitbread Flowers by 1968.

Ultimately the centralisation of the brewing industry resulted in a small number of very large breweries dominating the industry and the Campaign for Real Ale (CAMRA) came into being in the early 1970s to try to stem the tide of keg beer. Okay, you can take the mickey out of CAMRA and their stereotypical beards, beer bellies and dodgy knitwear, but it is these real ale

West Country Breweries became Whitbread in 1963. These plaques are a common sight in the Gloucester area.

stalwarts that have created the most successful consumer group in Europe and single-handedly saved our real beer and pub heritage.

The docks and railways brought the industrial revolution to Gloucester with a vengeance in the nineteenth century, and the population grew quickly as people moved into the city for work – in 1841 Gloucester's population was 14,000; by 1871 it was 40,000. Many new houses were built and pubs were important in these generally poor and overcrowded areas. The beerhouse thrived; cropping up in normal terraced houses they were often short-lived and frequently had no formal name.

Slum clearances began in Gloucester in the twentieth century. The Oxebode was cleared in the 1920s and Hare Lane followed in the 1920s–30s. Following the war, Gloucester Corporation set about further improvements to the city with some enthusiasm, culminating in the delivery of the Jellico Plan, commissioned by the city council to rejuvenate Gloucester and halt the post-industrial decline that it was suffering. The plan was delivered in 1962 and building was completed in the 1970s, including King's Square and the Eastgate Shopping Centre.

CAMPAIGN FOR REAL ALE

(Campaign for Real Ale)

King's Square, a product of the Jellico Plan completed 1972. It seemed like a good idea at the time.

Although the Jellico plan delivered perhaps the most significant development in the city, some of the worst pub-related crimes were the result of earlier projects under what were referred to as Gloucester Comprehensive Redevelopment Areas. There were two of these, one in Westgate and one in that area of Kingsholm unofficially known as Clapham, both of which had a high density of pubs. In many cases the brewers were only two happy to get rid of them in return for licences in the new out of town developments, but they are fondly remembered and the city centre seems a poorer place without them.

And so we come to the present day. Pubs as a social institution are suffering and they are closing at an alarming rate: a report in July 2009 stated that 52 pubs were closing across the country each week. To survive they are increasingly diversifying: live music, food and big screen TVs for watching sport are all common. There is also the new breed of disco-pub, blurring the lines between the pub and nightclub. Over recent years this has happened particularly in the lower part of Eastgate Street, which has become the centre of Gloucester's 'night time economy'. The pubs here thrive on the pre-nightclub crowd: they are lively and loud and the drinks are all brightly coloured with trendy names.

These latter are often criticised for encouraging drinking among the young, encouraging intemperate consumption through 'vertical drinking' and leading to violence and nuisance on the streets. Although there may be some element of truth in this, there are also echoes of the old temperance movement attitude: po-faced kill-joys who just disapprove of too much frivolity.

Adega, Northgate Street

REF: 1/300
MAP: A
STATUS: Building in different use
DATE: By 1722 to 1956
LOCATION: 25 Northgate Street

The Adega was originally called the Maiden Head Inn. It was located at 98 Northgate Street in the old street numbering and the first licensing record that I have found for it is from 1722. Records continue until at least 1849, after which it seems likely that it underwent a couple of name changes.

The name Tredegar Arms has been associated with the site from about 1860 to 1875, presumably after the town of that name in South Wales. However, it is not in *Bretherton's Directory* of 1869, but a pub called the Railway Guard is listed,

Northgate, Gloucester.

which may have been on the same site. By 1876 an inn called No.1 Vaults is recorded on the site.

The first mention of the Adega is found in *Smart's Directory* of 1883. It has been speculated that 'Adega' may be a corruption of 'Tredegar'. It was originally called Adega Vaults, later becoming just the Adega or Adega Inn. It may have been renamed the Victoria briefly about 1890.

By the early 1900s the landlord is recorded as Earnest Daniel Tandy, a name more recognisable for the fact that it was painted on the side of the Bull Inn in Bull Lane, where he was previously a landlord (see p. 44).

Following the street renumbering in the 1920s the Adega became 25 Northgate Street. In July 1923 it was owned by Arnold Perrett & Co. Ltd who valued the pub at £7,000, describing the accommodation as including a public bar, a jug and bottle department, smoke room, glazed covered yard with tap and furnace, first-floor accommodation, two attics and large cellars. The frontage to Northgate Street was 26ft including a passage at the side. They proposed to exchange it for The Duke's Head Inn, Hereford; No. 67 Cotterell Street, Hereford; The Red Lion Inn, Monkland, Herefordshire; and The Royal Forest Inn, Milend, near Coleford.

By 1928 the Adega was owned by the Cheltenham Original Brewery Company, who were considering an application to sell the property. By now they valued it at £9,500. Probably at about this time the buildings to the south of the Adega were rebuilt; Marks & Spencer now occupy nos 13–23 Northgate Street. Photographs suggest that the Adega shrank in size after this time, so it may have originally been at nos 23–25 (98–99 in old numbering), with the southern half being demolished to make way for the new building. Its licence lapsed in 1956.

There is a medieval carved oak screen on display in Gloucester Folk Museum, which is claimed to be from the Adega Inn. It is dated to 1550 and was given to the museum

Upper Northgate Street before the development of the west side. The Adega is the fourth building down on the left with the curved black sign outside.

NORTHGATE STREET, GLOUCESTER.

Above: Adega in the early 1950s shortly before it closed. Note that the frontage is only two windows wide, compared to four windows on the earlier picture.

Right: An oak screen from the Adega, now on display at the Gloucester Folk Museum. *(Darrel Kirby, used with permission of Gloucester City Museums)*

in 1936 by the brewery. It is unclear whether this means that the actual Adega building dated back that far, much less whether it was an inn at that time. There is some confusion, however, as the records state that it was removed when Boots the Chemists' was built on the site in the 1930s – Boots was a couple of doors further north than the Adega at no. 31, the site now occupied by Peacocks.

Avenue, Bristol Road

REF: 11
MAP: H
STATUS: Trading
DATE: By 1900 to date
LOCATION: 227, Bristol Road, GL1 5TH
CONTACT: 01452 423468

The Avenue is a good walk out from the town centre and is the most southerly pub covered in this book. Situated on the northern corner of Bristol Road and Tuffley Avenue it was built as a large hotel, possibly for the Stroud Brewery Company, by 1900. No longer a hotel, it is now simply known as the Avenue and is a tied house of Banks's of Wolverhampton, who bought it from Whitbread in the early 1990s. Appearing in CAMRA's *Good Beer Guide* from 1999–2000, it still does a fine pint of Banks's Bitter.

The pub retains two separate rooms; a lounge bar and a public bar, with the bar counter between the two. The public bar has a big screen TV showing live sports and when I visited early on a Saturday evening it was extremely lively. The lounge bar, although less raucous, was nonetheless quite busy, mainly with what appeared to be family groups, many of whom were eating.

The lounge reflects the Victorian origins of the pub with tall ceilings, traditional bar fittings and etched windows and it is decorated in traditional greens and reds with a typical patterned pub carpet. It has a pleasant community feel to it and offers quiz nights and occasional music.

Bar H2O, Eastgate Street

Bar H2O is on the corner of Eastgate Street and Nettleton Road. It was developed as the Courtyard in 1991 by the owner of Frankie's nightclub above. By 1996 it had been converted into an American style café bar called Dreams, with the former nightclub upstairs used as a function room. Now owned by Excelsior Leisure UK, Bar H2O opened in May 1999, specifically with an eye to the imminent opening of the nearby Liquid nightclub. It was planned to have an open-plan Mediterranean feel, and like the other pubs in this area is aimed at the pre-nightclub crowd.

REF: 18
MAP: F
STATUS: Trading
DATE: 1991 to date
LOCATION: 113 Eastgate Street, GL1 1QB
CONTACT: 01452 550523

The bar is square, not particularly big and dominated by an expanse of light wood flooring. Designed mainly for 'vertical drinking', there is minimal seating, mostly in the form of tall tables and stools. However, when I visited it was still quite early and the bar was quiet and the staff were welcoming and friendly.

Bell & Gavel (now Priory), St Oswald's Park _____

REF: 29/409
MAP: C
STATUS: Trading as Priory
DATE: 1958 to date
LOCATION: St Oswald's
Retail Park, GL1 2SR
CONTACT: 01452 523022

The Bell & Gavel was built by West Country Breweries on the west side of St Oswald's Road in 1958. It got a publican's licence in December of that year, removed from the Pheasant in Columbia Street, which was demolished as part of the Kingsholm Redevelopment. No doubt it was built with an eye to the arrival of the cattle market which was moved to the site in the 1960s from its original home in the area now occupied by the bus station.

The pub must have been rebuilt in about 1984, because the CAMRA *Real Ale in Gloucestershire Guide* for that year lists Stockyards, a 'modern "fun pub" built where the Bell & Gavel used to be.' They clearly weren't impressed, describing it as having a horrible exterior colour scheme and noting that after it opened a sign saying 'Public House' had to be added to the name sign. It was called the Bell & Gavel again by 1993.

The Bell & Gavel pub sign now in Geoff Sandles' collection. *(Geoff Sandles)*

Although the pub sign shows a hand bell and an auctioneer's gavel, according to the *Wordsworth Dictionary of Pub Names*, in earlier dialect 'gavel' referred to corn which had been cut and was ready to be made into sheaves. In rural areas a bell was rung to mark the beginning and end of the harvest. Although that may be the traditional meaning, given the proximity of the cattle market an auctioneer's gavel seems more appropriate.

Despite the fact that from the outside the building was modern and unattractive, inside it was very pleasant with rustic décor. It must have been very busy with trade from the cattle market in the early days and later a popular Saturday market was held on the site. In the 1990s a new Tesco superstore opened nearby, potentially pulling in yet more custom, but in April 2001 the Bell & Gavel closed.

The cattle market was closed down in 2005 and the site was redeveloped into St Oswald's Retail Park, which includes a B&Q store so big that it makes an aircraft hangar look like a garden shed. During this development the Bell & Gavel was demolished and a new Brewer's Fayre pub and restaurant was built in its place, opening on 28 November 2005 as the Priory Inn, named for the nearby St Oswald's Priory. In 2007 it was sold to Mitchells & Butlers and, presumably at this time, the name changed again to the Monkey Tree. At the end of 2009 it was converted to a Harvester restaurant and the name reverted to the Priory. As you would expect it is mainly geared towards food, but it sells several real ales and the new owners have stated their ambition to get into CAMRA's *Good Beer Guide*.

Berkeley Hunt Inn, Southgate Street _____

REF: 33
MAP: A
STATUS: Demolished
DATE: By 1836 to 1973
LOCATION: 37 Southgate
Street

The Berkeley Hunt Inn stood on the east side of Southgate Street between Commercial Road and Greyfriars. It was a plain, square, three-storey brick building, originally at no. 132, becoming no. 37 on renumbering.

The first reference I've found for the Berkeley Hunt is in *the Returns of Constables of the four wards as to the state of public houses during time of divine service* from 31 January 1836. At this time it was probably only a beerhouse. It is found in *Smart's Directory* by 1883 and it had a publican's licence by the 1950s. It was demolished in January 1973 and today the site is home to an unattractive modern brick office building.

On the opposite side of the road to the Berkeley Hunt Inn, on the corner with Blackfriars, was the similarly named Berkeley Arms (Ref 32, Map A). This appears

Southgate Street, Gloucester.

FRITH.
GLS.20.

in the licensing records earlier, in 1809, and the last reference to it is 1914. This building has also been demolished.

Both pubs are named for the famous aristocratic Gloucestershire family, the Berkeleys, who can trace an unbroken male line of descent back to Anglo-Saxon times. The manor of Berkeley, about 18 miles south-west of Gloucester, was given to Roger de Berkeley, Lord of Dursley, by William the Conqueror and it is one of the largest in England. The Berkeley Hunt can be traced back to the twelfth century. It hunted stag and fox until the late eighteenth century, then just fox. Of course these days the foxes are safe from molestation by dogs and men on horseback, but the Berkeley foxhounds, the oldest pack of foxhounds in the country, remain.

Berkeley Hunt is also, apparently, cockney rhyming slang for an extremely rude word. This is contracted to give the expression 'berk', so you may wish to tread more carefully with that seemingly innocent, almost affectionate, term of abuse!

Southgate Street, 1949. The Berkeley Hunt Inn is the tall building on the right. (Reproduced from a Frith & Co. postcard)

Black Dog Inn, London Road

The Black Dog Inn stood at no. 1 London Road, the point where Northgate Street ended and London Road began. The site is now marked by Black Dog Way, part of the inner ring road built in the 1960s.

The Black Dog Inn was around from at least 1722, when I first come across it in the licensing records, although it may be older. There is a single mention of a Black Dog in the West Ward in 1686, which could be this inn listed under the wrong ward.

On 24 July 1860 John Organ bought the premises from Henry and Richard George Weaver for £2,075. The deeds state that this purchase included a 'messuage or tenement commonly called or known by the name of the Black Dog Inn (not including such part or parts thereof as was or were formerly belonging to an inn called the Horse

REF: 39
MAP: A & C
STATUS: Demolished
DATE: By 1722 to 1965
LOCATION: 1 London Road

Plan showing location
and extent of Black Dog
Inn. *(Gloucestershire
Archives & Gloucester
City Council)*

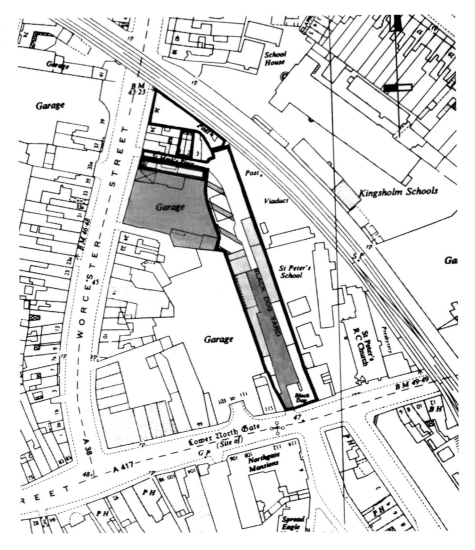

& Groom)'. The property also included a Rick Yard, part of which had been converted to a tan yard and a dwelling house and 'divers other erections and buildings'. Also included in the purchase were several other pieces of adjoining land, including a piece of land leading out onto Worcester Street.

The reference to the Horse & Groom is interesting. A pub by this name 'without the North Gate' is seen referenced back to about 1740 and in 1791 the Hereford 'waggon' set out from there. Later, a pub by the name of the Horse & Groom is listed in licensing records throughout the nineteenth century. Yet later still, a Horse & Groom existed on the opposite side of London Road to the Black Dog; this was a tiny pub tucked under the railway bridge at no. 12 (Ref 249, Map C) and survived into the mid-1970s. Although I have associated all licensing references with the later pub, this reference seems to suggest that there was another, larger, Horse & Groom adjacent to the Black Dog which had closed by 1860.

Thomas Organ purchased the Black Dog from John Organ in 1873 for £3,000, by which time a brew house is shown on the plans of the premises. Thomas was probably

John's son; he is described on the deed as already being an innkeeper and he was recorded as the brewer at the Black Dog. His son Richard later took over as brewer.

Thomas sold the inn to the Stroud Brewery company on 7 September 1909 for £4,800, by which time it is referred to as the Black Dog Hotel and it included a house at no. 3 St Mark's Place, a brewery yard, stables, coach house, loft, blacksmith's shop, coachbuilder's yard, outbuildings and garden. The onsite brewery ended with this purchase.

From about 1910, a great black dog, 8ft long and 4ft high, lay on the parapet. It was carved out of teak by Gloucester sculptor Arthur Levison Senior. The Levison family were famous wood carvers who were also responsible for carving the figure head of the tea clipper *Cutty Sark*.

The Black Dog that once sat on the parapet of the pub and can now be found in the Gloucester Folk Museum. *(Darrel Kirby, used with permission of Gloucester City Museums)*

The demolition of the Black Dog was considered a great loss by Gloucester drinkers, who seem to have fond memories of it. West Country Breweries, who by this time had taken over the Stroud Brewing Company, were less sentimental, however, and don't seem to have put up much of a fight. On 4 May 1965 their tied house director wrote to the town clerk saying, 'You informed us that your council may wish to purchase this house in say 2–5 years time . . . It seems to us that rather than prolonging the matter indefinitely it would be more satisfactory to close the house in the reasonably near future.' The correspondence also indicates that the purchase of the pub was not for the building of the inner ring road, but for car parking purposes.

The pub was closed by October 1965 and the sale was finally completed on 29 May 1968 for a purchase price of £25,000, and the pub was demolished shortly afterwards. This provided 100 car parking spaces in the yard, even though some premises continued to be leased there until the end of 1974, when the occupants were served notice to quit for phase II of the inner ring road.

The black dog sculpture was removed in May 1966 and was thought to have been destroyed, but in 1973 it was rediscovered in the derelict warehouse of the former Stroud Brewery by the curator of Stroud Museum. It was returned to Gloucester in 1996 and can now be seen in the Folk Museum.

Black Swan, Southgate Street _____

At no. 70 Southgate Street, on the corner with Commercial Road, is an impressive three-storey stone faced building which majestically follows the curve of the street. Now home to a block of twenty-two apartments, the building's heritage as a pub can still be seen from the West Country Ales plaque on the wall and 'Black Swan Hotel' still emblazoned above the central ground-floor windows.

An alehouse licence is found for an inn in Southgate Street by the name of the Black Swan by 1802, and it is probably older. Commercial Road was built in 1847, just inside the old South Gate, and in 1849–50 new offices were built for the Gloucester Savings Bank on the prominent triangular site on the south side. The Black Swan was rebuilt to a similar design by Hamilton and Medland at the same time. The Schedule of Listed

REF: 46
MAP: A & G
STATUS: Building in different use
DATE: By 1802 to 2004
LOCATION: 70 Southgate Street

Buildings describes the Grade II listed building as having a 'Symmetrical Italiante street façade, faced in ashlar.'

Originally a tied house of Godsell & Sons, by December 1970 the pub was owned by Whitbread, who demolished part of it to make a small car parking area and by 1973 had renamed it the Yeoman. An advertisement in the *Gloucester Guide* from the early 1970s boasts that 'The Yeomanry Lounge is comfortable and interesting, with a Full Dress Uniform of a Gloucester Yeoman on view and Authentic Colour Prints of Country Yeoman of many Countries adorning the Walls.'

The building was refurbished and reopened as the Black Swan in the 1990s. It was a great pub with regular live music and a range of real ales which earned it a well-deserved place in the CAMRA *Good Beer Guide* in 1995–6, 1998 and 2000–4, and was Gloucester CAMRA's City Pub of the Year in 2000. Unfortunately, despite the refurbishment it quickly started to look shabby and it closed on 1 August 2004. Its conversion to apartments was carried out by the Beswick Partnership, contracted by Enterprise Heritage, and they opened in spring 2007.

Blackfriars Inn, Commercial Road

REF: 47

MAP: G

STATUS: Closed

DATE: By 1879 to after 1974

LOCATION: 10 Commercial Road

Sitting on the north side of Commercial Road, just as it becomes the triangle, is a long-closed red-brick building. There is evidence that this was once a pub – the West Country Ales plaque can still be seen on the right of the building and the pillars on either side of the door retain a decorative hop and grape relief.

This was the Blackfriars Inn, obviously named for the Blackfriars monastic building which stands behind it. It dates back to at least 1879 and was originally a beerhouse. The photograph shows how it looked in about 1900, when the landlord was William Adams-Gainsford, the gentleman standing in the doorway. At this time you can see from the etched window that it was owned by Wickwar.

William Adams-Gainsford
outside the Blackfriars Inn
in about 1900.
(*Martin Parsons*)

By 1954 the pub had a beer and wine licence, with a full publican's licence issued in 1961. At some point, as attested by the plaque, the pub was taken over by West Country Breweries, subsequently becoming Whitbread. The last mention that I have found of the pub is from a *Kelly's Directory* entry in 1974.

Bristol Hotel, Bristol Road

The Bristol Hotel is an impressive three-storey building which curves gracefully round the corner of Bristol Road and Lysons Avenue. It has a small circular tower and the entrance from Bristol Road is through a large semi-circular archway, above which is a central recessed bay frontage with balcony.

REF: 69
MAP: H
STATUS: Trading
DATE: 1902 to date
LOCATION: 131, Bristol
Road, GL1 5SS
CONTACT: 01452 528232

James Uriah Godsell, of Godsell & Sons Brewery, made an application in 1902 for 'the provisional grant of a new licence to sell intoxicating liquors in a new house and premises to be called the Bristol Restaurant.' Now just called the Bristol, it is a sports venue bar.

Inside the Bristol there's more space than a whole episode of *Star Trek*: it has typical high Victorian ceilings and all of the internal walls have been removed. There's light, stripped wood flooring throughout and a dark wooden bar sits in the middle. To the right of this is a large empty area leading back to a skittle alley; to the left is a small stage with a large projector screen and equally large speakers. In the corner, in what was clearly once a cosy separate room, are a number of comfy leather sofas.

It was still quite early on the Saturday evening that I visited and so not particularly busy. It doesn't sell any decent ale and my friend's gloating that they sold his favourite cider was short-lived when he was told that the pump is just for show! The few customers were all clustered in the relatively small area in front of the bar, creating a somewhat deserted air to the rest of the place. The fact that it was early means that I am probably doing the Bristol a disservice. I imagine that later in the evening it turns into a disco and is packed out, fully utilising all of that empty space. I hope so, because to work well as a bar it needs more ambience and atmosphere. And more walls.

Brunswick, Park Road

REF: 75
MAP: F
STATUS: Closed
DATE: Early 1980s to 2009
LOCATION: 7 Park Road

The Brunswick was situated at 7 Park Road, just off Brunswick Road. It only became a pub in the early 1980s, before which it was a nightclub called Snobs.

Although off the beaten track of the city centre pubs it was a regular haunt for me in the mid- to late 1980s. It was known as the Frontier in 1983 and had become the Brunswick by 1993, but I remember it best as the Man in the Bowler Hat, the slightly bizarre name that it went by for some time in between those dates. It was a great music venue and a regular haunt for local bands such as our blues favourites

The Brunswick 2009, shortly after closure.

of the time, Maxwell Street. In fact, two of my best friends met in the Man in the Bowler Hat and remain happily married.

The bar was largely destroyed by fire in January 1998, but was rebuilt and continued as a popular music venue with a large function room upstairs called Snobs, in memory of the old nightclub. Its fortunes took a turn for the worse when the local college moved away from nearby Brunswick Road to the docks.

The Brunswick was leased to Places Trading Ltd by Enterprise Inns and, as is all too often the case, it seems that they could not meet the high demands of the pub company. On 25 April 2009 Places Trading called it a day and the pub was closed. It went on the market at £250,000 and at the time of writing is due to open as an Indian restaurant, making a nice change from flats and apartments which seem to be the usual fate of former pubs.

Butlers, Eastgate Street

Butlers is one of the pre-club 'venue bars' that line the lower part of Eastgate Street. From the outside it has a smart, modern black and chrome frontage which contrasts sharply with the ancient building in which it is located.

Originally next door to the Crown & Thistle (see p. 107), no. 99 was incorporated into the pub as an adjoining wine bar in the early 1980s. By 1993 the Crown & Thistle was owned by Devenish, who had separated the wine bar and opened it as Butlers of Gloucester. It had an eighteenth-century beamed annex called Jesters, which was later incorporated to form a second bar.

The CAMRA *Real Ale in Gloucestershire Guide* of 1993 describes it as a 'genuine old building well adapted as an alehouse by Devenish.' It sold real beer and was still doing so at the time of the 1996 guide.

Butlers was taken over at the end of 1997 by a twenty-three-year-old chap called Justin Hudson, who described it at the time as, 'A very old-fashioned traditional tavern.' He soon put an end to that with a £124,000 refurbishment to turn it into a 'disco pub'

REF: 87

MAP: F

STATUS: Trading

DATE: By 1993 to date

LOCATION: 99–101 Eastgate Street, GL1 1PY

CONTACT: 01452 304314

called Butlers Venue Bar. In 2001 it won a bronze award in the *Morning Advertiser* National Disco Pub of the Year. Ownership of the building passed to Punch Taverns through a series of mergers and acquisitions and in the summer of 2009 Hudson bought it from them for £1.3 million.

Inside, Butlers shows little sign of the building's heritage, with only the low ceiling giving it away. The bar is basically just a dance floor, with a large booth for the DJ and TV screens on the walls showing music videos. There is minimal furniture, which is smart and stylish, and overall it gives the impression of being more slick and upmarket than the other venues in Eastgate Street. Initially, despite the fact that I am by no means Butlers' target audience, I quite liked the concept of merging a pub and club. The problem is that it takes itself too seriously; getting past the bouncers feels more like crossing the border to a despotic police state than entering a pub. Inside it continues the theme, having more surveillance equipment than George Orwell's nightmares. This negative view is, admittedly, not entirely unbiased. In all of my field research around the pubs of Gloucester, this is the only venue where I met a hostile response. I was forcibly removed by the bouncer, on the orders of the owner, for having the temerity to write notes inside the premises, a crime captured by the many cameras. It probably comes as no surprise, therefore, that this is not a pub that I feel inclined to recommend!

Chambers, St Aldate Street

REF: 94
MAP: A
STATUS: Trading
DATE: 1999 to date
LOCATION: 27, St Aldate Street, GL1 1RL
CONTACT: 01452 417089

Located on the corner of St Aldate Street and Market Parade, Chambers was built on the site of the Pearce Pope Offices, known as St Aldate Chambers. It opened on 21 September 1999.

Chambers is modern inside and out. It's spacious with large TVs showing sport. It is busy at weekends, appealing to a modern crowd. It's pleasant enough, but has no real beer.

Crown & Thistle (now Zest), Eastgate Street _____

On the north side of the lower part of Eastgate Street, about half way between Brunswick Road and Bruton Way, is a pub called Zest. This occupies nos 101–3, which were clearly two separate buildings originally, both of which are very old.

Until the 1980s this part of Eastgate Street was the upper part of Barton Street, and what is now no. 101 Eastgate Street was no. 67 Barton Street, changing to no. 45 by 1939. This building was originally the Crown & Thistle, which may go back to the early eighteenth century. There is a suggestion that, as it lay beyond the East Gate, it catered for travellers arriving too late to get through the city gates. The pub name itself goes back even further than this, being a reference to when James VI of Scotland became James I of England in 1603. However, the first mention I have found for the pub is in *Pigot's Directory* of 1830.

REF: 140/615
MAP: F
STATUS: Trading as Zest
DATE: By 1830 to bee
LOCATION: 101–103 Eastgate St, GL1 1PY
CONTACT: 01452 502241

The Crown & Thistle achieved a listing in CAMRA's *Good Beer Guide* in 1982–6 and 1988. The 1984 CAMRA *Real Ale in Gloucestershire Guide* describes it as an 'up market real ale house with adjoining wine bar' and it had just been extended.

By 1993 the Crown & Thistle was owned by the Devenish Pub Company, who had separated the adjoining wine bar and opened it as Butlers of Gloucester (see p. 105). The fittings and decoration of the Crown & Thistle are described in the 1996 *Real Ale in Gloucestershire Guide* as creating 'a rural atmosphere in a pub that seeks to continue the alehouse tradition.' In June

Picture of Barton Street by Gwladys Davies showing the Crown & Thistle, probably in the 1960s. *(Gloucestershire Archives)*

The same area as that taken by Gwladys Davies, but this one taken in 2009: not much has changed. You can see that the original Crown & Thistle was between what is now Zest and Butlers.

2001 it became Zest. No. 101 seems to be shared, with Zest in the front part and Butlers behind.

As the name Zest suggests, it is no longer seeking to continue the alehouse tradition, becoming another pre-club venue. When I ventured into the Eastgate Street scene with a small posse of brave female friends in March 2009 we were not impressed by Zest, although my attitude may have been clouded by the bad experience that I'd had next door in Butlers just seconds before.

From the outside Zest looked very tatty, painted in white and bright blue. Inside was no better; it was dark and dingy with a carpet that stuck to your feet and cloudy plastic glasses. It didn't seem to know what it was, being part pub but with the ubiquitous DJ booth in the back and day-glo drinks behind the bar. The sad thing is, beneath all of this, if you squint, you can almost see the Crown & Thistle. The outside has since been given a makeover and now looks much better, so the inside may have improved too.

Dean's Walk Inn, Dean's Walk

REF: 145
MAP: C
STATUS: Trading
DATE: By 1844 to date
LOCATION: Dean's Walk,
GL1 2PX
CONTACT: 01452 415762

The Dean's Walk Inn is an ardent Gloucester rugby pub. Most of the rugby pubs are to be found clustered close to the ground on Kingsholm Road, but the Dean's Walk is a bit further out. It is tucked away alongside a dingy-looking Victorian railway bridge near the junction of Dean's Walk and St Catherine Street: you have to know it is there because you are unlikely to stumble upon it by accident.

If its distant location puts you in any doubt about its credentials as a rugby pub, these are soon dispelled when you see it: protruding from the roof is a large rugby ball and outside at the back of the pub is a painting of the Gloucester Rugby Ground 'Shed'. Even the pub sign shows the Dean in full religious regalia clutching a rugby ball – the Very Reverend Nick Bury, Dean of Gloucester, posed for the portrait in 2003.

According to Jean Clarke, whose parents owned the Dean's Walk Inn from 1932, and whose memories are recorded in *Ottakar's Local History Series: Gloucestershire*, the building housing the Dean's Walk was previously home to a blacksmith, a primer/painter and a paraffin shop.

At the beginning of its life as a pub it was just a beerhouse by the name of the Quart Pot. The first reference that I have found for it by this name is from 1844 when it belonged to St Nicholas Church and an application was made to rent it. Another later lease from 1887 shows it still owned by the church, but by this time it was referred to as Dean's Walk Inn. By the time Jean Clarke arrived in 1932, the Dean's Way council houses were almost new and she says the pub drew customers from surrounding streets, except (ironically) Dean's Walk, which was too posh.

The pub stood in its own grounds with St Catherine's Meadow at the bottom. There was no obstacle between the pub's garden and the River Severn, which meant that the ground floor was subject to regularly flooding. Jean reports that it regularly flooded up to 8 inches and in the severe floods of 1947 it was submerged in 2ft 11ins of water. At this time the pub was tied to the Cheltenham Original Brewery, which later became Whitbread, who closed the pub and in 1979 it was burnt down by squatters. It was rebuilt and enlarged by an entrepreneur and reopened in 1980 by the dean, the Revd Gilbert Thurlow. It earned itself a place in CAMRA's *Good Beer Guide* from 1982 to 1984 and the 1984 *Real Ale in Gloucestershire Guide* lists it as selling three real ales. These days the Dean's Walk only sells real ale on match days or special occasions.

Not being of a sporting nature, my experience of the Dean's Walk has always been to see live music, which takes place in the public bar. This is not a big room, and a decent band can generate an ear-drum splitting volume. When it is not full of a band, this bar normally houses a pool table. In the spirit of research, however, I felt that I should visit the rugby pubs on match day, and even go to a rugby match. I therefore visited with a sports-oriented friend, Geoff, in early in 2009, before going on to watch Gloucester beat Saracens 22–16. On this occasion we decided to sit in the lounge bar and were pleasantly surprised.

The bar retains the air of a traditional old pub and it's hard to believe that it is the result of such modern rebuilding. It is dark and welcoming with a flagstone floor, low timber-beamed ceiling and wooden partitions with stained glass creating cosy seating areas. The decoration is in traditional pub style, with metal advertising signs and pictures which look pleasingly authentic without going over the top. Best of all, there was a roaring real fire in the large red-brick fire-place: most welcome on a frosty January day.

In deference to its status as a rugby pub, the Dean's Walk has the obligatory flat screen TV showing sport, but this is located in a semi-partitioned area at the back of the bar, so is pleasingly unobtrusive to those, like me, who prefer to avoid it. There was a choice of two excellent real ales and behind the bar was a large stack of rolls cut from generous lengths of French bread. Although I like pub food and believe gastro-pubs have their place, in a decent, authentic boozer what you want to see is just good, simple filled rolls.

Dolphin Vaults, Northgate Street

REF: 156

MAP: A

STATUS: Demolished

DATE: By 1722 to 1908

LOCATION: Northgate Street

In Northgate Street, on the right-hand side as you walk away from the Cross, just beyond the Oxebode there was once a small road called Dolphin Lane. On the north corner of the lane, at no. 21 Northgate Street, was a simple, unremarkable brick-built pub called the Dolphin Inn or Vaults.

The first reference I have seen for the Dolphin comes from Dodd & Moss, who report that Thomas Maddockes at the Dolphin acted as agent for an estate called Hartpurys Farm in 1722. They also recount a later tale of Thomas Hartland, publican at the Dolphin, being indicted for insulting and assaulting one of the City Fathers, Alderman Blackwell, in 1759. The earliest definite alehouse licensing record I have found for the Dolphin in the North Ward is from 1806, when the licensee was John Hoskins. This was not the first Dolphin in Gloucester; there is also one listed in licensing records in the West Ward in 1680 and 1682, although it would not be unprecedented for this to be the same pub listed under the wrong ward.

On the opposite side of Dolphin Lane from the pub was a drapers shop called the Bon Marché. The store was started in 1889 by John Rowe Pope and became extremely successful. Business boomed and the store's expansion plans were aided when in March 1906 the Dolphin Inn, which at that time was leased to Smith's Brimscombe Brewery, was referred to the compensation authority 'as not being required to meet the wants of the neighbourhood.'

The Dolphin Vaults were closed in 1908 and demolished to make way for an extension to the Bon Marché in 1909. A further extension was added in 1914. Although the pub went, Dolphin Lane remained between the original store and the extension until it was officially closed in 1926. In 1931 the original part of the store was demolished and a large new building was put in its place as part of the Oxebode development. The store changed its name to Debenhams in the 1970s.

Northgate Street early in the twentieth century before the Bon Marché expanded. The Dolphin Vaults is the small square building on the left.

Gloucester, Northgate Street.

East End Tavern (Now TnT), Eastgate Street

Of all the complicated pub histories in Gloucester, this must be a fair contender as one of the worst! The East End Tavern was situated on the south side of Barton Street, now the lower part of Eastgate Street. As far as I can make out its early history goes like this: From about 1820 until 1861 there was a beerhouse called the Merry Fellow in Barton Street. In *Hunt's Directory* of 1849 it is listed at no. 23, but this can't be right because there was another pub there called the Hope Inn. It seems likely therefore that it was actually at no. 25 (although it could have been no. 43, which we will consider later). Whether it was previously the Merry Fellow or not, by 1871 no. 25 Barton Street was listed as the Ostrich. In 1876 the Original Shakespeare is listed in Barton Street and seems likely to have been on this site. Confused? You will be . . .

By 1879, no. 25 Barton Street was known as the Eastend Wine & Spirit Vaults, which by 1893 had been truncated to just the Eastend Vaults. By 1908 the street numbers were messed about with and it became no. 66 Barton Street and by 1939 the name is rendered slightly differently as the East End Vaults. By 1955 the name was changed again to the East End Tavern.

To add to the confusion, meanwhile there was another East End Tavern. The 1879 *Gloucester Directory* lists this at 43 Barton Street, in addition to the East End Wine & Spirit Vaults at no. 25. So, if the Merry Fellow (remember that?) was at no. 43 it was actually a precursor to this East End Tavern. No. 43 was on the opposite side of Barton Street on the corner with Station Road, just a couple of doors away from the Bell Inn. This East End Tavern disappeared by about 1885.

REF: 169/546

MAP: F

STATUS: Trading as TnT

DATE: By 1820 to date

LOCATION: 112, Eastgate Street, GL1 1QT

CONTACT: 01452 330808

TnT, formerly the East End Tavern.

Our original East End Tavern is described by the 1984 CAMRA *Real Ale in Gloucestershire Guide* as a 'good town boozer,' although at the time its only beer was the ubiquitous Whitbread PA. By 1993 things had changed dramatically: the street numbering had been messed with yet again to bring this part of Barton Street into Eastgate Street, so its address was 112 Eastgate Street, and it had been renamed to the Gate. This was not simply a name change, but an entire change of philosophy for the pub. It underwent a major refurbishment and, like most other pubs in the area, was turned into a student nightspot with disco and live music. It has now changed names again to TnT and styles itself as a 'café bar', providing lively pre-club entertainment. This is a mission that it takes very seriously without taking itself too seriously; it has an atmosphere ideal for young partygoers and hen nights and a pole on the dance floor which is used by enthusiastic customers once they've had enough to drink.

Despite being aimed at a young audience, Friday and Saturday nights are 'cheesy party music' nights, so even if old fogies like me can't keep up the pace, at least we recognise the music. On the Saturday night that, in the name of research, I braved the area with friends, this was without a doubt the most lively and fun place on the Eastgate Street 'strip'. Taking research to the limits, one of my friends even tried out the pole, but has requested anonymity (you know who you are!).

England's Glory, London Road

REF: 175

MAP: E

STATUS: Trading

DATE: By 1872 to date

LOCATION: 66–8, London Road, GL1 3PB

CONTACT: 01452 302948

Below: London Road looking east, with the New Inn on the right. *(Geoff Sandles)*

At the time of writing the England's Glory is the only pub open on London Road, but it was not always so isolated. It was originally known (rather unoriginally) as the New Inn and was flanked by the York House to the east and the Denmark Arms Inn to the west.

The New Inn was a beerhouse by 1872 and in the early days it brewed its own ale. By 1984 it was owned by Whitbread and its name was changed to England's Glory after the famous brand of matches manufactured by Moreland's in Bristol Road.

The England's Glory was virtually rebuilt internally in 1992, but the lounge bar is decorated in a traditional style and has a wonderful log fire, making it seem much older. It is now tied to Wadworth of Devizes and it earned a place in CAMRA's *Good Beer Guide* in 1999–2002 and 2004–5.

Famous Pint Pot, Bruton Way

REF: 178

MAP: F

STATUS: Trading

DATE: By 1861 to date

LOCATION: 74 Bruton Way, GL1 1EP

CONTACT: 01452 416840

The Famous Pint Pot is situated alongside the busy inner ring-road of Bruton Way, close to the Gloucester Leisure Centre now called GL1. It is a large, two-storey rendered building with a rustic, traditional interior with low ceilings, fake beams, rough plaster and old advertising signs. I have fond memories of the Pint Pot as, in the mid-1980s, before I should have been frequenting pubs and before I had fully embraced the joy of real ale, I used to go there to drink Merrydown Cider.

But I get ahead of myself. The Pint Pot started life as a beerhouse probably in about 1861 at 5 Cambridge Street. *Bretherton's Almanack and Gloucester Directory* of 1869 lists a beer retailer called Richard H. Bourn in Cambridge Street. In 1876 the name given is Thomas Bendall, but the pub is still not named. By 1879, the *Gloucester Directory* lists T. Bendall at the Locomotive in Cambridge Street, under the trade category of Inns and Taverns.

It was called the Locomotive because of its proximity to the Eastgate railway station, which stood where Asda is today. A planning application of 1952 shows it to be owned by the Stroud Brewery Co., who by 1963, when another planning application was submitted, had become West Country Breweries. Although directories continue to give the address for the Locomotive Inn as Cambridge Street until 1973, the planning paperwork gives the address as Station Road. Cambridge Street disappeared underneath the 1970s expansion of the Leisure Centre.

The closure of Eastgate station in 1975 didn't seem to cause too much inconvenience to the pub as building plans were passed for quite significant internal alterations and improvements in October of that year. Further internal alterations were granted in 1977.

One consequence of the disappearance of the Eastgate station was that the name, Locomotive Inn, no longer seemed so

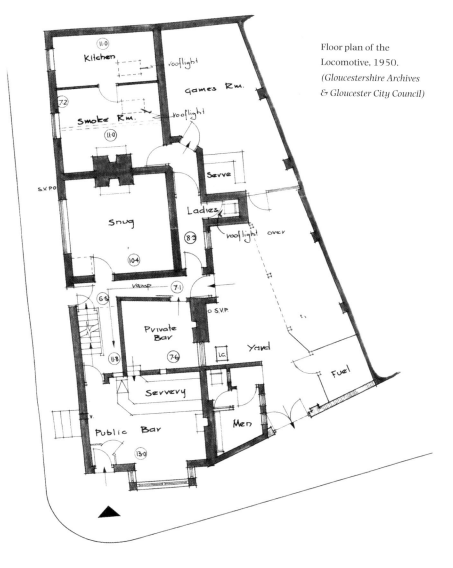

Floor plan of the Locomotive, 1950. *(Gloucestershire Archives & Gloucester City Council)*

appropriate, so by 1979, when there was some planning dispute about a proposed first-floor extension, it was referred to as the Pint Pot Inn, with the plans referring to it as the Famouse (sic) Pint Pot.

With the building of the inner ring road it changed address again to 74 Bruton Way. The Famous Pint Pot is now owned by Places Trading Limited, who also own Innteraction, the large nightclub next door, so at the weekend it caters largely for the pre-club crowd. However, perhaps surprisingly given this fact, unlike the disco pubs in Eastgate Street, the Pint Pot retains the atmosphere of a proper pub and even sells proper beer, so it also appeals to a much broader and more discerning clientele.

Greyhound Hotel, Eastgate Street

REF: 226
MAP: A
STATUS: Building in different use
DATE: By 1544 to 1935
LOCATION: 1 Eastgate Street

The Greyhound Hotel stood in the shadow of St Michael's Church at 1 Eastgate Street. Recorded from 1544, it appears in the earliest alehouse licensing records I have found from 1680. It is recorded as an inn in *Pigot's Directory* of 1830, but by *Bretherton's Directory* in 1869 it is listed as a hotel.

Eastgate Street looking away from the Cross in about 1914. The Greyhound Hotel is visible in the foreground on the right.

Advert from The *Ancient Order of the Foresters Guide to Gloucester* 1901. *(Gloucestershire Archives)*

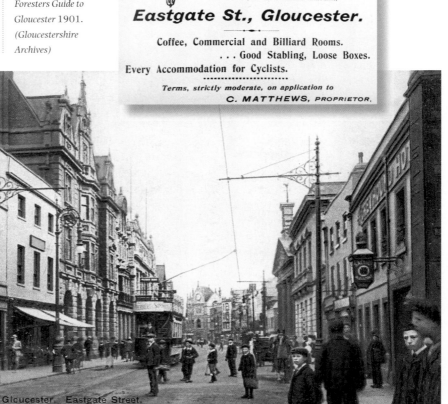

THE
Greyhound Hotel
(near the Cross and Cathedral),
Eastgate St., Gloucester.

Coffee, Commercial and Billiard Rooms.
. . . Good Stabling, Loose Boxes.
Every Accommodation for Cyclists.

Terms, strictly moderate, on application to
C. MATTHEWS, PROPRIETOR.

22238 Gloucester. Eastgate Street.

Eastgate Street, Gloucester. 18026

An advert from 1901 advertises 'Every Accommodation for Cyclists' but has no mention at all of beer. However, a postcard from about 1914 shows that by then it was owned by Salt & Co. of Burton upon Trent.

On 18 January 1918, the Greyhound Hotel was auctioned at the New Inn Hotel, described as, 'Very valuable and extensive Premises, freehold and fully licensed.' The property included two bars, a club room, drawing room, seven bedrooms and a yard with saddle room and three stables. It had a frontage of 48ft to Eastgate Street and totalled 780 square yards. At that time it was let to Alton Court Brewery Company Ltd.

What happened after this is unclear. Some reports suggest that the Greyhound was demolished in the 1920s; it doesn't appear in *Smart's Directory* of 1920, but it makes a reappearance by *Cope's Directory* of 1935. Botherways confectioners had operated next door to the Greyhound since at least 1908, and later postcards suggest that they took over the upper floor of the Greyhound, becoming Botherways Café, with the ground floor becoming retail premises.

This later became the Cadena Café, which by *Kelly's Directory* of 1939–40 was listed at 4–6 Eastgate Street in the new street numbering, with no. 2 (formerly no. 1) occupied by the tailors John Bright. The Cadena is fondly remembered; it was a popular place to eat and its bakery had a great reputation. It also boasted an excellent ballroom with dances every Wednesday and Friday night and tea dances on Saturdays.

St Michael's Church was demolished in 1956, leaving just the fifteenth-century tower. It was replaced by modern retail premises called St Michael's Buildings, but the adjacent buildings were retained. The Cadena Café continued until about 1970, but by 1972 the building was home to Hardy & Co. Furnishers. At the time of writing, the building is occupied by Currys Digital.

This later postcard shows Botherways Café in the former Greyhound building; this later became the Cadena Café.

Lamprey (now Westgate), Westgate Street

REF: 285/577

MAP: A

STATUS: Trading as Westgate

DATE: By 1920 to date

LOCATION: 56 Westgate Street, GL1 2NF

CONTACT: 01452 417113

The Lamprey was on Westgate Street near the corner with College Street, but its origins lie not only with a different name, but a different location. The story begins with the Gresham Hotel & Restaurant, located on the opposite side of Westgate Street at no. 32, on the corner with Berkeley Street. The first reference I can find to this dates to 1893, although it's probably older than that. By 1897 it was owned by the Stroud Brewery.

The Gresham was demolished to make way for an extension to the Shire Hall. It is last listed in *Smart's Directory* of 1908, although it is questionable whether it was still trading by that time.

Meanwhile, on the opposite side of the road near College Street at no. 135 was the Commercial hotel and restaurant. By 1920 it was listed with F.J. Smiley as manager. He was still there in 1927, by which time the name had become the Gresham Hotel & Restaurant and the street numbering had changed to put it at no. 56.

The Gresham Hotel was sold to the Cheltenham Original Brewery in 1931 and the name had changed to the Lamprey Hotel by 1941, when it is listed in *Kelly's Directory* with Capt. R. Heron as manager.

The lamprey was named for an ugly eel-like fish with royal connections and a long association with Gloucester. It has a jawless mouth ringed by teeth that help it to fasten itself into the flesh of other fish to feed from their blood. As unappetising as this sounds, royals have long enjoyed eating them and Henry I famously died from eating 'a surfeit of lampreys'.

King John instituted lamprey-keeping in Gloucester, where they were fished in the Severn, and from medieval times until 1836 it was customary for Gloucester to send a lamprey pie to the monarch at Christmas. Today lampreys are an endangered species, which probably explains why I have never seen this Gloucester delicacy, much less tried it. These pies are still presented to no doubt grateful monarchs on special occasions, including to Queen Elizabeth II after her coronation. Hopefully she liked it, because she got another for her silver jubilee in

The original Gresham Hotel in 1905, just before demolition.

(*Gloucestershire Archives*)

1977. The lamprey is such a strange and rare creature it seems unlikely that there is another pub anywhere with the same name.

The Lamprey Hotel was popular with business folk in the 1930s and during the Gloucester Assizes it was packed with legal types. However, by the 1990s it had become a failed disco pub, apparently with a brothel upstairs (something else I didn't try!). It was briefly turned into a successful Russian themed bar, but after only four weeks it was closed down by Whitbread for extensive rewiring and remained closed and boarded up for some time.

Like many a good DIY project, one thing obviously led to another because when the Lamprey reopened in June 1998, as the Lamprey Café Bar, the interior had been completely replaced and it had a new glass frontage. It was declared the regional Marketing Pub of the Year in 1999 at the Whitbread Pub Partnerships inaugural Excellence awards. It became Gloucester's first internet bar in August 2000 when a new bar was opened at the back with two state of the art touch-screen computers from which customers could send e-mails.

A Milton Keynes-based organisation called Therapy Co. took over the Lamprey shortly afterwards. This was their first venture and they decided that heritage and individuality had no place in their business philosophy and all their bars were to be called Therapy. And so it was that the Lamprey opened under this corporate banner in April 2002. Once again it was given a make-over – large screen TVs were introduced and there was regular drum and bass music.

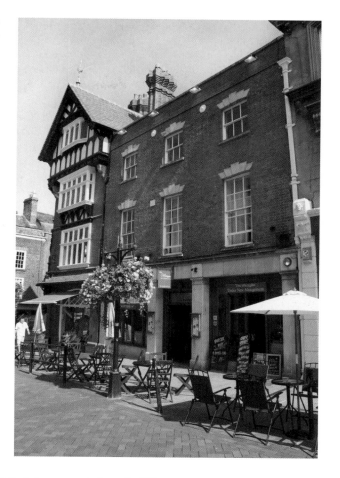

The Westgate, 2009.

Having broken away from any heritage in the name of the pub it now started to change its name so frequently it is hard to keep up. In June 2003 it became Haus, a schizophrenic establishment that styled itself as a coffee house, bar, restaurant and nightspot. This lasted longer than Therapy, but it was closed by April 2007. It opened again in August of that year as the Grill, the opening delayed by a month due to the serious floods that plagued Gloucestershire at that time. You barely had chance to finish your pint in the Grill, however, before it changed yet again in 2008 to the Westgate.

When I visited in June 2009 it was very nice, if quiet. It is very open, light and modern with a long bar down one side sprouting tall, shiny chrome keg beer fonts (there's no real ale). The manageress who I spoke to had been there since February and said that it tended to be busier in the day than in the evening: it had apparently been busy earlier with people watching tennis and rugby.

Since then the Westgate has had another change of owner, reopening in October 2009 under the management of James Wilkinson, who also owns the Orchard in Quedgeley. This time it retained the name and now offers wholesome food cooked freshly on site and a 'bar/ traditional pub for the over-25 market.'

Lemon and Parker, Eastgate Street

REF: 287

MAP: A

STATUS: Building in different use

DATE: 1882 to early 1970s

LOCATION: 15 Eastgate Street

One of the most popular and fondly remembered Gloucester pubs from the 1950s and 1960s was the Lemon and Parker in Eastgate Street. The rather unusual name comes from the surnames of its licensees, Arthur Sidney Lemon from Bristol and Gloucester man Mr Parker.

In about 1882 they took over George Barrett's wine & spirit merchants at no. 40 Eastgate Street and renamed it Lemon & Parker Wine & Spirit Merchants. They also had bonded stores at the docks and in Westgate Street. Parker died in 1887 and by 1908 it is shown in directories as Hardess G&A Wine & Spirit Merchants. This soon reverted and it was listed in directories as a public house as well as a wine and spirit merchants, known just as Lemon & Parker.

Eastgate Street, Gloucester.

View of Eastgate Street in about 1914, looking away from the Cross. Lemon & Parker Wine Merchants is next to the Gloucester Coffee House on the left of the picture. *(Gloucestershire Archives)*

The Lemon & Parker conservatory. *c.* 1901. *(Gloucestershire Archives)*

Following the street renumbering in about 1920 it became no. 15. The pub had a pleasant canopied drinking area to the rear with slatted benches, round bar tables and a great abundance of wisteria, ferns and other plants. In its heyday it had three bars and up to fifty bar staff and was one of the first pubs in the city to have live music. In 1963 it was refurbished and had the distinction of being the first city centre pub with a balcony. Being close to the Guildhall it was a popular meeting place before dances and other functions.

The Lemon & Parker Inn closed in the early 1970s and the site is now occupied by Waterstone's bookshop.

Malt & Hops, Longsmith Street

The Malt & Hops was the first pub that I ever drank in regularly. It was immediately behind the Golden Cross in Southgate Street (see p. 74) and there was a linking corridor between the two. However, whereas the Golden Cross was full of the noise and bustle of trendy people getting drunk before heading for a nightclub, the Malt & Hops was much more laid back.

Opened in the mid-1970s, it is claimed that the Malt & Hops was Gloucester's first dedicated real ale bar, although it only made CAMRA's *Good Beer Guide* once, in 1977. It was certainly nothing special from the outside; an ugly, square, flat-roofed building squeezed into the garden of the Golden Cross. Inside, however, it had a rustic, traditional look, with lots of wooden beams and pillars and booths along one wall.

Although when I started drinking there the clientele was generally young and it was popular with students, it nonetheless had staunch regulars. One booth in the corner was always frequented by the same group of people to the extent that they personalised it with postcards and other personal belongings.

As is often the way, the Malt & Hops fell into decline and it closed on 3 April 2001. It stood empty and derelict until it was finally demolished in 2008 when the garden of Robert Raikes' House, the former Golden Cross, was restored.

REF: 301
MAP: A
STATUS: Demolished
DATE: mid-1970s to 2001
LOCATION: Longsmith Street

Midland & Royal Hotel, Station Road

Behind the Gloucester Leisure centre, GL1, near to the busy Bruton Way ring road, is an impressive Victorian three-storey red-bricked building called Royal House, which currently houses Langley Wellington solicitors. However, the building's heritage as a drinking establishment can be seen from the West Country Ale plaques that are still in situ.

The location of the building at no. 28 Station Road, on the corner of Albert Street, was very close to the old Eastgate station of the Midland Railway which stood where Asda is now, and it was the Midland Railway that built it as the Royal Hotel in 1898.

In 1912 there is mention of a second hotel on the other corner of Albert Street at no. 29. This was an unlicensed hotel called the Midland Hotel and it disappeared to be replaced by offices called Midland Chambers by 1920. Subsequently, by 1923, the Royal Hotel became known as the Midland & Royal Hotel.

In about 1946, at which time the hotel was owned by the Cheltenham & Hereford Brewery Co., the skittle alley and a small section of the hotel were destroyed by fire. Being wartime, permission was needed from the Ministry of Works to carry out any

REF: 315/457
MAP: F
STATUS: Building in different use
DATE: 1898 to early 1979
LOCATION: 28 Station Road

Midland & Royal
Hotel in the 1930s.
(Gloucestershire Archives)

building work and a licence was granted for making good the hotel but not the skittle alley. In 1948 an application was made by the Biffyans Bowling Club to erect Nissen Huts as a temporary skittle alley, but this was still rejected due to labour requirements. Finally an alternative using a M.A.F. building was approved.

Following the war plans were submitted to provide a proper skittle alley in 1954, along with an application for a music and dancing licence. The name reverted to just the Royal Hotel in about 1959 and brewery acquisitions and mergers meant that the owners changed to West Country Breweries, then Whitbread Flowers. Despite the closure of the Midland Railway station in 1975, plans were passed to give the hotel a facelift in 1979, including converting the skittle alley to a restaurant. However, the hotel closed soon afterwards and was converted into office accommodation.

Northend Vaults, Northgate Street

REF: 347/562
MAP: A
STATUS: Trading as The
Vaults
DATE: By 1869 to date
LOCATION: 86, Northgate
Street, GL1 1SL
CONTACT: 01452 523560

The Northend Vaults is at 86–8 Northgate Street, immediately opposite the junction with Worcester Street. Under the original street numbering it was nos 44–5. It is a Grade II listed building which dates back to the late sixteenth or early seventeenth century, when it was a merchant's house. It was re-fronted in the eighteenth century, but behind that is the original timber-framed building.

The first mention that I have found for it as a pub is from 1869, when it was called the Northend Wine Vaults, owned by Dobell, Mott & Co. The 'Northend' part of the name was dropped for a time, and by 1912 it was owned by Godsell & Sons Ltd. By 1920 the name had once again become the Northend Wine & Spirit Vaults, which was shortened to the North End Vaults by 1939. Godsell & Sons were taken over by Stroud Brewery Company in 1928, eventually becoming Whitbread.

The Northend Vaults was next door to the extremely grand building of the Northgate Methodist Church, which was built in 1860. The church was demolished in the 1970s to make way for the horribly bland modern brick building that was originally built as a Tesco supermarket and now houses Wilkinsons, but somehow, miraculously, the Northend Vaults survived.

Northend Vaults next to the now sadly demolished Northgate Methodist Church. *(Reg Woolford)*

It didn't, however, escape the pub-theme trend of the 1990s. In February 1994 the front of the pub was shrouded in scaffolding as it was discovered to be gradually moving forward. Whitbread took this opportunity to refurbish the building as well as repair it, at a total cost of £115,000. It reopened in May 1994 as a Tut 'n' Shive, described by Whitbread as a 'traditional ale house with various wacky themes and attractions.' This didn't last long as in May 1996 it was refurbished again in a 24-hour challenge, returning it to a more traditional atmosphere. The Tut 'n' Shive label was dropped, but the theme madness didn't subside entirely as it became Ebenezer Riley's Northend Vaults. Thankfully, the Ebenzeer Riley branding was also eventually removed.

Prior to the re-theming, the Northend Vaults earned itself a place in CAMRA's *Good Beer Guide* for a couple of years in 1984 and 1987, but it never regained its former status for the beer drinker, despite the fact that my brother worked there for a short time. As I write at the end of 2009, in line with the current trend for short, pithy pub names, it is now known just as the Vaults.

The Vaults has definitely seen better days. It is not a large pub and it has a bit of a grungy air inside, which is a shame because if you look beyond that it is an impressive old building. When I visited on a Saturday night in November 2009 it had a disco blaring out, which was not only oppressively loud in the relatively confined space of the pub, but it also seemed out of place. The clientele didn't have the appearance of a disco crowd, and the pool table appeared to be a more appropriate attraction. I was impressed to find a real ale pump on the bar, boasting a very reasonably priced pint of Doom Bar, but then immediately disappointed to find that it had sold out.

The Northend Vaults, now just the Vaults, sandwiched between two modern monstrosities, giving a very different impression of the city as you approach from the north.

Park End, Parkend Road

REF: 376

MAP: H & I

STATUS: Trading

DATE: By 1872 to date

LOCATION: 18, Parkend Road, GL1 5AL

CONTACT: 01452 524624

The Park End Tavern was built by Mitchells & Butlers before 1872, when it is in licensing records as a beerhouse. It got an alehouse licence in 1874. There was a bowling green alongside the pub and the Gloucester Bowling Club was established there in 1897.

The *Real Ale in Gloucestershire Guide* for 1984 describes it as a gem of a pub with original wood and excellent engraved windows, selling Fussells Best Bitter. Subsequent guides report no real ale, a situation that remains true as I write, but it also remains a gem of a pub with a magnificent, huge wooden bar that should be listed. When I visited on a weekday evening it had a friendly, community atmosphere, including a table of men playing dominoes.

Prince Albert (now Fusion), Station Road

REF: 402/193

MAP: F

STATUS: Trading as Fusion

DATE: By 1867 to date

LOCATION: 1, Station Road, GL1 1EN

CONTACT: 01452 523246

The Prince Albert was located at 1 Station Road, on the corner with Whitfield Street. The first mention that I have for it is 1867, at which time it would have been ideally situated for both of the railway stations and the cattle market, which was located where the bus station is today.

In the early days the Prince Albert was supplied with beer from the Cirencester Brewery – possibly the only place that you could get these beers in Gloucester. Following a couple of mergers and takeovers, by 1960 the Cirencester Brewery was owned by Courage, and so was the Prince Albert. The pub closed in 1996 and remained boarded up for some time.

As you may be aware, Prince Albert is also the name of one of the more common male genital piercings, the thought of which makes my eyes water. This is more commonly referred to as a PA. Whether deliberately playing on this name or an unfortunate oversight, the pub reopened on 26 March 1999 as the PA Sports Café & Pub, owned by the Unique Pub Co. and Falcon Inns. By July 2001 this was shortened simply to PA.

Fusion, formerly known as the Prince Albert. The black and white photograph can't do justice to the lurid paintwork.

As is often the case with modern pub names, they don't hang around for long. By 2003 the name had changed again to Bar Spirit, specialising in Japanese food. Again it closed down, reopening in April 2007 as Jameson's, an Irish Theme pub. After only a year the pub was shut again, reopening in April 2008 after a complete refurbishment. This lasted even less time before the doors closed again.

Later, in 2008, it reopened with yet another new name: Fusion. The exterior of the impressive Victorian building was painted dark grey with purple woodwork and was bathed in lurid neon lighting, looking more like a nightclub than a pub. I set out to visit it in March 2009 but wasn't quick enough: it was closed again.

Following another revamp it reopened with the same name and colour scheme in August 2009, now owned by the pub company London Town, who focus on reopening pubs which they believe have a viable future with the right management and support. The new manager, Alex Fletcher, is confident and offers well priced food as well as beer.

Rising Sun, Eastgate Street

Located at 30 Eastgate Street in the original street numbering, the Rising Sun was a beerhouse just a couple of doors away from the Saracen's Head. It existed under that name by 1894 when it was a tied house of the Gloucester City Brewery.

Prior to that it was the City Wine Vaults from at least 1869, when the landlord was J. Phelps. By 1879 it had changed to Dunlop Mackenzie & Co. Wine & Spirit Merchants and J. Phelps shows up in the similarly named Eastend Wine & Spirit Vaults in Barton Street.

The *Ancient Order of the Foresters Guide to Gloucester* 1901 carries an advert for the Greenroom at 30 & 31 Eastgate Street, but this is the only mention that I have found for it, so presumably this was a short-lived name change for the Rising Sun. The proprietor Bro. W. A. King advertises 'Salt & Co.'s noted Ales and Stout on draught. Wines and Spirits of the best quality only at popular prices.' A postcard from 1904 shows the landlord as Fred Ireland and it is still owned by Salt & Co. of Burton upon Trent, but the name of the pub is not shown.

REF: 441
MAP: A
STATUS: Demolished
DATE: by 1869 to 1911
LOCATION: 30 Eastgate Street

Eastgate Street looking toward the Cross in about 1904. The Rising Sun is the building with the ornate arched windows on the right next to the American & Canadian Stores. The Saracen's Head can be seen three doors further down.

Gloucester, Eastgate Street.

The Rising Sun had closed by 1911 and the building was converted into the City Cinema. Three years later it underwent improvement and modernisation, reopening on 1 March 1915 as the Gloucester Hippodrome, the second cinema in the city (after the De-Luxe) to convert to 'talkies' in 1930. It became the Gaumont in April 1959, but despite continued popularity it was closed in April 1961 and remained empty until 1964, when it was demolished to make way for British Home Stores.

Seymour, Seymour Road

REF: 469
MAP: H
STATUS: Trading
DATE: By 1893 to date
LOCATION: 145, Seymour Road, GL1 5PT
CONTACT: 01452 523226

The Seymour is located on the corner of Seymour Road and Linden Road. From the outside it is an interesting and attractive stone-built pub with an impressive corner entrance with stone carvings. A crest on the top of the door entrance is badly weathered but it is believed to be a Godsell & Sons malt shovel clasped in hand emblem.

The first reference that I have found for the pub dates back to 1893 when the landlord was C.J. Ramstedt, and it was owned by the Ramsdedt family for well over forty years until at least 1939. Godsell & Sons owned the Seymour from at least 1927, and the crest would suggest that they originally had the pub built.

Being located away from the main road in a residential area, the Seymour is very much a local community pub. I visited on a Saturday evening with a group of friends, and the two girls in our party were not impressed to be met at the lounge bar door by a welcoming committee of what one of them later described as 'fat men wearing food stained t-shirts.' The greeting clearly didn't have the allure that the men hoped it would have for the ladies, instead causing them to beat a hasty retreat.

Luckily there is another way in, through the ornate main entrance on the corner, which brings you into the public bar. Whereas the lounge is carpeted, this part of the bar is very traditional looking with wooden floors, trestle seating, stained glass and very high ceilings typical of the Victorian period. Unfortunately, despite the signs on the window proclaiming the Seymour to be an 'Ale House', there was no real ale.

The pub has two pub signs, one showing a coat of arms, the other a bearded chap in Tudor attire. This relates to the person for whom the pub is named – Thomas Seymour.

He was born in about 1508 and historian David Starkey describes him as 'tall, well-built and with a dashing beard and auburn hair.' Also, apparently unlike the pub's clientele, 'he was irresistible to women.'

Thomas became Baron Seymour of Sudeley in 1547, by which time he had served with distinction in the war against France, briefly holding supreme command of the English Army before becoming admiral of the fleet. His sister was Jane Seymour, Henry VIII's third wife, and his brother Edward became Lord Protector of England. After the death of Henry VIII, Thomas married one of Henry's other wives, Catherine Parr.

Jealous of his brother's power, it seems that Thomas got up to all manner of skulduggery, eventually being sent to the Tower of London accused of thirty-three charges of treason. He was executed in 1549, dying 'dangerously, irksomely and horribly.'

Shakespeare, Northgate Street

The earliest mention that I have found for the Shakespeare in Northgate Street is 1820, when it is found in alehouse licensing records. However, Dodd and Moss list it in their book *Eighteenth Century Alehouses*, so it is clearly older, probably originating as a beerhouse. The pub was on the east side of Northgate Street, to the north of the Northend Vaults, at no. 49 in the original street numbering, later no. 96.

The Shakespeare was rebuilt by 1856 and during excavations a Romano-British votive tablet was found on the site, hinting of the importance of alcohol here long before this. The tablet depicts two figures, one of whom is Mercury, messenger of the gods, patron of travellers and wayfarers and god of trade, particularly the grain trade.

REF: 471
MAP: A
STATUS: Demolished
DATE: by 1820 to 1959
LOCATION: 96 Northgate Street

The other is thought to be Rosmerta, the Gaulish goddess of fertility and abundance and possibly a deity of the Dobunni and Hwicce peoples who occupied the Severn Valley immediately before and after the Roman occupation. On this tablet Rosmerta appears to be pouring a libation, or offering of a drink to a god, into a bucket. The same excavations revealed a Roman building, thought to be the temple in which this tablet was dedicated.

The pub was valued at £2,222 in 1900, by which time it was owned by the Stroud Brewery Company. It was closed in 1959 and demolished probably as part of the redevelopment of the area in the 1970s.

Votive tablet discovered on the site of the Shakespeare Inn, Northgate Street, on display in the Gloucester City Museum. *(Darrel Kirby, used with permission of Gloucester City Museums)*

Station Hotel, Bruton Way

REF: 504
MAP: A
STATUS: Trading
DATE: By 1856 to date
LOCATION: Bruton Way,
GL1 1DE
CONTACT: 01452 520022

The Station Hotel is an impressive three-storey Victorian building located just a stone's throw from the railway station on the corner of Bruton Way and Station Approach. Originally called the Wellington Hotel it has been around since at least 1856 and probably before that, about the time the railway arrived in Gloucester in the 1840s. The current building dates from 1880.

The Wellington Hotel is presumably named for the Duke of Wellington, who visited Gloucester the year after the Battle of Waterloo, although that was forty years before the first date that I have found for the hotel. The original address was George Street, which still exists as a small road running behind the hotel but was the main road before Bruton Way was built in the 1960s. Another hotel, the Gloucester, was located on the opposite side of George Street, owned by Arnold Perrett & Co. This closed in about 1957 and the building still exists but is now in commercial use.

Allied Breweries owned the Wellington Hotel in the 1980s and in 1984 the CAMRA *Real Ale in Gloucestershire Guide* lists it as the New Wellington Hotel. It was sold to the Chapman Group in April 2001, who renamed it the Station Hotel. Today the Station is hard to miss, painted bright yellow with blue doors and stonework around the bottom. The entrance from Bruton Way is through a small pillared porch-way which leads into a vast, open, modern interior with high ceilings. The bar is off to one side, leaving a large, open area with wooden floor that has the appearance of a dance floor, which perhaps it is in the evenings.

When I recently visited the Station after a rugby match it was, unsurprisingly, full of rugby fans on their way home. I was pleased to see a range of hand-pulls at the bar, but the large chap beside me, apparently in charge of the kitty for a group of lads who had the look of rugby players about them, was being far more adventurous. Before him was a line of glasses with identical contents looking innocently like cola, although I'm sure that I saw pickled eggs lurking in the bottom of some of them. He was busy topping them up with beer from a pint glass.

'What is that?' I asked, the revulsion perhaps all too clear on my face.

'A cheeky vimto,' he replied. 'I'm just making it a bit more interesting.'

'Ah,' I said, none the wiser. I looked it up when I got home. According to Wikipedia, a 'cheeky vimto' is one or two shots of ruby port and a bottle of Blue WKD. I'm glad I wasn't in his round!

Tabard (now Varsity), Northgate Street _____

The Tabard was situated at 53 Northgate Street, on the corner with Hare Lane. The earliest reference that I have found for the pub comes from records from Stratton, Davis & Yates, architects, who produced plans for proposed alterations to the 'Gloucester Spot', subsequently the 'Tabard', in 1924. It is unclear whether the name the Gloucester Spot was ever used, much less whether it was a pub.

Next door to the Tabard in Hare Lane was another, older pub called the King's Arms (see p. 49). These two pubs were amalgamated, probably in the late 1970s or early 1980s.

In the mid-1980s I frequented the Tabard occasionally. At this time it was notorious as a biker pub. The people drinking here were not young wannabee bikers like my friends and I, they were the real McCoy – older guys dressed in tatty, grease-caked denim and leather, with bike club patches proudly displayed on cut-off denim jackets.

REF: 521/561
MAP: A
STATUS: Trading as Varsity
DATE: By 1924 to date
LOCATION: 53, Northgate Street, GL1 2AJ
CONTACT: 01452 304357

Tabard Lounge and Snack Bar in about 1924. The King's Arms just sneaks onto the edge of the picture. Note also the superb tabard pub sign. *(Gloucestershire Archives)*

The interior of the Tabard bar in about 1924. *(Gloucestershire Archives)*

Varsity, formerly the
Tabard, 2009.

By the late 1980s or early '90s, things were very different. The pub became a trendy, youth oriented place. For a while it was called Cleopatra's and by 1993, perhaps in recognition of its origins, it was renamed Kings. In early 1999 the pub underwent a £500,000 facelift, reopening as King's Venue Bar.

About this time Kings was owned by the Laurel Pub Group, who in 2002 sold it to the Barracuda Pubs & Bars Company. It closed again for refurbishment, this time costing £650,000, before reopening in the autumn of 2002 as the Gate. The manager at the time, Katrina Nixon, described it as a high quality, contemporary pub with salvaged fittings, leather seating and mellow colour schemes.

By 2008 the pub changed names again to Varsity, to bring it in line with the rest of the Barracuda chain. Today it is a loud, lively bar mainly frequented by young people. It has large screen TVs dotted around showing sport, including possibly the biggest TV screen I've seen outside a cinema at the back of the pub. Although lively at the front of the pub, it gets noisier as you move backwards into the old King's Arms part, where it has a full on disco atmosphere.

Water Poet, Eastgate Street

REF: 569
MAP: F
STATUS: Trading
DATE: 1997 to date
LOCATION: 61–3, Eastgate
Street, GL1 1PN
CONTACT: 01452 783530

The Water Poet opened on 29 October 2007 as Gloucester's second J.D.Wetherspoon pub, the other being the Regal (see p. 72). The Water Poet building was once the TSB Bank but it started its life as a pub on 16 September 1997 when Regent Inns spent £3.5 million and four months converting it to the Old Bank (written as O£d Bank). Staying true to the bank ethos it was aimed at the suit and tie business market, but this didn't last long because on 1 October 1998 it opened as Spoofers Bar, which as the name suggests was aimed at more of a party crowd.

Despite the fact that it was barely a year since its last refurbishment, another £1 million was spent on Spoofers and it was officially opened by Gloucester Rugby

captain Pete Glanville. This lasted a bit longer, until June 2005 when it had another change of name to Zebra Bar. When J.D. Wetherspoon took over they spent yet another £970,000 developing it into the Water Poet.

The pub is named after the poet John Taylor, who was born in Gloucester on 24 August 1580 and educated at Crypt Grammar School. He was apprenticed to a London waterman, ferrying passengers across the Thames in a scull, hence he became known as the Water Poet. Watermen were used as a naval reserve, and Taylor served in Essex's fleet at Flores in 1596 and at the Siege of Cadiz in 1597. He had a sense of adventure and during his life undertook ten journeys around the UK and as far afield as Bohemia, which he used as inspiration for his poetry. He gave up working as a waterman to concentrate on poetry full time in 1622 and produced a total of 150 publications during his life. His poems include one of the first palindromes to be named as such, 'Lewd did I live & evil did I dwel', written in 1614. He died in December 1653.

Despite only being a couple of years old, the Water Poet has established itself as a CAMRA favourite. The pub has a good mix of modern and contemporary décor and is spacious and open. It has a wide range of beer which is well kept and, of course, like all Wetherspoons pubs, cheap. It prides itself on being 'a traditional alehouse' and always stocks three session ales and a number of local ales on tap. I have particularly enjoyed a couple of the regular Wetherspoon's beer festivals at the Water Poet, where the atmosphere has always been good and the selection of beers superb. It tied for Gloucester CAMRA's City Pub of the Year 2009, only losing out to the Pig Inn the City on a casting vote, but it earned an entry in the *Good Beer Guide* and is there again in 2010.

Its location puts the Water Poet at the head of the Eastgate Street 'night time economy' area – a welcome source of decent beer to steady you for the onslaught of fizz and madness to follow.

White Hart Inn, Bell Lane

REF: 585
MAP: A
STATUS: Demolished
DATE: By 1869 to 1966
LOCATION: 14 Bell Lane

Bell Lane was a narrow road running from Southgate Street to Queen Street, which ran parallel to Brunswick Road. In medieval times, Bell Lane was called Trauellone, or Travel Lane, and got the name of Bell or Bellman's Lane in commemoration of William Henshawe's Bell foundry that operated there in the sixteenth century. In the 1970s the un-lovely concrete Eastgate Shopping Centre was built over the top of Bell Lane and the main thoroughfare through it is called Bell Walk in its memory.

I don't imagine that Bell Lane was a very grand thoroughfare, although it can't have been too bad as it was home to Robert Raikes toward the end of his life, and later to

Thomas Addison, who built a folly in memory of his old neighbour in nearby Marylone, near Café René. Bell Lane was also home to two pubs, virtually opposite each other – The White Hart Inn and the City Arms.

The White Hart, on the south side of the lane, originally no. 10 then later 14, existed by 1869. It is possible that it existed earlier than this, but it is difficult to distinguish it from the older White Hart in Southgate Street (see p. 42). The stables of this older White Hart backed onto Bell Lane, but I have been unable to determine whether there is any connection between the two.

The last licensee was a boxer called Harry Hewlett who was at the pub for twenty-six years until he called

White Hart, 1963.
(Crown Copyright.
National Monuments
Record (NMR))

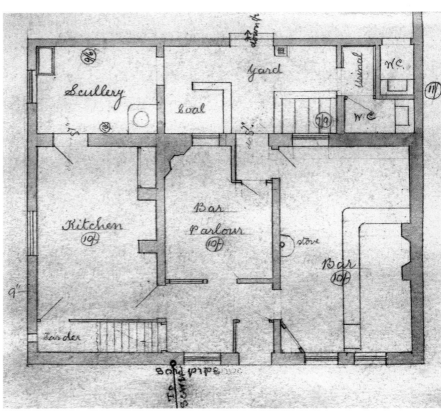

Floor plan of the City
Arms. (Gloucestershire
Archives)

it a day in 1964. In sixteen years as a boxer he claimed never to have been knocked out, warned or disqualified. He was so well known that the White Hart was known to regulars just as 'Harry's'.

The City Arms (Ref 100, Map A) was almost opposite on the north side of the lane, originally listed as no. 9 and later as no. 7 Bell Lane. It is possible that it existed as a beerhouse from the eighteenth century, but the first reference that I have for it in the alehouse licensing records is from 1802. It was purchased by the Gloucester Bell Hotel Company (limited) in 1865 – the committee were authorised to purchase it for a price not exceeding £700.

Both the City Arms and White Hart were demolished in about 1966–7 in preparation for the building of the Eastgate Shopping Centre.

Windmill, Eastgate Street

The Windmill is located at 83 Eastgate Street. It has an interesting and attractive exterior in a mix of styles. It is basically a square, brick two-storey building with small paned glass windows on the ground floor and has what I think of as an art-deco appearance, but I'm no expert on these things and may be entirely wrong about that!

It started life as a pub as Brunel's Wine Bar in 1984, being renamed the Windmill in 1987. It was bought by Marston's Brewery in 1994, who sold it on to Greene King in 1999. By 2002 it moved into private ownership.

Like most of the pubs in this part of Eastgate Street, the Windmill was a disco-pub catering for the young, pre-nightclub crowd. However, in 2006 it was refurbished by pub regulars and volunteers into a café bar. It closed again early in 2009, reopening in April having been converted to Fever nightclub, playing 1970s, '80s and '90s music.

REF: 602
MAP: F
STATUS: Trading as Fever nightclub
DATE: 1984 to 2009
LOCATION: 83-85, Eastgate Street, GL1 1PN
CONTACT: 01452 500370

Lower Westgate Street and the Westgate Comprehensive Redevelopment Area

When I bump into someone at the bar and tell them about my research for this book, if they are over a certain age they will almost inevitably give the same response: 'Do you know there used to be x number of pubs in Westgate Street? I can name them for you if you like . . .'. The number of pubs stated varies, but the gist is that it was a lot. It is only Westgate Street that inspires such a strong knee-jerk reaction to reminisce.

Until the early 1960s Westgate Street ran in an uninterrupted line right down to Westgate Bridge. The area beyond the junction with The Quay, where the ring road now cuts through, was known as the Island. This dates back to the days when a third arm of the Severn cut through roughly where the junction is and was crossed by the Foreign Bridge.

For many centuries Westgate Street, or Westyatstret, was the busiest and most important of Gloucester's highways, forming an important link in the main trading routes from London and Bristol to South Wales. The cathedral would also have been important to the life of Westgate Street, and would have attracted many devout and thirsty pilgrims. Most significant of all, however, was the proximity of The Quay. Before the docks were built in the nineteenth century this is where the port was and where there are sailors and port workers, there are pubs.

Beginning in the late nineteenth century people started drifting out of the city to the suburbs. Many of the properties in this area were also badly affected by the extensive floods of 1947, when water came up as far as the Shire Hall. This was a tragedy for the area, but it is only thanks to the *Citizen*'s photographs of the floods that we have any pictures at all of many of these pubs.

Slum cottages in Harris Court off Westgate Street – only quaint when viewed from a historical distance! (Reflections of Clapham Group/ Bernard Polson)

This all made the area ripe for redevelopment under the post-war improvements. Designated the Westgate Comprehensive Development Area it comprised 13 acres bounded by Westgate Street, St Mary's Square and Archdeacon Street. Beginning in 1952 the development removed the existing 'obsolete' property, replacing it with flats, maisonettes and shops. This got rid of a lot of pubs.

Development continued with the ring road completed around St Bartholemew's Hospital in 1961 and buildings to the east of that demolished in the 1970s and 1980s, leaving the area west of St Nicholas Church a largely soulless and pub-less place.

Admiral Benbow, Lower Westgate Street

REF: 2
MAP: B
STATUS: Demolished
DATE: by 1736 to 1907
LOCATION: Westgate Street

The Admiral Benbow was located in Lower Westgate Street 'near Foreign Bridge' just before the junction with The Quay. It was on the south side of the road and to the east was Little Quay Court or Turnstile Alley.

The pub was named Admiral Benbow by about 1858 – prior to that it was known as the Masons Arms, which appears in licensing records since at least 1736.

Admiral Benbow
photographed by
Sidney Pitcher.
*(Gloucestershire
Archives)*

The Admiral Benbow is a popular pub name, possibly because it was the fictional home of Jim Hawkins in *Treasure Island*. Whether it is deliberate or coincidental, there is a link between *Treasure Island* and Gloucester: Robert Louis Stevenson based the character of Long John Silver on the poet and writer William Ernest Henley, who was born in Eastgate Street. The admiral was also a real person, although he doesn't seem to have had any direct connection with Gloucester. He was born in about 1653 in either Shropshire or Shrewsbury and joined the Royal Navy in 1678. He worked his way up through the ranks spending most of his career either hunting and killing pirates or fighting the French. It was while fighting the French that he was injured in 1702 and was taken to Port Royal in Jamaica, where he died and was buried.

The whole building of the pub and an adjoining shop protruded out into Westgate Street, clearly causing something of an obstruction. The owners, Stroud Brewery, gave up the licence in February 1907 on the understanding that they could purchase a piece of land at the junction of Linden Road and Stanley Road. The building was demolished in 1909.

Boot, Lower Westgate Street

The Boot existed in the Island at no. 28 Lower Westgate Street since at least 1736, when it is found in the alehouse licensing records. An advert from 1879 boasts, 'fine home brewed ales. Wines and Spirits of the finest brands.'

In 1925 it was referred to the compensation authority. The owners, Ind Coope, 'had considered the question of structural alterations and were of the opinion that the only thing that could be done was to rebuild.' Whether this rebuilding took place is unclear, but the Boot was still listed in directories in 1935.

REF: 60

MAP: B

STATUS: Demolished

DATE: By 1736 to after 1935

LOCATION: 28 Lower Westgate Street/the Island

All that now remains of the Boot is the pub sign, housed in the Gloucester Folk Museum. *(Gloucester City Museums)*

Duke, Lower Westgate Street _____

REF: 160/164

MAP: B

STATUS: Demolished

DATE: by 1736 to 1936

LOCATION: 178 Lower
Westgate Street/the Island

This is yet another pub name which caused me much confusion. A pub called the Duke appears in alehouse licensing records by 1736. By 1806, and probably earlier, there are two pubs of that name listed. By 1827 some clarity is given as they are referred to as the 'Duke on the Island' and the 'Duke on The Quay'.

I have seen both of these pubs referred to in various places as the Duke of Gloucester, but it is only the one on The Quay (Ref 161/162, Map B) that seems to have formally gone by that name. It is listed in *Pigot's Directory* of 1830 and appears on the Public Health map of 1851 by that name, although Causton's Map of 1843 still shows it as just the Duke Inn. On 15 August 1890 the Duke of Gloucester was conveyed to the Cheltenham Original Brewery along with Star Inn, Quay Mill and cottages in Quay Lane, all for £3,090. It was submitted for compensation in 1905 and presumably closed shortly thereafter.

Meanwhile, the Duke on the Island is still known as just the Duke in *Pigot's Directory* of 1830. The first record I have of an expansion of this name is *Hunt's Directory* of 1847, when its allegiance is to another county as the Duke of Sussex. It also appears by this name on the Public Health map of 1851 and keeps going until at least 1936. It is now buried under the Westgate Galleria.

Leather Bottle, Archdeacon Street _____

REF: 286

MAP: B

STATUS: Demolished

DATE: by 1682 to 1959

LOCATION: 17 Archdeacon
Street

Archdeacon Street in
the floods of 1947.
The Leather Bottle can
be seen on the left.
(Gloucester Citizen)

The Leather Bottle was a nondescript brick-built pub at 17 Archdeacon Street, off Westgate Street. The road was named Leather Bottle Lane for a time. Once a tied house of Smith & Sons, Brimscombe Brewery, Stroud, the Leather Bottle was later acquired by the Bristol Brewery Georges & Co. Ltd.

It is first found in the licensing records way back in 1682, and the name is a reminder that bottles used to be made from leather rather than glass. At this time the licensee was Samuel Webly; another Webly, Katherine, was licensee at the Oxbody at the same time, but I don't know if that is coincidence or whether they were related.

The Leather Bottle continued trading right up until it found itself slap bang in the middle of the Westgate Comprehensive Redevelopment Area. The first phase of the scheme included the realignment and reconstruction of Archdeacon Street between Westgate Street and the north side of St Mary's Square and the Leather Bottle had to be acquired and demolished to facilitate that.

The Gloucester Brewers' Association represented Georges & Co.'s interest along with their own pubs affected by the development. The City Architect stated that, 'The arrangement with the Gloucester Brewers' Association is that their properties in the redevelopment areas will be acquired on the basis of the unlicensed value, on the understanding that the corporation will eventually offer one new site for every three licensed premises so acquired.'

The licence was put in suspension on 6 October 1959.

Old Dial, Westgate Street

The Old Dial was originally at 93 Westgate Street and following renumbering became 150 Westgate Street. It was on the corner of Westgate Street and Swan Lane, with the White Swan on the opposite corner.

Looking back at the history of the Old Dial is difficult: it was originally called the Dial, but the curse of unimaginative pub names strikes again and there were two pubs called the Dial in the West Ward, both of which had an alehouse licence in 1806 and one as far back as 1736.

One of these pubs was in St Mary's Square (Ref 148, Map B), but it changed its name to the Sundial from 1807 to 1812, but then reverted to the Dial and continued trading. The last record I have for it is 1876.

The other Dial, which I believe to be the older one, was on the site of the later Old Dial in Lower Westgate Street. This traded as the Dial until 1821, after which it appears to have been renamed the Crown & Anchor which it traded as until at least 1836. By 1847, there is no record in *Hunt's Directory* of the Crown & Anchor, but the Old Dial makes its first appearance.

By the 1950s the Old Dial, now owned by Cheltenham & Hereford Breweries Ltd, found itself in the Westgate Comprehensive Redevelopment Area. The brewery was happy to sell the pub to the Gloucester Corporation as they had been allowed to transfer the licence to a bright, shiny new house at Matson, and the pub closed on 28 March 1956. However, there was some haggling over the £900 that the Corporation offered them for it in May 1957. Clearly they had previously been in negotiation to purchase a site at the new cattle market and felt that the suggested price, 'seems to bear no relation to what you recently asked us for the Cattle Market site, when both should be valued on the same basis.'

REF: 358
MAP: B
STATUS: Demolished
DATE: By 1736 to 1956
LOCATION: 150 Westgate Street

Looking up Westgate Street during the 1947 floods. The Old Dial is on the edge of the shot on the left, next door to the White Swan.
(Gloucester Citizen)

Square & Compass, Westgate Street _____

REF: 489

MAP: B

STATUS: Demolished

DATE: By 1871 to 1964

LOCATION: 168–70
Westgate Street

The Square & Compass stood on the corner of Westgate Street and Priory Road. It was originally numbered 82 to 84 Westgate Street, becoming 168–70 following renumbering in the 1920s.

The first reference that I have found for the Square & Compass is 1871, when it was a beerhouse. As can be seen from the photograph, thanks to the floods of 1947, it was by this time owned by Stroud Brewery. The landlord at this time was Bill Miller, who ran the Square & Compass from at least 1936 until 1957.

The last landlords were Alf and Myrtle Bignall, who took over in 1959. It wasn't until their time that the pub acquired a full publican's licence, in December 1961. Unfortunately it didn't survive much beyond that as it was demolished in 1964 to make way for improvements and the building of the new ring-road – the site is now near or under Royal Oak Road.

On the closure of the Square & Compass Alf and Myrtle moved to the Beehive in Millbrook Street. Alf was president of the Gloucester Shove Ha'penny League for many years.

Floods of 1947 again.
(Gloucester Citizen)

White Swan, Westgate Street _____

REF: 600

MAP: B

STATUS: Demolished

DATE: By 1807 to 1972

LOCATION: 148 Westgate
Street

The White Swan was located at 148 Westgate Street, 94 in the old numbering convention. It was on the opposite corner of Westgate Street and Swan Lane to the Old Dial. Like the Old Dial, the White Swan was in Phase 2 of the Westgate Comprehensive Redevelopment Area plans.

The first mention that I have found for the White Swan is from 1847, but it seems likely that it is the same pub previously known just as the Swan, which had an alehouse licence by at least 1807, and after which the road is named.

The White Swan was a 'substantial double-fronted brick-built premises well placed in a busy main thoroughfare,' according to Wintle's Forest Brewery of Mitcheldean who owned it for a time. It was situated next door to the architecturally superb listed

Demolition is well
advanced in this picture
of Westgate Street, but
the Duke of Norfolk's
House is still standing
and the White Swan
can be seen next door.
(Gloucestershire Archives)

building known as the Duke of Norfolk's Lodging House, or more properly, Eagle House. This Grade II listed building was described by the Georgian Group in 1965 as, 'one of the two or three surviving domestic buildings of architectural importance in the city.'

The Duke of Norfolk's House caused the City Corporation considerable problems. Recognising its importance and architectural merit, the City Corporation tried very hard to find a tenant willing to carry out the necessary work to restore it so that it could be incorporated within the Westgate development. The city architect fired off letters in all directions trying to find a buyer, including to West Country Breweries, who by this time owned the White Swan, trying to convince them to use it in a major redevelopment of the pub. Their response, on 22 March 1967, was, 'This structure . . . would be a bit uneconomical to incorporate as part of the pub, and looking ahead this was not quite the "image" that we would wish to put to the public . . . Much as the Brewery would like to assist the City in retaining its more historical and interesting buildings, we have now-a-days to be even more commercially minded than perhaps in the past.'

So with all avenues exhausted, in February 1968 the decision was made to demolish. There were howls of protest, the loudest coming from the Society for the Protection of Ancient Buildings, so not unreasonably, the corporation said if they were so concerned perhaps they could find a tenant. So they gave it a damned good go, but all they succeeded in doing was delaying things by another three years, during which time the building deteriorated to a point where it was unsafe. Eventually, on 9 September 1971, listed building consent was given for demolition, which commenced on 27 September 1971.

This of course left the White Swan a bit isolated, so it was compulsory purchased from the brewery, who by this time was Whitbread Flowers Ltd. The pub and yard was valued at £16,000 and it was demolished in 1972.

Kingsholm & Clapham

GLOUCESTER RUGBY

Kingsholm is the oldest part of Gloucester, being the site of the original Roman fort set up by the late AD 40s. The fort stayed at Kingsholm until about 68 AD when it was dismantled and the Romans moved on to what is now modern Gloucester. The Saxons followed the Romans in occupying Kingsholm and in the tenth century a great timber hall was built there, known as 'Aula Regis', literally King's Hall, from which the area's name was derived.

In more recent times Kingsholm has become synonymous with rugby. Gloucester RFC was started in 1873, with the ground moving to Kingsholm in 1891, being built on what was then known as the Castle Grim estate. The pubs around the area are therefore very rugby oriented.

To the south and east of Kingsholm Road, sandwiched in the fork between Worcester Street and London Road, is a residential area of terraced houses. This is all that is left of a fondly remembered Kingsholm parish unofficially known as Clapham. The brainchild of George Worrall Counsel in the 1820s, Clapham consisted of ten streets of purpose-built tiny, identical, back-to-back two-up, two-down terraced houses with lean-to sculleries and backyard privies. They were built to house workers, mainly coming from the Midlands, attracted by Gloucester's growing industry around the docks and railway. Like Lower Westgate Street, Clapham had more than its share of pubs.

As the Industrial Revolution waned, poverty and unemployment became rife, and in the 1950s the council decided something had to be done to 'help' the people living in what they saw as squalid conditions. They initiated the Kingsholm Redevelopment and between 1956 and 1957 the bulldozers moved in and Clapham was no more.

Sherbourne Street, Clapham, celebrating the Queen's coronation in 1952, shortly before the bulldozers moved in. (Reflections of Clapham Group/Bernard Polson)

Fortune of War, Kingsholm Road _____

The first reference that I have found for the Fortune of War on Kingsholm Road is from the *Returns of Constables of the four wards as to the state of public houses during time of divine service* from 31 January 1836. It is likely that it was a beerhouse at this time as it does not appear in licensing records.

The Fortune of War was on the south end of the terrace known as Kingsholm Buildings, with the Kingsholm Inn on the north corner. By 1847 it was probably known as the Beehive, which appears in *Hunt's Directory* of that year, and in 1851 the Public Health map shows it as the Soldiers Return. It was again known as the Fortune of War by *Bretherton's Directory* of 1869.

It was tied to Godsell, who surrendered the licence sometime after 1935. They intended to re-use the licence for a new property on the corner of Calton Road and Ladysmith Road to be called the Calton Hotel.

REF: 186
MAP: C & D
STATUS: Building in different use
DATE: By 1836 to 1935
LOCATION: 2 Kingsholm Road, GL1 3AT

Kingsholm Inn, Kingsholm Road _____

The Kingsholm Inn is at 8 Kingsholm Road, on the corner with Sweetbriar Street. Due to its location almost opposite the Kingsholm rugby ground, like the other pubs in the area it is closely associated with rugby. This is immediately apparent from the outside as the predominantly cream-coloured building has bright red signage and paintwork, reflecting the famous cherry and white colouring of Gloucester Rugby. A large sign proclaims the Kingsholm Inn to be 'Gloucester's Premier Rugby Pub' and the pub sign itself depicts three Gloucester Rugby players, probably the three 2003 World Cup winners Trevor Woodman, Andy Gormarsall and Phil Vickery.

One of the pub signs also gives its alternative name in brackets: the Jockey. It is still occasional known by this name, which is apparently a hangover from the days before the rugby ground arrived in 1891, when there was a small racecourse on the site. There was a pub by the name of the Horse & Jockey in Sweetbriar Street in the 1850s but there is no evidence of a link with the Kingsholm.

Inside, the rugby theme continues with a huge amount of rugby memorabilia. If you visit on match day it is packed to the rafters with Gloucester fans and moving is barely an option, much less taking a look round, so it is worth visiting at a quieter time. All around the pub are glass cases with rugby shirts donated by various generous benefactors, and taking up most of one wall is a large glass cabinet containing numerous rugby club ties.

This is all overlaid on top of what is basically a traditional, old-fashioned looking pub. It has low ceilings and more dark timber than you can shake a stick at. Alongside all of the rugby stuff are the normal trappings of a traditional pub: horse brasses, old pictures of livestock, flowers and fruit and slightly chintzy plates and jugs. Toward the back of the pub is a pool table, and most importantly of all, unlike most of the other rugby pubs, the Kingsholm sells real ale.

REF: 277
MAP: C & D
STATUS: Trading
DATE: By 1842 to date
LOCATION: 8 Kingsholm Road, GL1 3AT
CONTACT: 01452 530222

Kingsholm Road looking north with the Kingsholm Inn on the right. *(Geoff Sandles)*

I have seen a date for the Kingsholm Inn given as early as 1842, although it is not named on Causton's Map of 1843. It was certainly in existence by 1847, when it is mentioned in *Hunt's Directory*, and it is shown on the Public Health map of 1851. It was at the northern end of a terrace called Kingsholm Buildings and appears to have extended into the next door building at some point.

There is also an 1863 reference to the Kingsholm Brewery, which may be related to the Kingsholm Inn, although by 1896 it was owned by Arnold Perrett & Co. and was later a tied house of Godsell & Sons of Salmon Springs, Stroud. Today it is owned by Discovery Inns.

Queen's Head Inn, Kingsholm Road

REF: 414

MAP: C

STATUS: Trading

DATE: By 1847 to date

LOCATION: 68 Kingsholm Road, GL1 3BQ

CONTACT: 01452 413374

The Queen's Head is almost next door to the White Hart/Teague's Bar and is obviously just as sport oriented, as can be deduced from the large banners proclaiming 'Live Sport' hanging from the exterior and, on match days, the rugby shirts for sale outside. It is quite a small Victorian red-brick pub with a gabled roof and ornate sign giving the pub's name below the first floor window. The exterior appearance is not improved by the single-storey extension added to the side of the building with a rudimentary wooden shelter built in front of it, clearly designed to keep the smokers dry.

The extension provides a pool room, with the main building housing a small single bar. On the match day that I visited the pool room was empty, but the main bar was packed with predominantly large, middle-aged men in rugby shirts. The bar is comfortable enough with a 1960s-type traditional feel to it. The décor includes some rugby paraphernalia, but is nothing like in the same league as the Kingsholm or Teague's, and the TVs showing sport, as promised on the banners outside, were much smaller, older and less obtrusive than those in Teague's.

The Queen's Head dates back to at least 1847, when it appears in *Hunt's Directory*. Detailed plans from 1916 suggest it was rebuilt at this time. The Queen's Head was a beerhouse, once a tied house of Smith & Sons Brimscombe Brewery and later Bristol Brewery Georges & Co. Ltd, which became Courage in 1961. It didn't get a publican's licence until 29 May 1962. It was later acquired by Ushers of Trowbridge and is now owned by Innspired. The Queen's Head appeared in CAMRA's *Good Beer Guide* in 1978, but unfortunately now has no real beer.

Queen's Head on match day, January 2009.

White Hart Inn, Kingsholm Road

The White Hart is a fine large red-brick Victorian pub, the centre of which rises impressively in steps to a point with a moulded white hart in the centre. Located directly opposite the Shed end of the Gloucester Rugby stadium, it is now known as Teague's Bar, as it is owned by former Gloucester Rugby legend Mike Teague: where better to go for a drink on match day?

Inside, Teague's Bar is high ceilinged, bright and much more modern looking than the other pubs near the ground. The bar is absolutely packed with rugby paraphernalia, pictures and shirts; it has flat screen TVs liberally distributed throughout the bar so that you need not miss a minute of sport while having a pint either before or after the game. I visited before the game on a match day and it was full of people in Gloucester shirts and animated rugby conversations. One thing it lacked was any decent beer.

The origins of the current building are displayed above the right-hand bar entrance, where there's a magnificent stone carving with the words 'Ind, Coope & Co. Ltd' beneath an ornamental crest of Britannia – Ind Coope's trademark – and the date 1898. However, the pub dates back further than that: some references list it as far back as 1820, and it certainly appears in *Pigot's Directory* of 1830, which lists Hannah Wright as landlady.

REF: 586
MAP: C
STATUS: Trading
DATE: By 1830 to date
LOCATION: 48 Kingsholm Road, GL1 3BH
CONTACT: 01452 413374

Clapham

The pubs in Clapham were mostly small terraced properties, no more than beerhouses. It is difficult to be sure when many of these pubs came and went as they did not appear in licensing records. I can't even be certain whether those I have listed are separate pubs, changes of name or even just tricks of the memory. Considering that the demolition of Clapham is relatively recent history, records and memories of these pubs often seem to conflict and become confused.

I have seen mention of the Bunch of Grapes (1859), the Black Lion (1850–68) and the Rose & Crown, all in Columbia Street, but can find no information on them so I am unclear whether these were separate pubs or alternative names for other pubs. The same goes for the Carpenters Arms (1850) in Alvin Street, and on Suffolk Street, as well as the Suffolk Arms (by 1847–1949) there seems to have been the Suffolk Inn.

Many of the pubs disappeared before the Kingsholm Redevelopment. Because there were so many pubs in such a small area a number were referred for compensation as no longer being needed. These included the Columbia House Inn in Columbia Street and the King William in Alvin Street, both of which existed by 1836 and were referred for closure in 1905 and closed in 1906. The Stag's Head, also in Alvin Street, followed. It survived referral in 1913 but was referred again in 1919, when it was not so lucky and it closed in 1920. The New Inn in Columbia Street, which existed by 1852 and was

The Clapham area shown on Causton's Map, 1843.
(Gloucestershire Archives)

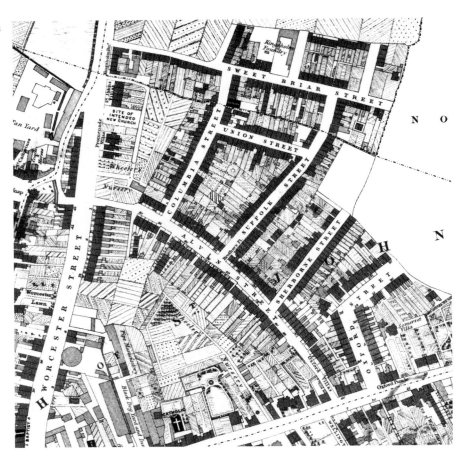

mentioned in the referral as being only fifty yards from the Stag's Head, was also gone by about 1930.

So, by the time it came to the Kingsholm Redevelopment only five pubs are named as seeking compensation: the Magnet (by 1865 to 1959) in Union Street, the Pheasant (by 1839 to 1958) in Columbia Street, the Duke of York (by 1879 to 1956) and the Suffolk Arms (by 1847 to 1959) in Suffolk Street, and the Anchor (by 1857 to 1956) in Sweetbriar Street. At the end of 1937 it was estimated that these five licensed house would cost £2,250 each. They all closed, starting with the Anchor on 10 June 1956 and ending with the Magnet on 28 April 1959. In some cases the licence was removed to another house: the Pheasant's went to the new Bell & Gavel at the cattle market and the Magnet's to the Beehive, presumably in Millbrook Street which until that time was just a beerhouse. Most of the pubs did not get £2,250 when they were demolished; the Anchor, for instance, owned by the Stroud Brewery Company, got only £1,350.

One pub somehow managed to survive the redevelopment the White Lion on Alvin Street hung on until January 1967.

The Anchor. *(Reflections of Clapham Group/Bernard Polson)*

White Lion. *(Reflections of Clapham Group/ Bernard Polson)*

Barton & Tredworth

Originally Eastgate Street ran only as far as the East Gate, on the corner of what is now Brunswick Road. Building didn't begin outside the East Gate until after 1778, creating a fashionable residential area known as Bertonstret (Barton Street). This area of Upper Barton Street, from the old East Gate to the inner ring-road, was renamed to become part of Eastgate Street in the 1980s and is not covered in this chapter.

Settlement further out on Barton Street started in the thirteenth century and in the 1590s it extended beyond the bend in the road where the India House now stands. Outer Barton Street was a green suburb; by 1801 the parishes of Barton St Mary and Barton St Michael together had 136 houses with a population of 697. The Blenheim Gardens, later renamed Vauxhall Gardens, were opened here in 1812. To the south of Outer Barton Street was the village of Tredworth.

As a result of Gloucester's expansion in the nineteenth century, terraced housing was built throughout Barton Street to provide better working-class housing, all built to the same plan: two up, two down with a washhouse and outside privy at the back. By the time of the census in 1881 the parishes of Barton St Mary and Barton St Michael together had grown to a population of 13,818 with 2,986 houses, more than twenty times that of just eighty years before. At the same time Tredworth began to expand. The High Street was the main shopping area and to a great extent Tredworth was self contained.

Unlike Clapham, Barton and Tredworth continue to thrive. Although the privies have now moved inside, it is still one of the poorer areas of the city and the most culturally diverse, with 46 languages spoken and 25 different faiths. When I visited the pubs in the area with some friends on a Saturday evening in April 2009 we found that they retained a kind of old-fashioned community feel that you don't find in the city centre. In the main the drinkers in these pubs are regulars: they know each other and they know the bar staff, many of whom have been at the pub for many years. Virtually all of the pubs have skittles teams, darts teams or football teams, and, perhaps as a consequence, at a time when pubs are suffering from reduced trade, they were almost all busy.

Duke of Wellington, Tredworth Road

REF: 165
MAP: I
STATUS: Trading
DATE: By 1869 to date
LOCATION: 72 Tredworth Road, GL1 4QR
CONTACT: 01452 523981

The Duke of Wellington is situated at 72 Tredworth Road, opposite the end of the High Street, in an ordinary looking two-storey building. Apparently there has been a pub on the site for 400 years, but the name certainly doesn't go back that far as the title wasn't bestowed on the first Duke of Wellington, Arthur Wellesley, until 1814, just before his involvement in the Battle of Waterloo in 1815. The first mention that I have found of the Duke of Wellington (the pub that is) is from 1869, when it was a beerhouse. The current building definitely appears to be Victorian.

In the 1880s it had its own brewery, but it was later owned by Godsell & Sons which became Stroud Brewery and then Whitbread. It is now owned by Punch Taverns. Interesting facts about the Duke of Wellington include: it retained a 'men only' bar until the 1970s, it is said to be haunted and, for reasons I perhaps don't want to know, according to the 1993 CAMRA *Real Ale in Gloucestershire Guide*, it is known locally as the 'Stinkpot'. I detected nothing malodorous there on my visit.

The pub consists of a single bar which has been knocked through from several

different rooms. The central area is dominated by a dark wood bar with an open entrance to the pool room on the right, which has been knocked through into the next-door building. The walls around the pool table are decorated with the classic pictures of dogs playing pool, as well as old music and film pictures, which are also dotted around the rest of the pub mingled in with Gloucester Rugby pictures.

It was early evening when I visited and the pub was reasonably busy with what appeared to be locals and regulars. There was a mixed age group, including a family with young children playing on the pool table. Basically, the Duke of Wellington is a good local boozer.

Golden Heart, High Street, Tredworth

The earliest reference that I have found for the Golden Heart is as a beerhouse in 1870, and in the early days its address was given as Barton Terrace. About the turn of the twentieth century it was owned by Godsell & Son of Stroud who rebuilt it.

The Golden Heart is an impressive two-storey Victorian building at 85 High Street, taking up the corner of Tredworth High Street and The Laurels. The lower storey is painted in red and cream with the upper storey remaining plain brick. The canopy over the front door retains an ornamental plasterwork Godsell & Son emblem. Through a series of takeovers and mergers, Godsell's became West Country Breweries in 1958, and there is one of their brewery plaques to the left of the entrance.

Inside is a large, open single bar with the bar counter running along the right-hand wall. The atmosphere of the pub when I visited on a Saturday evening was loud and lively, with a predominantly young clientele. Overseeing things is an old-time pub matriarch; a friendly lady called Wendy, who has run the Golden Heart with her son Mike for fourteen years. Despite her age and diminutive size, Wendy keeps good order in the pub and seems to be respected by her potentially rowdy punters.

At the rear of the bar is a separate large skittle alley and function room called Porky's. The pub's football team is also called Porky's, named for the 1982 film, and their pictures adorn the walls. At the time of our visit they had been unbeaten all season in the Premier division of the Gloucester & District Sunday Football League and were playing in the final the following day, where their winning streak continued with a 7–0 win against Leonard Stanley. In keeping with the Porky's theme, the function room boasts a large collection of pigs of various sorts that gives the collection at the Pig Inn the City a run for its money.

While in the function room, Wendy showed us one of the pub's games. This consists of a large cylindrical block of wood, which she said had been made from a ship's mast, into the top of which nails had been driven. The game was to compete to see who could drive a nail into the wood with the fewest blows. The loser, of course, bought the drinks. I suspect there are some local chippies that do very well playing that game!

REF: 210

MAP: I

STATUS: Trading

DATE: By 1870 to date

LOCATION: 85 High Street, GL1 4SY

CONTACT: 01452 501414

Great Western, Alfred Street

REF: 214

MAP: I

STATUS: Trading

DATE: By 1876 to date

LOCATION: 91 Alfred Street, GL1 4BU

CONTACT: 01452 538888

The Great Western is a bit off the beaten track at the far end of Alfred Street on the corner of Windmill Parade. It is a pleasant, traditional looking Victorian back street boozer which once overlooked the Great Western Railway goods yard, but in 1989 its view was obscured by the building of Metz Way, the Eastern Radial Road. Now Alfred Street ends in a dystopian vision of a large concrete flyover which overshadows the pub.

Originally called the Plough Inn and later the Plough Hotel, the pub has existed since at least 1876 when it is found in *Bretherton's Directory*. It is sometimes listed with Windmill Parade as its address. Originally tied to Smith & Sons Brimscombe Brewery, it was sold to Wintles Forest Brewery, Micheldean, in 1915. This was bought out by the Cheltenham Original Brewery in 1930, eventually becoming Whitbread.

Because of its location near the railway sidings overlooking the Great Western Railway goods yard, it was felt appropriate to rename the pub the Great Western as part of the GWR 150 celebrations in 1985. Ironically it was only a few years later that it was isolated from the railway by the building of Metz Way.

Today the Great Western is owned by Admiral Taverns, who seem to have taken the wise but unusual decision to leave it well alone. It has been run by landlady Lyn Mann for twenty-four years and it retains a wonderfully traditional charm. You enter from the street into a passageway, with a door on the right leading to the unspoilt lounge bar, with lots of dark wood and leather seating. A second door leads off the corridor a little further down into a room containing a pool table with the bar counter between the two rooms. The Great Western is also one of the few pubs in the area that sells real ale.

At the time of my visit it was quieter than many of the other pubs in the area, with just a small number of locals in. Both Lyn and the locals were very friendly and welcoming and once they knew that I was there for the purposes of pub research they regaled me with numerous stories and memories of old Gloucester pubs.

The Great Western – a great traditional pub in the shadow of the Metz Way flyover.

At the back of the pub the Great Western has a final surprise: if there was such a thing as a good pub garden competition, the Great Western would be a serious contender. Being amid terraced housing I expected little more than a courtyard for smokers, but instead there is a lovingly tended garden divided into small 'rooms'. In the evening the whole thing is beautifully lit giving a grotto-like effect.

By the end of our visit my friends and I had all been entirely won over by the Great Western – a good traditional pub run in a traditional way; long may it continue.

India House, Barton Street

The India House is located in the fork between Barton Street and India Road and claims to be the only pub of that name in Britain. Its address was originally 101 Lower Barton Street, but is now 227 Barton Street.

Reference to the India House can be found in city deeds as far back as 1780, but the first mention that I have found for it in licensing records or street directories is 1830, when it appears in *Pigot's Directory*. It seems likely that India Road is named for the pub rather than vice-versa as in the late nineteenth century it is referred to as India House Lane.

By the 1950s the pub is referred to as the Olde India House and later Ye Olde India House, but now it seems to have reverted back to simply the India House. By the 1980s it was owned by Whitbread and was acquired by Arkell's of Swindon in 1991. It is a large two-storey pub with a single-storey extension to the front.

On the Saturday evening of my visit it had a live band playing in the bar and the place was packed. I had the opportunity to talk to one of the regulars, an opportunity that arose from having to talk my way out of trouble when his suspicions were raised by my note-taking. He told me that the pub retained a good community spirit and had both a skittles team and a darts team.

The India House also has a long association with boxing and has a gym upstairs. Local boxing legend Hal Bagwell trained at the India House. Born in 1920, Bagwell began boxing in 1937 as a lightweight. He is popularly credited as having the longest winning streak in boxing history: from 1938 to 1948 he is said to have had 180 fights without defeat – 175 wins and 5 draws. He died in May 2001.

REF: 254
MAP: I
STATUS: Trading
DATE: By 1780 to date
LOCATION: 227 Barton Street, GL1 4JE
CONTACT: 01452 413218

(Geoff Sandles)

Laburnum Hotel, High Street, Tredworth _____

REF: 279

MAP: I

STATUS: Building in other use

DATE: 1842 to mid-1970s

LOCATION: 2 High Street, Tredworth

The Laburnum Brewery was on the corner of the High Street and Ryecroft Street. Any connection with the yellow flowering tree of the same name is unclear, but presumably this is a reflection of the fact that in the past there was more greenery in Tredworth High Street than there is today.

A beerhouse licence was granted to the Laburnum Brewery in 1872, although the first directory entry I have found for a house of this name listed under Inns & Taverns is in the *Gloucester Directory* of 1879. The address was given as Barton Terrace and the landlord was John Apperley. Earlier directories dating back to 1869 list John Apperley as a brewer and beer retailer, but do not give the name Laburnum Brewery.

An advert from 1894 suggests that the brewery dates back earlier than that, claiming that it was established in 1842. It is probably not a coincidence that this is the first date that I have found for the Laburnum Inn (Ref 280, Map I). This was a smaller terraced property on the east side of the High Street, for which *Hunt's Directory* of 1847 also gives the address as Barton Terrace, so the Laburnum Brewery may have started here.

By 1898 the Laburnum Brewery was owned by Arnold Perrett & Co., who on Friday 6 May of that year instructed Bruton Knowles Co. to sell 'the whole of the valuable fixtures and fittings of the Laburnum Brewery, Ryecroft Street, Gloucester,' by auction.

By 1908 the Laburnum Inn is listed as 15 High Street and the Laburnum Brewery has become the Laburnum Hotel at 2 High Street, with G.H. White as proprietor. The Laburnum Hotel continued to be listed as a public house until 1949, after which it disappears from directories until reappearing in 1959 listed under hotels. By this time it had a publican's licence. By 1972 it was known as the Ryecroft Hotel. When it ceased trading is unclear, but the building is now in use as the Ryecroft Bail Hostel.

The Laburnum Inn also continued until at least the mid-1970s, but is now a private house.

New Victory Inn, Tredworth Road

The New Victory Inn dates back to at least 1872, when its address is given as Barton Terrace, along with the Golden Heart, but its modern address is 103 High Street.

The 'New' part of the New Victory Inn is presumably to distinguish it from the other Victory Inn which already existed further down Tredworth Road (see p. 154). The New Victory is a two-storey building with what appears to be an over-sized façade. It is more frequently called the Little Vic, from which you may deduce that

REF: 339
MAP: I
STATUS: Trading
DATE: By 1872 to date
LOCATION: 103 High Street, Tredworth, GL1 4SY
CONTACT: 01452 309444

it is significantly smaller than the Victory Inn, which is known as the Big Vic. The New Victory was owned by Godsell & Sons in 1900 when it was valued at £57 10s 10d. Originally a beerhouse, the Little Vic didn't get a publican's licence until 1960.

It must be something of a record that the New Victory was owned by the same family for over 70 years from 1912, when Thomas Townsend took control, until 1983 when his brother Jim, who had run it since 1954, called it a day.

During the 1950s and '60s the New Victory was something of a sporting pub and was the headquarters of the Tredworth Rugby Football Club as well as hosting successful clubs in darts, shove ha'penny, crib and even angling. In the 1950s the Tredworth Road Walk was established at the Little Vic. Initially just for fun, this developed into a competitive race. It was revived in 1974 and still takes place on Easter Monday, starting from the Little Vic.

A delightfully old-fashioned, unspoilt pub, the Little Vic is entered via a small covered passageway from the High Street. The passage goes through to the pub garden at the back and two doors lead off it. The first has a sign saying 'Saloon & Off Sales', although this is the pool room. Just inside the door is an old hatch for off-sales, which I haven't seen in any other pubs in the city. The sign over the second door says 'Games Room'. This is a small room with a bar running along the length of the right-hand wall and a dartboard on the back wall. The Little Vic doesn't sell real ale, but it does sell cider, referred to by the regulars as 'rough', but we weren't adventurous enough to try that.

Plough Inn, Upton Street

REF: 396
MAP: I
STATUS: Trading
DATE: By 1879 to date
LOCATION: 9 Upton Street, GL1 4JT
CONTACT: 01452 382540

The Plough Inn is situated at the north end of Tredworth High Street at 9 Upton Street, on the corner with St James Street. The earliest reference that I have found for the pub is from 1879. It is a two-storey building with bay windows on the ground floor. At some point since the early twentieth century the simple brick building has been rendered and is now painted cream and blue.

It was sold by Whitbread in 1991 but continued trading for some years before closing down. It reopened in May 2008 after being derelict for some years. It is now owned by Punch Taverns and until recently was managed by licensee Rachel Jones, who has a heritage of running pubs in the area – her parents ran the Blenheim Inn in Barton Street and her uncle was landlord at the County Arms in Millbrook Street. On taking over, Rachel said, 'The Plough Inn is going to be a traditional, friendly pub where everyone can relax and enjoy themselves.'

Although Rachel has moved on, her vision appears to have remained intact. There is a front and a back room, decorated and furnished in a traditional style, with a single bar in the middle to serve both. The clientele seemed to be a fairly mixed age group consisting mainly of locals and regulars. When I visited, the Plough had both real ale and two varieties of cider on hand pump.

Robin Hood, Hopewell Street

Hopewell Street is a terraced street just off Barton Street. A short way down, on the right as you approach from Barton Street, one of these terraced houses has a surprisingly ornate green tiled exterior with 'Stroud Brewery Ales & Stout' prominent in raised lettering. The green glazed tiles only extend to the ground floor, the upper floor is in brick but has a central white panel which reads 'Ye Olde Robin Hood Inn'.

REF: 445
MAP: I
STATUS: Building in other use
DATE: By 1872 to late 1970s
LOCATION: Hopewell Street

The pub existed from at least 1872 when it appears in licensing records as a beerhouse. Previously it was probably the Hopewell Inn, briefly renamed to Cox's Beerhouse in 1872 before becoming the Robin Hood. I'm not aware of any connection between Gloucester and the legendary outlaw, but this was the second pub of that name to open in the mid-nineteenth century, the other being in Bristol Road. The *Wordsworth Dictionary of Pub Names* may provide the answer with the theory that the name spread with the Ancient Order of Foresters, a Friendly Society formed in 1834.

This Robin Hood was rebuilt by the Stroud Brewery Company in 1908, at which time it presumably received its exuberant exterior. It is not clear why the brewery was prepared to spend so much money on an ordinary back street pub. It was closed under Whitbread ownership probably in the late 1970s or early 1980s. Although the pub exterior remains it is now in other usage.

Vauxhall Inn, Barton Street

REF: 563
MAP: I
STATUS: Building in other use
DATE: By 1832 to 2008
LOCATION: 174 Barton Street

(Gloucestershire Archives)

The Vauxhall Inn in Lower Barton Street, on the corner of Vauxhall Road, was a Victorian gem of a pub. It was built in 1876 by Mitchells & Butlers of Cape Hill, Birmingham, to replace a pub of the same name on the site. No expense was spared in its construction; built in the Arts and Crafts style, it had the classic M&B glazed ceramic tiled exterior on the ground floor with intricate ornamental baroque detail and acid-etched windows with the M&B monogram. Above the ground-floor windows the ceramic tiles are inscribed with 'The Vauxhall Inn' and 'Wines and Spirits'. The building is Grade II listed and described as, 'a particularly good example of late [nineteenth-century] pub architecture.'

The Vauxhall Inn was at no. 64 Lower Barton Street, becoming 174 Barton Street on renumbering. When the original Vauxhall Inn was built is unclear, but it was clearly named for the adjacent Vauxhall Pleasure Garden (see p. 143). The first record of an alehouse licence that I have found for the Vauxhall Inn dates from 1872, but it is shown on Causton's Map of 1832 as the Vauxhall Inn and Gardens. In 1859 it was described as the Vauxhall and tea gardens and at one time it had its own private zoo attached to the premises. The Vauxhall Gardens were built on from

1863, but a bowling green survived behind the Vauxhall inn until the mid-twentieth century.

The 'Vauxhall Inn & Pleasure Grounds' were offered for sale by auction by Messrs Bruton, Knowles and Bruton on 7 June 1878. The inn is described as 'containing on the ground floor entrance hall; well-fitted bar; bar parlour; tap-room; smoking-room . . . club-room . . . kitchen; China Pantry &c.' It also boasted a 'spacious and well-arranged brewery, tun, malt & store rooms, coach house, stabling for six horses, loose box and a capital hay loft.' In the rear, the 'extensive pleasure grounds' included a lawn, summer house, aviary, a range of arbours and a skittle alley with slate floor. The property had recently been connected to the city sewers.

Over recent years the Vauxhall had a troubled time and in May 2008 it closed. It has now been converted into Barton Street's first supermarket, called the Vauxhall Mart. It is not a faceless corporate entity, but instead sells a range of English, African-Caribbean, South Indian and Bangladeshi foods to cater for the multi-cultural inhabitants of the area. Obviously the conversion to a supermarket has resulted in the interior of the pub being completely gutted, but the exterior has been preserved.

Victoria House (now One Eyed Jacks), Barton Street

One Eyed Jacks is on the corner of Barton Street and Victoria Street. The exterior of the two-storey building has an over-sized façade and is painted cream and brown, with small wooden framed window panes on the ground floor and a single-storey extension to the right. The pub sign shows the jack of spades.

The pub has been in existence since at least 1847, when it was known as the Victoria, presumably in honour of the monarch at the time. It became the Victoria House, although the 'House' part of the name seemed to come and go. Its original address was 28 Lower Barton Street, becoming 136 Barton Street on renumbering.

REF: 565/366
MAP: I
STATUS: Trading as One Eyed Jacks
DATE: By 1847 to date
LOCATION: 136 Barton Street, GL1 4EN
CONTACT: 01452 530054

One Eyed Jacks, the current incarnation of the Victoria House Inn.

Victoria House Inn,
1973. *(Gloucester Citizen)*

Papers relating to a valuation in February 1908 indicate that at that time the Victoria House was owned by Ind Coope & Co. Ltd of Burton upon Trent. It was later owned by West Country Ales, as evidenced by a plaque to the left of the entrance, who later became Whitbread.

The Victoria underwent refurbishment and opened as Molly Malone's, Gloucester's first Irish music theme pub, on 12 September 1990, complete with the wacky theme-pub trappings common at the time. This didn't last very long as it was refurbished again in 1995, this time to a mock Victorian style. Despite the Victorian styling, it didn't revert to its original name, but instead opened as One Eyed Jacks.

The pub is currently owned by Places Trading Ltd and the Victorian styling isn't a major feature of the interior now. It has a central bar, with a pool table on the left and seating on the right, leading back a deceptively long way into a skittle alley. A second small room leads off to the left behind the bar.

When I visited, the pub was reasonably busy without being packed. The clientele were of a mixed age group and also seemed to be a mix of regulars and more casual pub drinkers. This was the last pub that we visited on our 'research trip' around the Barton and Tredworth pubs: it retains some of the feeling of a community pub that was so prevalent further into Barton and Tredworth, and the landlady, Pat Hurley, was made 'Mayor of Barton' in 2007, an ancient tradition where a 'mock mayor' is elected by the Court Leet of Barton St Mary to support and promote the local community. However, as a result of its closer proximity to the city centre and the nightclubs of Eastgate Street, this is less pronounced and it feels less personal somehow. It treads a fine and difficult line between being a community pub and a town pub.

Victory Hotel, High Street, Tredworth

REF: 568
MAP: I
STATUS: Trading
DATE: By 1859 to date
LOCATION: 167 High Street,
Tredworth, GL1 4TD
CONTACT: 01452 530165

The Victory Hotel is a large red-brick building at 167 High Street, on the corner with Ducie Street. It existed by 1859 and was originally called the Victory Inn, changing to Hotel in 1925, undeterred by the fact that it offers no accommodation. It is commonly referred to as the 'Big Vic' to distinguish it from the later New Victory Inn, or 'Little Vic' further up the High Street (see p. 149).

The pub is apparently named for HMS *Victory*, as depicted on the pub sign. The theme is continued inside, with pictures and paraphernalia relating to HMS *Victory* in evidence throughout the pub. The reason for the association with Nelson's flagship at Trafalgar in this part of Gloucester is unclear (there is also a Trafalgar chip shop just around the corner in Tredworth Road). Although Gloucester is a port, it is a bit far inland to have any real association with famous ships and sea battles. The HMS *Victory* was commissioned in 1778, which is too historic to be associated with the pub, but the Battle of Trafalgar was more contemporary, being just over fifty years before the first date I have for the pub, in 1805.

Inside, the Victory has a single large open bar, with the bar counter along the right wall and a pool table on the left. At the time of my visit, despite being early, it was very busy, with a lively, mixed clientele and loud but good music playing. At the far end of

the bar is a door leading to a large skittle alley, where the reason for the heightened excitement was apparent. Five or six dartboards were set up along the alley at which people were practicing. Along the back wall was a long table groaning under the weight of trophies waiting to be handed out. We had happened to turn up on the night of the annual tournament for the Gloucester darts league. Having played around the pubs and clubs of Gloucester all season, every year the teams all descend on the Big Vic for prize-giving and to play for individual honours. As well as darts and skittles, the pub also has a football team, called Big Vic, doing well in Division 1 of the Gloucester & District Sunday Football League.

Windmill Inn, Millbrook Street

Until the sixteenth century there were a number of areas of open field outside Gloucester. One of these was Windmill Field, which covered a large area extending south-eastwards from Wotton to the Twyver at Coney Hill.

In 1839 Charles Meadows, a painter from Gloucester, purchased a 'piece or parcel of land or ground formerly part of a field called Windmill Field . . . in the hamlet of Wotton St Mary near the city but in the county of Gloucester including one half part of the new road.' He also took a mortgage on property on the land.

Charles Meadows died in 1848 and the benefactors of the will, his brother George (a perfumer) and a friend, William Horne (a cooper), were forced to auction the estate to pay off outstanding debts. A Mr George Merrett and Mr Frederick Hanman each purchased adjoining parts of the estate. In 1854 Merrett sold his part of the estate to Hanman's son, Charles Fredrick Hanman, a tailor; this consisted of a 'messuage or tenement situate in Asylum Road . . . and known by the name of the Windmill Inn and

REF: 603
MAP: I
STATUS: Demolished
DATE: By 1854 to 1984
LOCATION: Millbrook Street

now in the occupation of Thomas Brewer.' How long it had been an inn is not clear. Frederick Hanman died in 1872, leaving his estate, including the cottage adjoining the Windmill, to his son Charles. By 1882 a brewery and a club house had been added to the inn.

In 1890 Charles Hanman sold the Windmill and adjoining cottage to Messrs Henry Mitchell & Co. Ltd, who later became Mitchells & Butlers. By this time the road name had changed from Asylum Road to Millbrook Street, and Windmill Parade adjoined it at the north-east. At various times the pub's address was also given as Windmill Terrace and Alfred Street.

The Windmill was very close to the Horton Road rail crossing. One of the locals at the nearby (and still open) Great Western told me that there used to be a line down the middle of the main bar of the Windmill; workers from the Great Western Railway drank on one side of it, the Midland Railway men drank on the other side.

The property was closed in 1984 and bought in 1989 by the County Council, who demolished it to make way for the construction of the Eastern Radial Road, Metz Way.

6

The Pub Crawls

A great deal of the research for this book was done in the Gloucestershire Archives and in my office at home, surrounded by books, newspapers and the internet. However, I felt that I couldn't write about Gloucester's pubs if I hadn't sampled them, so over the course of 2009 I set out to experience them all first hand.

To do this I devised eight different pub crawls and invited friends to join me on them. These friends selflessly stepped up to the challenge and, by and large, a good time was had by all. By the time you read this it is likely that more pubs will have opened and closed, but if you fancy giving it a go for yourself, these are the routes that I took:

Route 1:   *The Rugby Pubs*

Date:	Saturday 3 January 2009
The Drinkers:	Geoff
The Pubs:	**Dean's Walk Inn**, Dean's Walk; **Coach & Horses**, St Catherine Street (closed, now reopened); **White Hart/Teague's Bar**, Kingsholm Road; **Queen's Head**, Kingsholm Road; (Rugby Match); **Kingsholm Inn**, Kingsholm Road; **Station Hotel**, Bruton Way
Comments:	The rugby match is of course optional, but on match day the pubs all have a great atmosphere so it does add to the spirit of the thing. These pubs are all very rugby oriented except the Station, which could have fitted into a number of routes but was convenient here and doing it after the match meant it was full of fans preparing to travel home.

Route 2:   *The Docks*

Date:	Saturday 7 February 2009
The Drinkers:	Geoff, Steve, Ed, Chris
The Pubs:	**Fosters on the Docks**, the Docks; **Inn on the Docks**, Llanthony Road; **Baker Street**, Southgate Street; **Nelson**, Southgate Street; **Tall Ship**, Southgate Street; **Whitesmiths Arms**, Southgate Street; **Curry – Namaste**, Clarence Street
Comments:	We started this route at lunchtime, so the pubs may have presented a different face during the day than they would in the evening. The pubs all sold real ale and have the feel of traditional, genuine pubs. I hope they will benefit from The Quays development, not be spoiled or killed because of it.

Ed and Steve, Baker Street.

Steve, Geoff and Ed, Whitesmiths Arms.

Route 3:   *East*

Date:	Saturday 14 March 2009
The Drinkers:	Sal, Jan, Clare
The Pubs:	**Fusion** (closed, see North); **Sloanes**, Brunswick Road; **Water Poet**, Eastgate Street; **Windmill** (closed, now Fever); **Butlers**, Eastgate Street; **Zest**, Eastgate Street; **Bar H2O**, Eastgate Street; **TnT**, Eastgate Street; **Famous Pint Pot**, Bruton Way; **Innteraction**, Bruton Way (nightclub)

Sal, Jan & Clare in Sloanes.

Comments:	Not for the faint-hearted – this is the heart of the night-time economy. Even if you are not into the nightclub scene, Sloanes, the Water Poet and Pint Pot are all worth a visit as they have a more traditional feel. I felt about twenty years too old for the others but apart from a bad experience in Butlers, it was still fun – TnT in particular.

Route 4:   *Centre*

Date:	Saturday 28 March 2009
The Drinkers:	Sharon, Andy, Jane, Rob, Lin, Paul, Kate, Mike, Cat
The Pubs:	**New Inn**, Northgate Street; **Old Bell**, Southgate Street; **Cross Keys**, Cross Keys Lane; **Robert Raikes' House**, Southgate Street; **Café René**, Marylone
Comments:	A great bunch of pubs grouped close together in the city centre, providing a mix of history and good beer. We ate in the New Inn – I would now highly recommend the Old Bell instead, but the restaurant wasn't open at the time of this visit. Café René offers an opportunity to drink late, although there is a small fee if you turn up after 11 p.m.

Route 5: *Barton and Tredworth*

Date: 18 April 2009

The Drinkers: Geoff, Steve, Simon, Scott, Chris, Theo

The Pubs: **Duke of Wellington**, Tredworth Road; **Victory Hotel**, High Street; **New Victory Inn**, High Street; **Golden Heart**, High Street; **Plough**, Upton Street; **India House**, Barton Street; **Great Western**, Alfred Street; **One Eyed Jacks**, Barton Street; **Water Poet**, Eastgate Street (an extra bonus from Route 3); **Curry – Hilltop**, Worcester Street

Comments: This route is the furthest from the centre, necessitates the most walking and has the greatest number of pubs in it. Quite a challenge, but one my chosen drinkers were well equipped to handle. Excellent community pubs with traditional atmosphere, catering mainly for locals and regulars. The down side is that most don't sell real ale. The Great Western is off the beaten track but a hidden gem, so don't miss it.

Route 6: *West*

Date: Saturday 27 June 2009

The Drinkers: Paul, Sal, Jan, Clare, Martin, Rob, Jenny

The Pubs: **Pig Inn the City**, Westgate Street; **Dick Whittington**, Westgate Street; **Old Crown**, Westgate Street; **Westgate**, Westgate Street; **Fountain**, Westgate Street; **Union**, Westgate Street; **Crackers**, Bruton Way (nightclub)

Comments: A good selection of some of the best and most historic pubs in the city, including Gloucester CAMRA's pub of the year 2009 and 2010, the Pig Inn the City. Good drinking pubs and a good drinking crowd meant I had a great time but forgot to do the research! The evening ended in an unplanned opportunity to re-live my youth at Crackers Rock Night: I'm glad I did as it closed a couple of weeks later.

Pig Inn the City beer garden. Left to right: Martin, Sal, Paul, Clare, Jenny, Jan, Rob.

Route 7: *South*

Date: Saturday 18 July 2009

The Drinkers: Russell, Steve, Lyndsay, Brigitte

The Pubs: **Avenue**, Bristol Road; **Bristol Hotel**, Bristol Road; **Seymour**, Seymour Road; **Linden Tree**, Bristol Road; **Curry – Baburchi**, Bristol Road

Comments: This is a long walk out of town rewarded by only a very sparse selection of pubs. A mixed bag with the Avenue and Seymour having a community feel and the Bristol apparently becoming a disco-pub. The Linden Tree, however, is always worth the walk being one of the best pubs in Gloucester for real ale. The curry house was also excellent.

The Linden Tree: Russell, Steve, Lyndsay, Brigitte.

Route 8:   *North*

Date:	Saturday 14 November 2009
The Drinkers:	Sharon, Paul, Andy, Jane, Rob, Lin, Geoff, Steve, Scott, Russell, Steve, Brigitte, David, Sarah
The Pubs:	**York House** (closed); **England's Glory**, London Road; **Victoria Inn**, Oxford Street (closed); **Welsh Harp**, London Road (closed); **Vaults**, Northgate Street; **Imperial**, Northgate Street; **Varsity**, Northgate Street; **Fusion**, Station Road (closed for refurbishment); **Chambers**, St Aldate Street; **Regal**, King's Square; **Curry – Hilltop**, Worcester Street
Comments:	A real mixed bag and a great variety of styles from the Victorian gem of the Imperial to the modern, raucous party atmosphere of the Regal. It is a shame that England's Glory is so isolated in London Road now, but it is a good pub and worth the walk. The Hilltop, one of my favourite curry houses, is handy to this route and opens past midnight to provide something to soak up the beer.

My long-suffering wife Sharon (with my pint!) and Lin in the Regal.

A huge gathering in the England's Glory for the last research pub crawl. Left to right: Steve, another Steve, Scott, Paul, Lin, Sharon, Russell, Jane, Andy, Rob, Geoff.

Strays and Orphans

Coach & Horses, St Catherine Street – Thursday 10 December 2009
Priory, St Oswald's Park – Friday 5 March 2010
Park End, Parkend Road – Thursday 10 December 2009
Pelican, St Mary's Street – Thursday 10 December 2009

7

Maps

The following maps identify the location of all pubs where known. The pubs are identified by the number given in the List of Pubs in Chapter 8. Where there is more than one number given this indicates different pub names associated with the site – the most recent is given first.

I have attempted to map the pubs onto the modern street plan, but as Gloucester's road layout has changed significantly over recent years this is sometimes difficult to do. These are only hand-drawn maps and may not be precisely accurate.

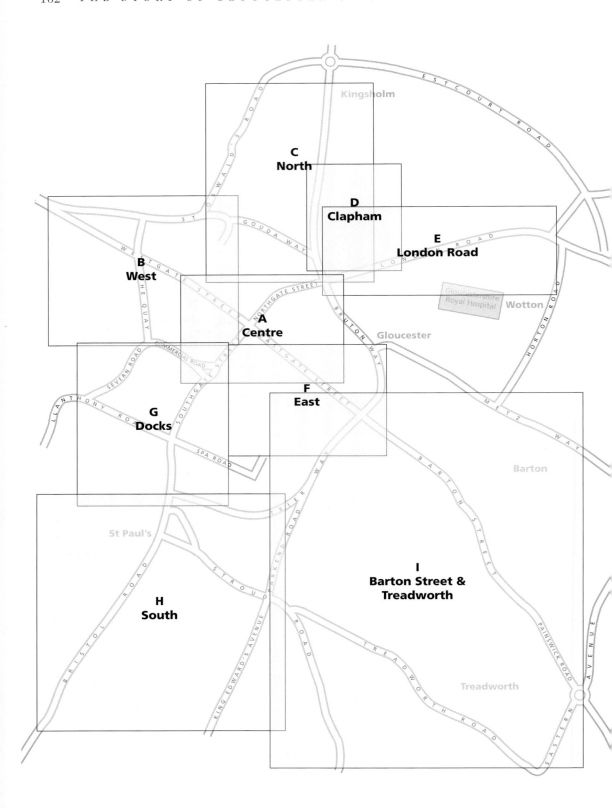

Map A: Centre

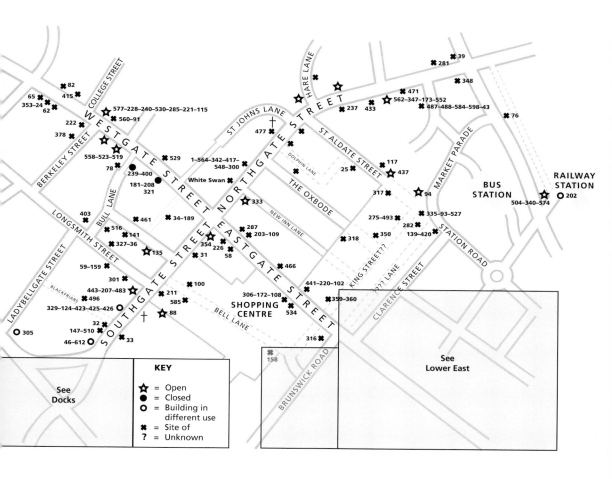

KEY

☆ = Open
● = Closed
○ = Building in different use
✖ = Site of
? = Unknown

Map B: West

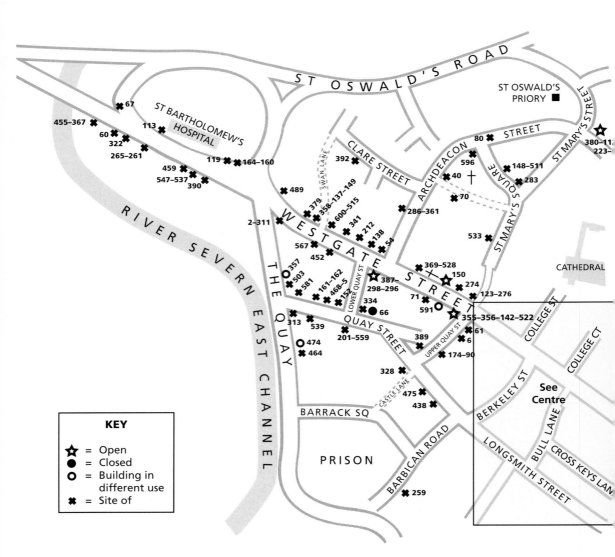

KEY

☆ = Open
● = Closed
○ = Building in
     different use
✖ = Site of

Map C: North

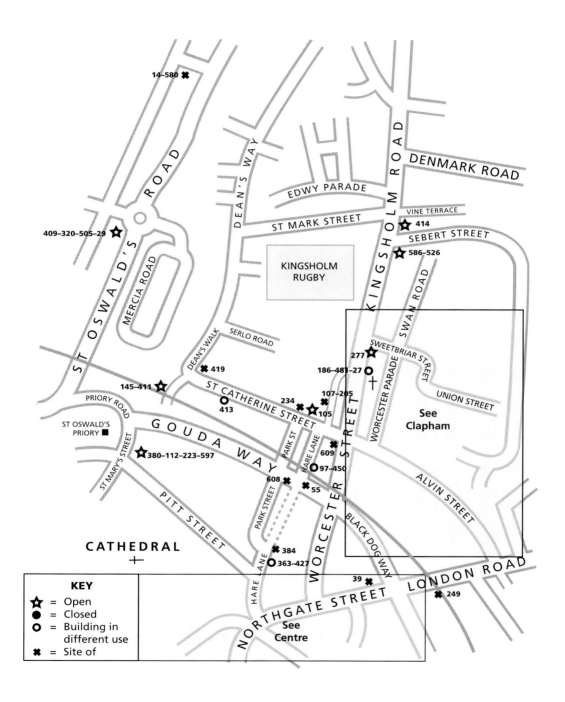

KEY
☆ = Open
● = Closed
○ = Building in different use
✖ = Site of

Map D: Clapham

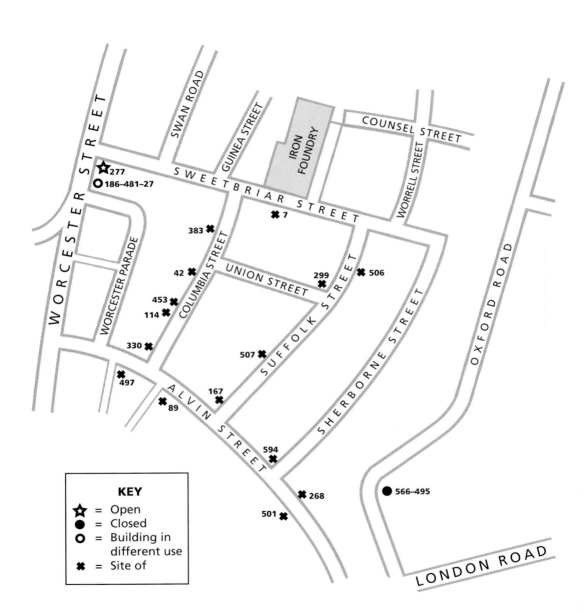

KEY

☆ = Open
● = Closed
○ = Building in different use
✖ = Site of

Map E: London Road

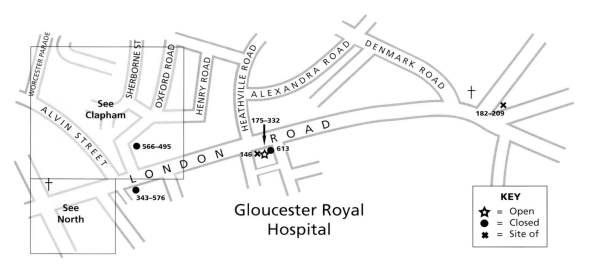

Map F: East

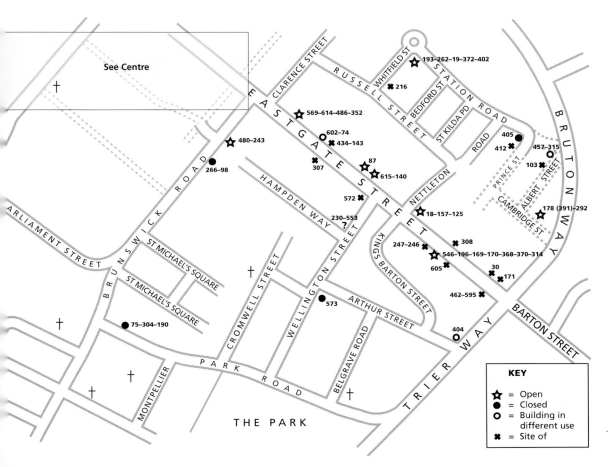

Map G: Docks

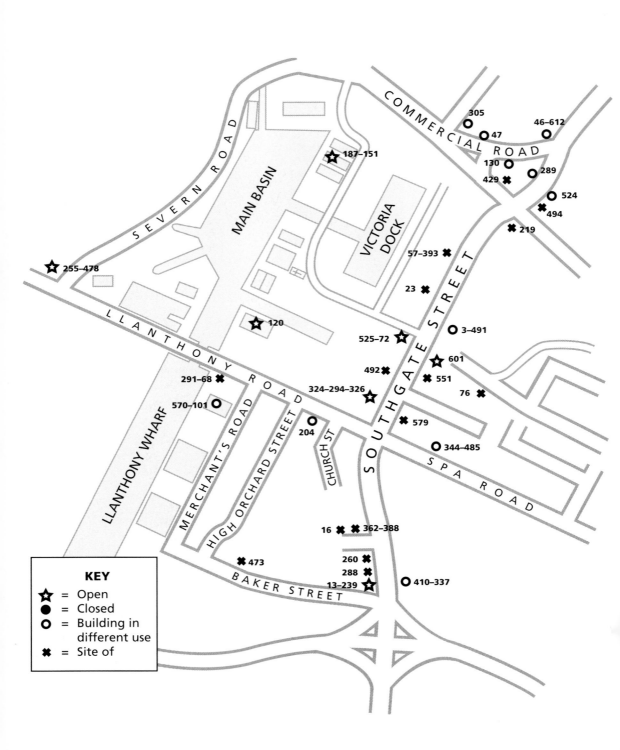

Map H: South

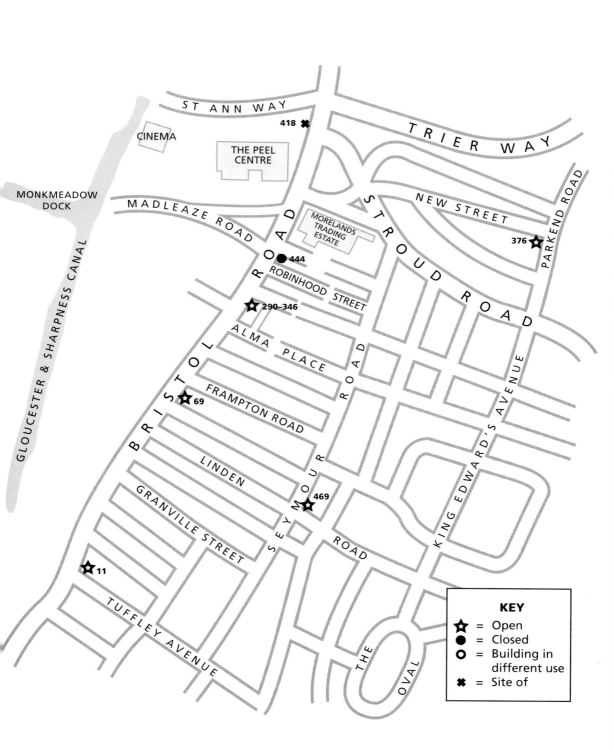

KEY

☆ = Open
● = Closed
○ = Building in different use
✖ = Site of

Map I: Barton & Tredworth

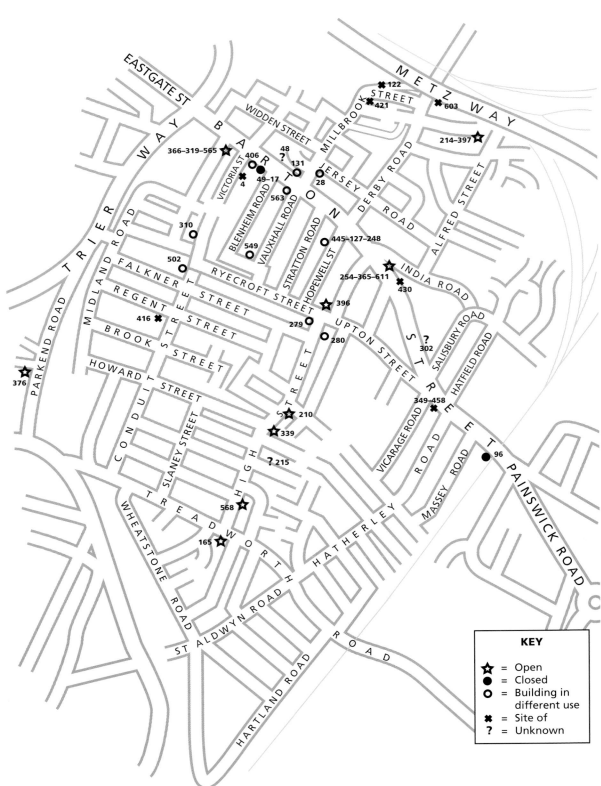

KEY

☆ = Open
● = Closed
○ = Building in different use
✖ = Site of
? = Unknown

8

List of Pubs

This is a full alphabetical list of all the pubs.

Street numbering is often quite complicated as many streets have been renumbered on many occasions, but here I give the most common appearances.

Dates are generally first and last references that I have found for the pub, not necessarily the full period in which they existed.

Status: O = open & trading
          N = trading under different name
          B = building in different use
          D = demolished
          X = previous name for pub now closed or in different use
          Unk = Unknown

Page numbers in bold indicate a main entry; numbers in normal type indicate where the pub is listed under an alternative name. Page numbers in brackets indicate a passing reference made to the pub.

For maps see Chapter 7.

Ref	Pub Name	Old No.	New No.	Street	From	To	Status	Comments	Page	Map
1	Adega Inn	98	25	Northgate Street	1883	1956	B	Previously the Maiden Head. Tredegar Arms and No.1 Vaults. Also called Adega Vaults. See also Railway Guard and Victoria. Licence lapsed 1956.	**94**	A
2	Admiral Benbow	77		Westgate Street	1858	1907	D	Previously the Masons Arms.	**132**	B
3	Albion Hotel	111	77	Southgate Street	1831	1935	B	Rebuilt on site of the Squirrel. New Squirrel opened at no. 79.	88	G
4	Alma Inn	1	1	Victoria Street	1872	1978	D	1872–4 referred to as Alma Brewery.		I
5	Anchor			Quay Street	Unk	Unk	D	No further information. Based on location, may have changed name to Severn Trow.		B
6	Anchor	13		Upper Quay Street	1871	1936	D			B
7	Anchor Inn	44		Sweetbriar Street	1857	1956	D	Closed 10 June 1956.	143	D
8	Angel			Lower Westgate Street/ the Island	1680	1736	D			
9	Angel & Crown			North Ward	18C	18C	Unk	No further information.		
10	Army & Navy			Wotton	1858	1858	Unk			
11	Avenue		227	Bristol Road	1900	date	O		**96**	H
12	Bacchus			Unknown	18C	18C	Unk	No further information.		
13	Baker Street		230	Southgate Street	1984	date	O	Previously the Hauliers Arms.	**79** (88)	G
14	Baker Street Tavern			St Oswald's Road	1993	1996	D	Previously Wheelwrights. Closed 27 March 1996.		C
15	Bakers Arms			West Ward	18C	1836	Unk			
16	Ball			Church Street	1857	1872	D		(80)	G
17	Bar 88		156	Barton Street	1992	1995	X	Name changed to Blenheim Inn.		I
18	Bar H2O		113	Eastgate Street	1999	date	O	Opened May 1999. Previously Courtyard and Dreams American Café Bar.	**97**	F
19	Bar Spirit		1	Station Road	2003	2007	N	Previously Prince Albert. Name changed to Jameson's, now Fusion.	122	F
20	Barbers Pole			Westgate Street (Lower)	1869	1869	D			
21	Barley Mow			Hare Lane	1740	1935	D			A
22	Barley Mow			The Quay	1869	1869	D			
23	Barley Mow	63	130	Southgate Street	1870	1984	D	Demolished in November 1988 as part of Gloucester Docks regeneration.		G
24	Bear	40	73	Westgate Street	1455	1722	D	Name changed to Old Bear.	(23)(26) 29 (49)	A
25	Beaufort Arms	14		St Aldate Street	1857	1936	D			A
26	Beedle			Unknown	18C	18C	Unk	No further information.		
27	Beehive		2	Kingsholm Road	1842	1851	X	Name changed from Fortune of War and reverted. See also Soldiers Return.	139	C/D
28	Beehive	10A	12	Millbrook Street	1870	1981	B	Also listed as 2 Jersey Road. Now a house.	(136)(143)	I
29	Bell and Gavel			St Oswald's Road	1958	2001	D	Name changed to Stockyards and reverted. Closed 3 April 2001. Demolished with building of St Oswald's Retail Park. Priory built on site.	**98** (143)	C
30	Bell Inn	46	91	Barton Street	1769	1939	D	Site now occupied by GL1 swimming pool.	(111)	F
31	Bell Inn	92	11	Southgate Street	1544	1967	D	Closed 29 September 1967. Demolished 1973 for building of Eastgate Shopping Centre.	**35** (38)(72)	A
32	Berkeley Arms	27		Southgate Street	1809	1914	D		98	A
33	Berkeley Hunt Inn	132	37	Southgate Street	1836	1973	D		**98**	A
34	Bicester Arms			Mercers Entry	1867	1877	D	Probably previously the Fox.		A
35	Bishop Blaize			Barton Street	1820	1830	Unk			
36	Black Boy			Longsmith Street	1680	1731	D	Name changed to New Bear.	(50)	A
37	Black Bull			Unknown	18C	18C	Unk	No further information.		
38	Black Dog			West Ward	1686	1686	Unk	Possibly London Road inn listed in wrong ward.	(99)	

Ref	Pub Name	Old No.	New No.	Street	From	To	Status	Comments	Page	Map
39	Black Dog Inn		1	London Road	1722	1965	D	Closed by October 1965. Demolished 1968. Site now under Black Dog Way.	**99**	A/C
40	Black Horse			Archdeacon Street	1836	1859	D			B
41	Black Horse			Southgate Street	1680	1753	Unk			
42	Black Lion			Columbia Street	1850	1868	D		(142)	D
43	Black Spread Eagle			Market Parade	1682	1747	D	Name changed from Spread Eagle and reverted. Also listed as Black Eagle and White Spread Eagle.	40	A
44	Black Swan			Bear Land	1722	1811	D			
45	Black Swan			Eastgate Street	1680	1702	Unk			
46	Black Swan	35	70	Southgate Street	1802	2004	B	Rebuilt 1847 with Commercial Road. Name changed to Yeoman 1970s–90s, but reverted. Closed 1 August 2004, now apartments.	**101**	A/G
47	Blackfriars Inn		10	Commercial Road	1879	1974	B		**102**	G
48	Blenheim (House) Arms	167		Barton Street (Lower)	1820	1920	Unk			I
49	Blenheim Inn		156	Barton Street (Lower)	1996	2008	C	Previously Bar 88.	(150)	I
50	Blue Anchor			Westgate Street (Lower)	1852	1861	D			
51	Blue Angel			Unknown	18C	18C	Unk	No further information.		
52	Blue Bell			West Ward	1680	1722	Unk			
53	Blue Bowl			London Road	1722	1722	Unk			
54	Blue Boy			Westgate Street	1850	1869	D			B
55	Boar's Head			Hare Lane	1682	1700	D			C
56	Boatman			The Quay	1455	1503	D		**22** (30)	
57	Boatman's Pleasure			Southgate Street	1850	1856	D	May be same as Pleasure Boat.		G
58	Bolt			Eastgate Street	1682	1759	D		43	A
59	Bolt			Longsmith Street	1680	1859	D	Name changed to Ducie Arms.	**43**	A
60	Boot Inn	28		Lower Westgate Street/ the Island	1736	1935	D		**133**	B
61	Booth Hall Tap		11	Upper Quay Street	1871	1945	D			B
62	Boothall (Hotel)	41	71	Westgate Street	1455	1956	D	Closed 28 March 1956. Site now occupied by Shire Hall buildings.	**22** (29)	A
63	Bowl			North Ward	1736	1736	Unk			
64	Bowling Green			South Ward	1722	1936	Unk			
65	Brewers Arms			Westgate Street	1871	1907	D	Closed June 1907.	(22)	A
66	Brewery			Quay Street	1996	2001	C	Closed 3 April 2001.		B
67	Bridge (End) Inn			Lower Westgate Street/ the Island	1836	1935	D			B
68	Bridge Inn			Llanthony Road			D	Alternative name for Llanthony Bridge Inn.	85	G
69	Bristol Hotel		131	Bristol Road	1902	date	O		**103**	H
70	Britannia		17	St Mary's Square	1836	1953	D	Removal declared final 3 November 1953.		B
71	British Brig			Westgate Street	1850	1850	D			B
72	British Flag	69	134	Southgate Street	1870	1984	N	Name changed to Tall Ship.	89	G
73	British Lion	3		Sebert Place	1870	1873	D			
74	Brunels Wine Bar		83	Eastgate Street	1984	1987	B	Name changed to the Windmill. Now Fever nightclub.	131	F
75	Brunswick		7	Park Road	1993	2009	C	Previously the Frontier and the Man in the Bowler Hat. Closed 25 April 2009. Due to reopen as an Indian restaurant.	**104**	F
76	Brunswick Arms			Albion Street	1850	1900	D			G
77	Buck's Head			Lower Westgate Street/ the Island	18C	18C	D	No further information.		

Ref	Pub Name	Old No.	New No.	Street	From	To	Status	Comments	Page	Map
78	Bull Inn			Bull Lane	1682	1910	D	Closed 1910. Demolished 1952.	**43** (95)	A
79	Bull's Head			North Ward	18C	18C	Unk	No further information.		
80	Bull's Head			St Mary's Square	1836	1918	D			B
81	Bunch of Grapes			Columbia Street	1859	1859	D		(142)	
82	Bunch of Grapes	125	74	Westgate Street	1836	1878	D			A
83	Butcher Row			North Ward	1736	1736	Unk			
84	Butcher Row			Westgate Street	1736	1736	Unk			
85	Butchers Arms			Bell Lane	1836	1871	D			
86	Butchers Arms			Westgate Street	1720	1836	Unk			
87	Butlers Venue Bar		99	Eastgate Street	1993	date	O	Partly occupies the former Crown & Thistle.	**105** (107)	F
88	Café René			Marylone	1998	date	O	Previously the Inner Court and Greyfriars. See also Courtyard Tapas Bar & Restaurant.	**63** (72)	A
89	Carpenters Arms			Alvin Street	1850	1851	D		(142)	D
90	Castle Inn/Tavern			Upper Quay Street	1832	1849	D	Destroyed by fire 1849. Probably site of later Elephant & Castle.		B
91	Cathedral Tavern	138	50	Westgate Street	1867	1867	X	Name changed from Upper George and probably reverted.	60	A
92	Catherine Wheel	27	53	Westgate Street	1502	1672	N	See also Katherine Wheele. Previously Savage's Inn. Name Changed to the Fountain.	25	A
93	Cattle Market Inn							See New Market Inn.		A
94	Chambers		27	St Aldate Street	1999	date	O	Opened 21 September 1999.	**106**	A
95	Chappell House			North Ward	1722	1722	Unk			
96	Chequers Inn		24	Painswick Road	1822	2008	D	Demolished 2009.		I
97	Cherry Tree			Hare Lane	1850	1850	D	Possibly the same site as the Rose & Crown.		C
98	Chicago Rock Café			Brunswick Road	1997	2000	X	Former Pickfords/Linbar store. Name changed to Jumpin' Jaks.		F
99	Chopping Knife			South Ward	1679	1686	Unk			
100	City Arms	9	7	Bell Lane	1802	1966	D	Demolished 1966–7 for building of Eastgate Shopping Centre.	131	A
101	City Barge			Merchants Road	1985	1993	X	Name changed to Waterfront.	**81**	G
102	City Wine Vaults	30		Eastgate Street	1869	1876	D	Name changed to Rising Sun.	123	A
103	Clarence Inn			Albert Street	1861	1896	D			F
104	Cleopatra's		53	Northgate Street	1989	1990	N	Amalgamation of King's Arms and Tabard. Cleopatra's in late 1980s/early 1990s. Name changed to King's, later Gate, now Varsity.	127	A
105	Coach & Horses	4	2	St Catherine Street	1806	date	O	Possibly same as Golden Cock. Confusion with Cock at Alngate as both North Ward.	**44**	C
106	Cock			Northgate Street	1722	1820	Unk	Possibly same as Golden Cock. Confusion with Cock at Alngate as both North Ward.		
107	Cock at Alngate			St Catherine Street	1722	1811	D	Possibly same as Golden Cock. Confusion with Cock in Northgate Street as both North Ward. Address sometimes given as Hare Lane.		C
108	Coffee House	5	10	Eastgate Street	1806	1835	D	Two Coffee Houses in East Ward in alehouse licensing records. One probably changed to Eastgate Vaults.		A
109	Coffee House	41	13	Eastgate Street	1806	1835	D	Two Coffee Houses in East Ward in alehouse licensing records. One probably changed to Gloucester Coffee House next to Lemon & Parkers.	(118)	A
110	Coffee House			South Ward	1806	1835	Unk	Two listed 1806–7 and 1817–23.		
111	Coffee House			West Ward	1806	1835	Unk	Two listed 1807–12 and 1815–16.		
112	College Arms		4	St Mary's Street	1993	2007	N	Name changed from Pelican and reverted.	51	B/C

Ref	Pub Name	Old No.	New No.	Street	From	To	Status	Comments	Page	Map
113	Colliers Arms			Westgate Street (Lower)	1850	1872	D			B
114	Columbia (House) Inn			Columbia Street	1836	1906	D		(142)	D
115	Commercial	135	56	Westgate Street	1906	1920	N	Name changed to Gresham Hotel. Later Lamprey, now Westgate.	116	A
116	Commercial Inn		11	Baker Street	1871	1974	D			
117	Commercial Tavern			St Aldate Street	1850	1851	D			A
118	Compasses			North Ward	1736	1736	Unk			
119	Coopers Arms	43	180	Lower Westgate Street/ the Island	1806	1960	D	Extinction of licence, 13 February 1960.		B
120	Coots Café Bar			Llanthony Warehouse, The Docks	2008	date	O		**82**	G
121	Cork			North Ward	1680	1736	Unk			
122	County Arms		65	Millbrook Street	1872	1997	D	Closed 9 September 1997. Demolished March 1998. Flats built on site.	(150)	I
123	County Shades	117	92	Westgate Street	1869	1935	D	Previously the King's Head Tap. part of the King's Head Hotel.	38	B
124	County Tavern			Southgate Street	1984	1993	X	Bar in the New County Hotel.	39	A
125	Courtyard		113	Eastgate Street	1991	1993	N	Opened as adjunct to Frankie's nightclub above. Name changed to Dreams American Café Bar. Now Bar H2O.	97	F
126	Courtyard Tapas Bar & Restaurant			Marylone	2002	2002	N	Name changed from Café René and reverted.	63	A
127	Cox's Beerhouse			Hopewell Street	1872	1872	X	Possibly previously the Hopewell Inn and later Robin Hood.	151	I
128	Crispin & Crispianno			West Ward	1736	1744	Unk			
129	Crispin & Pierre			Unknown	18C	18C	Unk	No further information.		
130	Criterion Inn		5	Commercial Road	1893	1993	B	Later the Criterion Hotel – Bed & Breakfast.		G
131	Cromwell's Head		175	Barton Street	1872	1982	B	Now a shop.		I
132	Cross			East Ward	1686	1686	Unk			
133	Cross Keys			Lower Westgate Street/ the Island	1680	1736	Unk			
134	Cross Keys			North Ward	1736	1736	Unk			
135	Cross Keys Inn			Cross Keys Lane	1720	date	O		**45**	A
136	Crow			Unknown	18C	18C	unk	No further information		
137	Crown & Anchor			Westgate Street	1822	1836	D	Previously the Dial and later Old Dial.	135	B
138	Crown & Sceptre	105	122	Westgate Street	1684	1871	D			B
139	Crown (Hotel)			Market Parade	1872	1965	D	Previously the Railway Inn.		A
140	Crown & Thistle Inn		101	Eastgate Street	1830	2001	N	Name changed to Zest.	**107**	F
141	Crown Inn			Cross Keys Lane	1680	1900	D		(31)	A
142	Crown Inn			Westgate Street (Lower)	1455	1680	D	Name changed to Old Crown. See also Tabard.	(23) 30	B
143	Curriers Arms			Barton Street	1736	1835	D	Possibly name changed to Red Rover Inn.		F
144	Cutlers Arms			North Ward	1736	1736	Unk			
145	Dean's Walk Inn			Dean's Walk	1887	date	O	Previously the Quart Pot.	**108**	C
146	Denmark Arms Inn		64	London Road	1871	1919	D		(112)	E
147	Dial			Southgate Street	1806	1869	D	Shown as Sundial in *Pigot's Directory* 1830.		A
148	Dial			St Mary's Square	1806	1876	D	Name changed to Sundial from 1807 to 1812 and reverted. Also Sundial in *Pigot's* 1830.	135	B
149	Dial	93	150	Westgate Street	1736	1821	D	Name changed to Crown & Anchor, then Old Dial.	135	B
150	Dick Whittington		100	Westgate Street	1982	date	O		**66**	B
151	Doctor Foster's			Kimberley Warehouse, Docks	1993	2004	N	Name changed to Fosters on the Docks.	83	G

Ref	Pub Name	Old No.	New No.	Street	From	To	Status	Comments	Page	Map
152	Dog			Quay St	18C	18C	D			B
153	Dog in the Green			Northgate Street	1736	1820	Unk			
154	Dog's Kennel			Unknown	18C	18C	Unk	No further information.		
155	Dolphin			West Ward	1680	1682	Unk		(110)	
156	Dolphin Inn/Vaults	21		Northgate Street	1722	1908	D	Closed in 1908. Demolished 1909 to make way for Bon Marché extension.	**110**	A
157	Dreams American Café Bar	113		Eastgate Street	1996	1999	N	Previously Courtyard, now Bar H2O.	97	F
158	Druid's Head			Queen Street	1850	1850	D			A
159	Ducie Arms			Longsmith Street	1869	1906	D	Previously the Bolt.	43	A
160	Duke	44		Lower Westgate Street/ the Island	1736	1836	D	Referred to as the Duke on the Island. Name changed to Duke of Sussex.	**134**	B
161	Duke			Quay Street	1806	1827	D	Referred to as the Duke on the Quay. Became Duke of Gloucester by 1830.	134	B
162	Duke of Gloucester			Quay Street	1830	1905	D	Previously the Duke.	134	B
163	Duke of Marlborough's Head			West Ward	1722	1722	Unk			
164	Duke of Sussex	44	178	Lower Westgate Street/ the Island	1847	1936	D	Previously the Duke.	134	B
165	Duke of Wellington		72	Tredworth Road	1869	date	O		**144**	I
166	Duke of Wellington			Westgate Street	1815	1836	Unk			
167	Duke of York		3	Suffolk Street	1851	1956	D	Closed 17 June 1956.	(143)	D
168	Eagle			North Ward	1680	1680	Unk	Possibly same as Spread Eagle, although that is also listed.	(40)	
169	East End Tavern	25	66	Barton Street	1955	1984	N	Previously Eastend (Wine) Vaults. Name changed to Gate, now TnT. Modern address is 112 Eastgate Street.	**111**	F
170	Eastend (Wine) Vaults	25	66	Barton Street	1879	1954	N	Originally probably the Merry Fellow beerhouse, then the Ostrich and the Original Shakespeare. Known as Eastend Wine & Spirit Vaults, Eastend Wine Vaults, Eastend Vaults and East End Vaults. Name changed to Eastend Tavern, then Gate, now TnT.	111	F
171	Eastend Tavern	43		Barton Street	1879	1885	D	Not to be confused with East End Tavern at no. 66.	(111)	F
172	Eastgate Vaults	5	10	Eastgate Street	1879	1939	D	Probably one of Coffee Houses in alehouse licenses from 1806. Initially Eastgate Wine & Spirit Vaults. Name changed to Market House.		A
173	Ebeneezer Riley's Northend Vaults		86	Northgate Street	1996	1996	N	Previously Northend Vaults and Tut 'n' Shive. Reverted to Northend Vaults, now the Vaults.	120	A
174	Elephant & Castle			Upper Quay Street	1871	1913	D	Probably on site of earlier Castle Inn/Tavern. Closed 23 December 1913.		B
175	England's Glory		66	London Road	1984	date	O	Previously New Inn.	**112**	E
176	Excelsior Inn	6	4	George Street	1936	1967	D	Closed 29 January 1967.		A
177	Falcon			West Ward	1682	1686	Unk			
178	Famous Pint Pot		74	Bruton Way	1979	date	O	Previously the Locomotive Inn at 5 Cambridge Street.	**112**	F
179	Fish			South Ward	1680	1686	Unk			
180	Fishguard Arms			Barbican Alley	1864	1864	D			
181	Fleece Hotel	10	19	Westgate Street	1497	2002	C	Known as Golden Ffleece in seventeenth century. Closed October 2002.	**17** (69)	A
182	Fleece Inn			Wotton Pitch	1736	1974	D	Previously the Golden Fleece. Demolished in August 1964 and continued in portacabin. Site now occupied by flats.		E
183	Fleece Tap			Westgate Street	1891	1891	Unk	Presumably associated with Fleece Hotel.		

Ref	Pub Name	Old No.	New No.	Street	From	To	Status	Comments	Page	Map
184	Flower de Luce			Southgate Street	1680	1736	Unk			
185	Foresters Arms			Northgate Street	1869	1869	Unk			
186	Fortune of War Inn		2	KingsholmRoad	1836	1935	B	Also known as the Beehive and the Soldiers Return.	**139**	C/D
187	Fosters on the Docks			Kimberley Warehouse, Docks	2004	date	O	Previously Doctor Fosters.	**83**	G
188	Fountain Inn	27	53	Westgate Street	1672	date	O	Previously known as Savage's Inn and Katherine Wheele.	(11)(18) **25**(30)	A
189	Fox			Mercers Entry	1736	1859	D	Probably name changed to Bicester Arms.		A
190	Frontier		7	Park Road	1983	mid-1980s	X	Previously Snobs Nightclub, later Man in the Bowler Hat and Brunswick.	104	F
191	Full Moon			North Ward	1722	1736	Unk			
192	Furriers Arms			Unknown	18C	18C	Unk	No further information.		
193	Fusion		1	Station Road	2008	date	O	Previously Prince Albert, PA, Bar Spirit and Jameson's.	122	F
194	Gallon Bottle/ Pot			West Ward	18C	18C	Unk	No further information.		
195	Game Cock			Archdeacon Street	1869	1869	D			
196	Gate		112	Eastgate Street	1993	late 1990s	N	Previously East End Tavern. Name changed to TnT.	111	F
197	Gate		53	Northgate Street	2002	2007	N	Previously the Tabard, Cleopatra's, Kings. Name changed to Varsity by 2008.	127	A
198	General Wolf			West Ward	18C	18C	Unk	No further information.		
199	George			Westgate Street				See Upper George and Lower George.		
200	Glaziers Arms			South Ward	1736	1736	Unk			
201	Globe Inn		1	Quay Street	1822	1962	D	Previously the Union Jack. Closed 5 February 1962.		B
202	Gloucester (Family) Hotel		19	George Street	1833	1957	B		(126)	A
203	Gloucester Coffee House	41	13	Eastgate Street	1850	1946	D	Probably one of Coffee Houses in alehouse licensing records from 1806. Next door to Lemon & Parkers. Carlton Restaurant by 1949, Dewhurst butchers shop by 1955.	(118)	A
204	Goat Inn			Llanthony Road	1851	1955	B		**84**	G
205	Golden Cock			Hare Lane	1830	1830	D	Probably same as the Cock at Alngate.		C
206	Golden Cock			Northgate Street	1763	1852	Unk	Probably same as the Cock.		
207	Golden Cross		38	Southgate Street	1975	2008	N	Previously the Dirty Duck Restaurant. Changed to Robert Raikes's House 2008.	74(119)	A
208	Golden Ffleece	19	10	Westgate Street	1673	1673	X	Earlier name for the Fleece Hotel.	17	A
209	Golden Fleece			Wotton Pitch	1726	1736	D	Name shortened to Fleece.		E
210	Golden Heart		85	High Street	1870	date	O		**145**	I
211	Golden Heart Inn			Southgate Street	1680	1763	D		**37**(38)(42)(64)	A
212	Golden Heart Inn		100	Westgate Street	1720	1935	D	Possibly two pubs with the older one on the Island.		B
213	Golden Lion			North Ward	1680	1722	Unk			
214	Great Western		91	Alfred Street	1985	date	O	Previously the Plough.	**146**	I
215	Great Western			Moreton Street	1847	1874	Unk			I
216	Great Western			Whitfield Street	1847	1871	D			F
217	Green			South Ward	1682	1682	Unk			
218	Green Dragon			Archdeacon Lane	1722	1722	D			
219	Green Dragon		26	Southgate Street	1683	1868	D	Demolished 1868 for expansion of infirmary.	**48**	G
220	Greenroom	30		Eastgate Street	1901	1901	D	Temporary name change from Rising Sun.	123	A
221	Gresham Hotel	135	56	Westgate Street	1927	1935	N	Previously Commercial Hotel, renamed after closure of Gresham on opposite side of road. Name changed to Lamprey. Later Therapy, Haus, Grill and now Westgate.	116	A

Ref	Pub Name	Old No.	New No.	Street	From	To	Status	Comments	Page	Map
222	Gresham Hotel	32		Westgate Street	1893	1905	D	Corner of Berkeley Street. Demolished to make way for Shire Hall extension. Moved across road to site of later Lamprey Hotel.	116	A
223	Grey Pelican			North Ward	1686	1686	N	Previously one of two Pelicans. Possibly temporary rename of the Pelican, but see also the White Pelican.	51	B/C
224	Greyfriars			Marylone	1987	1998	N	Previously Inner Court. Name changed to Café René. See also Underground.	63	A
225	Greyhound			The Quay	1720	1736	Unk			
226	Greyhound Hotel	1		Eastgate Street	1544	1935	B	Later the Botherways then Cadena Café. Currys Digital currently on site.	**114**	A
227	Griffin			West Ward	1680	1682	Unk			
228	Grill		56	Westgate Street	2007	2008	N	Previously the Gresham Hotel, Lamprey, Therapy and Haus. Name change to Westgate.	116	A
229	Half Moon			Northgate Street	1680	1736	Unk			
230	Hampden Inn			Wellington Street	1889	1893	Unk	Previously Uncle Tom's Cabin.		F
231	Hand & Lock of Hair			East Ward	1736	1736	Unk			
232	Hand & Pen			West Ward	1679	1681	Unk			
233	Hare & Hound			North Ward	1736	1736	Unk			
234	Hare & Hounds			St Catherine Street	1850	1861	D			C
235	Harp			Parish of St Catherines	1801	1801	Unk			
236	Harp			Westgate Street (Lower)	1802	1822	Unk			
237	Harrow Inn		74	Northgate Street	1686	1859	D			A
238	Hatt & Feather			West Ward	1736	1736	Unk			
239	Hauliers Arms Inn		230	Southgate Street	1852	1984	N	Name changed to Baker Street.	79 (88)	G
240	Haus		56	Westgate Street	2003	2007	N	Previously the Gresham Hotel, Lamprey and Therapy. Name change to Grill, now Westgate.	116	A
241	Heart of Oak			Columbia Street	1860	1860	D			
242	Hog in Armour & Black Boy			Berkeley Street	1735	1739	D			
243	Hogshead		3	Brunswick Road	1999	2003	N	Opened in former Jennings Printers on 3 January 1999. Name changed to Sloanes.	75	F
244	Hogshead			Unknown	18C	18C	Unk	No further information.		
245	Hole in the Wall			Unknown	18C	18C	Unk	No further information. (Presumably not an early reference to a cash point!)		
246	Hope & Anchor	23		Barton Street	1842	1842	D	Name changed to Hope Inn.		F
247	Hope Inn	23	62	Barton Street	1847	1974	D	Previously the Hope & Anchor.	(111)	F
248	Hopewell Inn			Hopewell Street	1870	1871	X	Probably changed name to Cox's Beerhouse and then Robin Hood.	151	I
249	Horse & Groom Inn		12	London Road	1740	late 1970s	D		(100)	C
250	Horse & Jockey			Sweetbriar Street	1850	1856	D		(139)	
251	Horse & Groom			East Ward	1736	1736	Unk			
252	Horseshoe			North Ward	1736	1736	Unk			
253	Imperial Inn	82	59	Northgate Street	1877	date	O	Previously the Plough Inn.	**48**	A
254	India House Inn	101	227	Barton Street (Lower)	1780	date	O	Also Olde India House and Ye Olde India House.	**147**	I
255	Inn on the Docks		28	Llanthony Road	2008	date	O	Previously the Sir Colin Campbell – reopened 17 October 2008.	**84**	G
256	Inner Court			Marylone	late 1970s	1987	N	Name changed to Greyfriars then Café René.	63	A
257	International Hotel		5	Commercial Road	1872	1883	Unk			

Ref	Pub Name	Old No.	New No.	Street	From	To	Status	Comments	Page	Map
258	Ivy Green			Archdeacon Street	1851	1881	D			
259	Ivy Green			Barbican Alley	1850	1869	D			B
260	Jack			Southgate Street	1861	1861	D		(80)	G
261	Jack Tar		205	Lower Westgate Street/ the Island	1850	1851	D	Name probably changed to Jolly Tar.		B
262	Jameson's		1	Station Road	2007	2008	N	Previously the Prince Albert, PA and Bar Spirit. Name changed to Fusion.	122	F
263	Joiners Arms			North Ward	1799	1836	Unk			
264	Jolly Sailor			South Ward	1799	1836	Unk			
265	Jolly Tar			Lower Westgate Street/ the Island	1869	1871	D	Probably previously Jack Tar.		B
266	Jumpin' Jak's			Brunswick Road	2000	2006	C	Previously Chicago Rock Café. Closed 27 August 2006. Planning permission to demolish.		F
267	Katherine Wheele	27		Westgate Street	1502	1672	N	See also Catherine Wheel. Previously Savage's Inn. Name changed to Fountain.	25	A
268	King William	14	32	Alvin Street	1836	1906	D		(142)	D
269	Kings		53	Northgate Street	1993	1996	N	Amalgamation of King's Arms and Tabard. Previously Cleopatra's. Name Changed to Gate, now Varsity.	127	A
270	King's Armes			East Ward	1680	1680	Unk			
271	King's Arms		3	Hare Lane	1786	late 1970s	N	Amalgamated with Tabard next door, now part of Varsity.	**49**	A
272	King's Arms			Lower Westgate Street/ the Island	1680	1736	D	West Ward. Mentioned in deeds as 'formerly the Packhorse between the bridges,' so presumably on the Island.		
273	King's Arms			Suffolk Street	1852	1852	D			
274	King's Head			Westgate Street	1520	1865	D	See also King's Head Tap/County Shades.	(36)(37) **38** (67)	B
275	King's Head Inn		27	King Street	1869	1885	D	Probably previously St Aldate House.		A
276	King's Head Tap			St Mary's Street	1831	1847	D	Part of King's Head Westgate Street. Later the County Shades.	39	B
277	Kingsholm Inn		8	Kingsholm Road	1842	date	O		**139**	C/D
278	Labour in Vaine			West Ward	1680	1686	Unk			
279	Laburnum (Brewery) Hotel		2	High Street	1842	1967	B	Brewery originated 1842 but may have originally been at Laburnum Inn. Later Ryecroft Hotel, now bail hostel.	**148**	I
280	Laburnum Inn		15	High Street	1842	1978	B	Now a private house.	148	I
281	Lamb			Northgate Street	1682	1736	D			A
282	Lamb Inn			Market Parade	1851	1957	D			A
283	Lamb Inn			St Mary's Square	1802	1897	D			B
284	Lamp Post			Unknown	18C	18C	Unk	No further information.		
285	Lamprey	135	56	Westgate Street	1941	2002	N	Previously the Gresham Hotel. Name changed to Therapy, then Haus, Grill and now Westgate.	**116**	A
286	Leather Bottle		17	Archdeacon Street	1682	1959	D	Sometime referred to as Old Leather Bottle. Licence was put in suspense 6 October 1959.	**134**	B
287	Lemon & Parker	40	15	Eastgate Street	1882	1974	D	Previously George Barrett's wine & spirit merchants. Waterstone's now on site.	**118**	A
288	Leopard Inn		200	Southgate Street	1871	1966	D	Closed 7 September 1966.	(80)(88)	G
289	Lifeboat Inn	37	74	Southgate Street	1867	1879	B			G
290	Linden Tree		73	Bristol Road	1984	date	O	Previously the Norfolk House Hotel.	**68**	H
291	Llanthony (Bridge) Inn			Llanthony Road	1847	1974	D	Known as Llanthony Bridge Inn, Llanthony Inn or just Bridge Inn. Closed 1974. Demolished 2008 in building of Gloucester Quays.	(69) **85**	G

Ref	Pub Name	Old No.	New No.	Street	From	To	Status	Comments	Page	Map
292	Locomotive Inn		5	Cambridge Street	1879	1974	N	Beer retailer since at least 1861, but pub not named. Name changed to Famous Pint Pot.	112	F
293	Loft		1	Bull Lane	2007	2009	C	Previously Poets Wine Bar. Loft opened November 2007.		A
294	Lord Nelson Inn	88		Littleworth	1830	1830	N	Previously the Nelson's Head Inn. Shortened to the Nelson and address became Southgate Street.	86	G
295	Lord Raglan			Albert Street	1856	1856	Unk			
296	Lower George	60	121	Westgate Street	1535	1997	N	Originally just the George, but confused as two in West Ward – see also Upper George. Name changed to Mad O'Rourkes, now Pig Inn the City.	**27** (60)	B
297	Lower Star			Unknown	18C	18C	Unk	No further information.		
298	Mad O'Rourkes		121	Westgate Street	1997	late 1990s	N	Previously Lower George. Name changed to Pig Inn the City.	27	B
299	Magnet		29	Union Street	1865	1959	D	Licence removed to Beehive Inn, Millbrook Street 28 April 1959.	(143)	D
300	Maiden Head Inn	98		Northgate Street	1722	1849	B	Name changed probably to Tredegar Arms and No 1 Vaults, then the Adega. See also Railway Guard.	94	A
301	Malt and Hops			Longsmith Street	mid-1970s	2001	D	Closed 3 April 2001. Demolished 2008.	**119**	A
302	Malt Shovel	269		Barton Street	1847	1913	Unk	Closed 23 December 1913.		I
303	Maltsters Arms			Northgate Street	1870	1871	Unk			
304	Man in the Bowler Hat		7	Park Road	1980s	1980s	X	Previously Frontier. Name changed to Brunswick.	104	F
305	Mariners Arms			Ladybellegate Street	1847	1935	B	Early reference to Mariners Arms & Custom House Inn. Now the Gloucester Royal Naval Association Club.		A/G
306	Market House		10	Eastgate Street	1945	1957	D	Previously Eastgate Vaults. Closed for sale of intoxicants 2 October 1957.		A
307	Marquis of Bute Inn	10		Barton Street	1871	1887	D			F
308	Marquis of Granby Inn	53	75	Barton Street	1820	1957	D			F
309	Masons Arms			Sweetbriar Street	1866	1866	D	Also Masons Arms in North Ward in eighteenth century, but seems unlikely to be the same.		
310	Masons Arms		82	Victoria Street	1872	1974	B	Converted to flats.		I
311	Masons Arms	77		Westgate Street (Lower)	1736	1852	D	Masons Arms & Swansea House in 1849 and 1852. Name changed to Admiral Benbow.	132	B
312	Mermaid			North Ward	1680	1686	Unk			
313	Mermaid		9	Quay Street	1680	1935	D			B
314	Merry Fellow	25		Barton Street	1820	1861	N	Probable precursor to East End Tavern at 25 Barton Street, but could be no. 43.	111	F
315	Midland & Royal Hotel		28	Station Road	1923	1959	X	Previously the Royal Hotel and reverted. Now offices.	**119**	F
316	Military Arms		2	Brunswick Road	1870	1871	D	Site now occupied by Boots.		A
317	Milkmaid		36	St Aldate Street	1836	1936	D			A
318	Mitre			Oxebody Lane/Mitre Street	1680	1879	D		50	A
319	Molly Malone's		136	Barton Street	1990	1995	N	Originally Victoria House. Name changed to One Eyed Jacks.	153	I
320	Monkey Tree			St Oswald's Retail Park	2007	2009	N	Previously the Priory and reverted. On the site of the Bell & Gavel.	98	C
321	Monks' Retreat	19		Westgate Street	1927	2002	C	Undercroft beneath the Fleece Hotel.	(17) **69** (86)	A
322	Nag's Head	26		Lower Westgate Street/ the Island	1722	1908	D			B
323	Nag's Head			Northgate Street	1680	1736	Unk			
324	Nelson Inn	88	166	Southgate Street	1847	date	O	Previously the Nelson's Head Inn and the Lord Nelson Inn.	**86**	G
325	Nelson's Arms			West Ward	1815	1815	Unk			

Ref	Pub Name	Old No.	New No.	Street	From	To	Status	Comments	Page	Map
326	Nelson's Head Inn	88		Southgate Street	1815	1820	N	Name changed to Lord Nelson Inn. then the Nelson Inn.	86	G
327	New Bear			Longsmith Street/Bolt Lane	1767	1856	D	Previously the Black Boy. Demolished 1868.	(50)	A
328	New Bear			Quay Street	1647	1726	D		(30) **49**	B
329	New County Hotel	21	44	Southgate Street	1937	2008	B	Previously the Ram Hotel and the Ram & County Hotel. Became New County Hotel 30 January 1937. Closed 2 June 2008. Opened as Mystiques Hotel & Restaurant, 12 December 2009.	39	A
330	New Inn	9		Columbia Street	1852	1930	D		(142)	D
331	New Inn			East Ward	1722	1835	Unk			
332	New Inn		66	London Road	1872	1974	N	Name changed to England's Glory.	112	E
333	New Inn		16	Northgate Street	1430	date	O	Rebuilt on site of inn dating from 1350.	(11) **14** (31) (68)	A
334	New Inn			Quay Street	1848	1851	D			B
335	New Market Inn			Market Parade	1841	1874	Unk	Also referred to as Cattle Market Inn. Probably the same as Telegraph Inn.		A
336	New Oxbody			North Ward	1722	1722	Unk	Appears distinct from Oxbody Inn.		
337	New Pilot		159	Southgate Street	1869	1999	X	Name changed to Professor Moriarty's.	(80) **87**	G
338	New Starr			West Ward	1736	1736	Unk			
339	New Victory Inn		103	High Street	1872	date	O		**149** (154)	I
340	New Wellington Hotel			Bruton Way	1984	1984	N	Temporary name for Wellington Hotel.	126	A
341	Newfoundland		144	Westgate Street	1850	1850	D			B
342	No.1 Vaults	98		Northgate Street	1876	1879	X	Probably previously Maidenhead and Tredegar Arms. Name changed to Adega.	94	A
343	No.36		36	London Road	2007	2008	C	Previously the Welsh Harp. Closed 1 January 2008.	61	E
344	Norfolk Arms			Spa Road/Norfolk Street	1869	1905	B	Rear of Ribston Hall/Gloucester Spa Hotel. Probably previously Spa Hotel Tap. Referred for compensation 14 December 1905.		G
345	Norfolk Arms			Upper Quay Street	1813	1836	D	Previously probably one of the two Coffee Houses listed in West Ward and known as Norfolk Coffee House.		
346	Norfolk House Hotel		73	Bristol Road	1836	1984	N	Name changed to Linden Tree.	68	H
347	Northend Vaults	44	86	Northgate Street	1869	2009	N	Early references as Northend Wine Vaults. Name changed to Tut 'n' Shive then Ebeneezer Riley's Northend Vaults, but reverted. Now changed to the Vaults.	**120**	A
348	Northgate Hotel		2	London Road	1869	1974	D	Demolished in 1980.		A
349	Oak Inn		350	Barton Street	1872	1993	D	Probably Roal Oak 1879. Closed 1 January 1993.		I
350	Oddfellows Arms			Oxbody Lane	1836	1910	D	Submitted to compensation authority for closure in 1909.		A
351	Old Acquaintance			Wotton	1841	1841	D			
352	Old Bank		61	Eastgate Street	1997	1998	N	Opened 16 September 1997 in old TSB Bank. Name changed to Spoofers Bar, then Zebra Bar, now Water Poet.	128	F
353	Old Bear	40	73	Westgate Street	1722	1927	D	Previously the Bear. Shire Hall now on site.	(22) **29** (49)	A
354	Old Bell		9a	Southgate Street	1912	date	O	Originally used as function rooms for the Bell in next door.	(35) **70**	A
355	Old Crown Inn		81	Westgate Street	1990	date	O	Opened in building on the site of part of the original (Old) Crown Inn.	**30**	B
356	Old Crown Inn			Westgate Street (Lower)	1680	1760	D	Previously the Crown. Mostly demolished. Later Old Crown established on part of site in 1990 and still trading.	**30**	B

Ref	Pub Name	Old No.	New No.	Street	From	To	Status	Comments	Page	Map
357	Old Custom House Wine Lodge			The Quay	1968	1974	B	Presume this was actually in old custom house – now flats.		B
358	Old Dial	93	150	Westgate Street	1847	1956	D	Originally the Dial, then Crown & Anchor. Closed 28 March 1956.	**135** (136)	B
359	Old Folk at Home			King Street	1908	1908	D	Probably same as Old House at Home.		A
360	Old House at Home		3	King Street	1859	1935	D	Referred to compensation authority in 1934. Demolished in King's Walk development. See also Old Folk at Home.		A
361	Old Leather Bottle		17	Archdeacon Street			D	See Leather Bottle.	134	B
362	Old Pilot			Southgate Street	1864	1909	D	Previously the Pilot Inn. Referred to the compensation authority on 8 March 1909.	(80) 87	G
363	Old Raven Tavern		1	Hare Lane	1955	1955	B	Presumably opened in restored Raven Tavern building, now an old people's centre.	52	C
364	Old Unicorn			North Ward	1736	1736	Unk	Probable later name for the Unicorn.		
365	Olde India House	101	227	Barton Street	1954	2009	N	Variation on India House. Also Ye Olde India House – now reverted.	147	I
366	One Eyed Jacks		136	Barton Street	1995	date	O	Previously Victoria House and Molly Malone's.	**153**	I
367	Original Royal Forester			Lower Westgate Street/ the Island			D	Name changed to the Royal Forester.		B
368	Original Shakespeare	25		Barton Street	1876	1876	N	Probable early name for East End Tavern, now TnT.	111	F
369	Original Ten Bells	113		Westgate Street	1859	1873	D	Previously Ten Bells.		B
370	Ostrich	25		Barton Street	1871	1873	N	Probable early name for East End Tavern, now TnT.	111	F
371	Oxbody Inn			Oxebody Lane/ Mitre Street	1680	1927	D		**50** (134)	A
372	PA (Sports Café & Bar)		1	Station Road	1999	2003	N	Previously Prince Albert, opened as PA 26 March 1999. Name changed to Bar Spirit, then Jameson's, now Fusion.	122	F
373	Pack Horse			Hare Lane	1812	1812	Unk	Application for licence to reopen House.		
374	Packhorse			Lower Westgate Street/ the Island				Dates unknown, but before 1680. King's Arms in West Ward described as 'formerly the Packhorse between the bridges', so assume on the Island.		
375	Painters Arms			Unknown	18C	18C	Unk	No further information.		
376	Park End Tavern		18	Parkend Road	1872	date	O		**122**	H/I
377	Park Tavern			Barton Street	1869	1869	Unk			
378	Parrott Inn	15	10	Berkeley Street	1720	1885	D			A
379	Paul Pry			Westgate Street	1850	1850	D			B
380	Pelican		4	St Mary's Street	1679	date	O	See also White Pelican and Grey Pelican. Name change to College Arms in early 1990s, but reverted.	**51**	B/C
381	Penn and Sword			Unknown	18C	18C	Unk	No further information.		
382	Penny Pot Cellar			Unknown	18C	18C	Unk	No further information.		
383	Pheasant	49	49	Columbia Street	1839	1958	D	Removal of licence to Bell & Gavel Granted 2 December 1958.	(98) (143)	D
384	Phoenix			Hare Lane	1850	1850	D			C
385	Pied Bull			North Ward	1680	1686	Unk			
386	Pied Horse			West Ward	1680	1722	Unk			
387	Pig Inn the City		121	Westgate Street	Late 1990s	date	O	Previously Lower George and Mad O'Rourkes.	**27** (129)	B
388	Pilot Inn			Bristol Road/High Orchard	1856	1859	D	Name changed to Old Pilot.	87	G
389	Pilot Inn			Upper Quay Street	1850	1861	D			B
390	Pineapple Inn	174		Lower Westgate Street/ the Island	1869	1920	D			B

Ref	Pub Name	Old No.	New No.	Street	From	To	Status	Comments	Page	Map
391	Pint Pot Inn		74	Bruton Way				See Famous Pint Pot.	112	F
392	Plasterers Arms			Clare Street	1836	1907	D	Closed 24 December 1907.		B
393	Pleasure Boat			Southgate Street	1853	1853	D	May be same as Boatman's Pleasure.		G
394	Plough	82		Northgate Street	1722	1876	N	Name changed to Imperial Inn.	48	A
395	Plough Inn			Smith Street	1632	1705	D	Smith Street is early name for Longsmith Street.		
396	Plough Inn		9	Upton Street	1879	date	O		**150**	I
397	Plough Inn			Windmill Parade	1876	1985	N	Renamed the Great Western in 1985. Address now given as 91 Alfred Street.	146	I
398	Plume of Feathers			North Ward	1682	1722	Unk			
399	Plume of Feathers			West Ward	1680	1686	Unk			
400	Poets Wine Bar		1	Bull Lane	2005	2007	X	Opened 13 July 2005. Name change to Loft.		A
401	Portcullis Inn			Three Cocks Lane	1649	1720	D		(57)	
402	Prince Albert		1	Station Road	1867	1996	N	Renamed PA Sports Café & Bar then Bar Spirit, Jameson's and now Fusion.	**122**	F
403	Prince Albert Inn	13	18	Longsmith Street	1870	1906	D			A
404	Prince Arthur			Arthur St/Park Road	1870	2004	B	Closed 1 January 2004. Now Pizza Delivery company.		F
405	Prince of Wales		25	Station Road	1842	2002	C			F
406	Princes Plume	40	148	Barton Street (Lower)	1869	1990	B	Closed 30 March 1990. Now Al-Murad ceramic tiles shop.		I
407	Princes Plume			Westgate (Causeway)	1843	1858	D			
408	Princess Royal			Westgate Street	1874	1879	Unk			
409	Priory Inn			St Oswald's Retail Park	2005	date	O	Opened 28 November 2005. Built on site of Bell & Gavel. Name changed to Monkey Tree and reverted.	98	C
410	Professor Moriarty		159	Southgate Street	1996	2001	B	Previously the New Pilot. Closed 3 April 2001. Now the Vaughan Centre.	87	G
411	Quart Pot		86	St Catherine Street	1844	1877	N	Name changed to Dean's Walk Inn and address now given as Dean's Walk.	108	C
412	Queen's Head		19	Prince Street	1842	1920	D			F
413	Queen's Head		53	St Catherine Street	1736	1970	B			C
414	Queen's Head Inn	32	68	Kingsholm Road	1847	date	O		**140**	C
415	Queen's Head Inn		66	Westgate Street	1850	1859	B	Later Butties then Teapots café. Building recently restored.		A
416	Raglan Arms		50	Regent Street	1866	1998	D	Closed 3 March 1998. Demolished 2002.		I
417	Railway Guard			Northgate Street	1867	1872	X	Possible name changed from Tredegar Arms and reverted. Later Adega.	94	A
418	Railway Inn	10	6	Bristol Road	1842	1974	D	Demolished late 1970s/early 1980s. Site now occupied by Peel Centre.		H
419	Railway Inn		2	Dean's Walk	1871	1939	D			C
420	Railway Inn			Market Parade	1850	1859	D	Later Crown Hotel.		A
421	Railway Tavern			Twyver Street	1869	1879	D	Address given as Twyver Road, Millbrook Street and Windmill Road – presume all the same pub.		I
422	Raindeer			North Ward	1736	1736	Unk			
423	Ram & County Hotel	21	44	Southgate Street	1936	1937	X	Previously the Ram Hotel. Name changed to New County Hotel.	39	A
424	Ram Inn			Northgate Street	1525	1865	D	Rebuilt in 1525, possibly on site of inn mentioned in the Rental of 1455. Demolished 1865.	**21**	A
425	Ram Inn	21	44	Southgate Street	1680	1935	X	Listed as Hotel by 1847. Name changed to Ram & County Hotel.	39	A
426	Ram Inn Tap			Southgate Street	1850	1850	X	Probably part of Ram Hotel.		A
427	Raven Tavern			Hare Lane	1641	1641	B	May refer to Raven Tavern in Southgate Street – uncertain whether inn of this name actually existed in Hare Lane.	52	C

Ref	Pub Name	Old No.	New No.	Street	From	To	Status	Comments	Page	Map
428	Raven Tavern			Southgate Street	1682	1686	Unk	Confusion with Raven Tavern in Hare Lane.	52	
429	Red Cow			Kimbrose	1836	1871	D			G
430	Red Lion		229	Barton Street	18C	1984	D		(54)	I
431	Red Lion			Hare Lane	1703	1722	D		54	
432	Red Lion			Littleworth	18C	18C	D		(54)	
433	Red Lion Inn	84	41	Northgate Street	1722	1920	D	Closed 1920. Demolished mid-1970s.	**54**	A
434	Red Rover Inn	33	69	Barton Street	1842	1914	D	Possibly previously the Curriers Arms.		F
435	Red White & Blue			Westgate Street	1862	1868	Unk			
436	Reform Tavern			Barton Street	1836	1867	Unk			
437	Regal		33	St Aldate Street, King's Square	1996	date	O	Former Regal/ABC Cinema.	**72** (128)	A
438	Reindeer			Bear Land	1836	1879	D			B
439	Reindeer			Northgate Street	1734	1734	Unk			
440	Ring of Bells			West Ward	1736	1802	Unk	Possibly the same as Six Ring of Bells.		
441	Rising Sun	30		Eastgate Street	1894	1911	D	Previously City Wine Vaults. See also the Greenroom. Closed by 1911 and converted to City Cinema, later Hippodrome. Demolished 1964. BHS now on site.	**123** A	
442	Rising Sun			St Mary's Parish	1720	1736	Unk			
443	Robert Raikes's House		36	Southgate Street	2008	date	O	Restored 2008, incorporating nos 36–8. No. 38 previously the Golden Cross. See also Southgate Vaults.	**74**	A
444	Robin Hood		39	Bristol Road	1869	2008	C		(151)	H
445	Robin Hood			Hopewell Street	1872	1974	B	Probably previously Hopewell Inn and Cox's Beer House.	**151**	I
446	Roebuck			Barton Street	1820	1836	Unk			
447	Roebuck		90	Northgate Street	1722	1867	D			A
448	Rolling Pin			West Ward	1683	1686	Unk			
449	Rose			West Ward	1736	1736	Unk			
450	Rose & Crown		76	Hare Lane	1879	1936	B	Possibly previously the Cherry Tree. Building still exists near railway bridge.		C
451	Rose & Crown			Market Parade	1871	1871	D			
452	Rose & Crown	67	135	Westgate Street	1679	1850	D	Seen in West Ward licensing records 1679–81 then as beerhouse in 1850 – may be different pub.		B
453	Rose & Crown			Columbia Street	1850s	1850s	D		(142)	D
454	Rose & Crown			Tredworth	1863	1870	Unk			
455	Royal Forester			Lower Westgate Street/ the Island	1873	1920	D	Previously the Original Royal Forester.		B
456	Royal George			Lower Westgate Street/the Island	1836	1874	D			
457	Royal Hotel		28	Station Road	1898	1979	B	Known as Midland & Royal Hotel 1923–59.	119	F
458	Royal Oak			Barton Street (Lower)	1879	1879	D	Probably same as Oak.		I
459	Royal Oak	14		Lower Westgate Street/ the Island	1736	1910	D			B
460	Royal Standard			Northgate Street	1867	1870	Unk			
461	Rummer			Cross Keys Lane	1822	1822	D			A
462	Running Horse Inn		38	Barton Street	1861	1907	D	Probably previously the White Lion. Closed 24 December 1907.		F
463	Sailors Home			Ladybellegate Street	1859	1876	D	Opened as a hostel. May have changed name to Southgate Vaults, although some overlap.		
464	Salmon			The Quay	1850	1851	D			B
465	Salutation			South Ward	1682	1686	Unk			
466	Saracen's Head	34	25	Eastgate Street	1680	1961	D	Extinction of licence 5 April 1961. Demolished 1964 C&G and BHS now on site.	**55**	A
467	Savage's Inn	27		Westgate Street	1455	1502	N	Name changed to Katherine Wheele, now the Fountain.	(11) 25	A

Ref	Pub Name	Old No.	New No.	Street	From	To	Status	Comments	Page	Map
468	Severn Trow			Quay Street	1806	1856	D	May have previously been the Anchor.		B
469	Seymour		145	Seymour Road	1893	date	O		**124**	H
470	Shades			Unknown	18C	18C	Unk	No further information.		
471	Shakespeare Inn	49	96	Northgate Street	1820	1959	D	Closed 1959, demolished 1974.	**125**	A
472	Shears			West Ward	1680	1680	Unk			
473	Ship & Castle			Baker Street	1850	1879	D		(80)	G
474	Ship Inn			The Quay	1680	1984	B	Closed 1984, building now used by county council.		B
475	Shipwrights Arms			Bear Land	1867	1884	D			B
476	Shoulder of Mutton & Cauliflower			Hare Lane	1731	1731	Unk			
477	Shuttle			West Ward	1682	1686	Unk			
478	Sir Colin Campbell		28	Llanthony Road	1861	date	N	Name changed to Inn on the Docks.	84	G
479	Six Ring of Bells			West Ward	18C	18C	Unk	No further information – possibly same as Ring of Bells.		
480	Sloanes		3	Brunswick Road	2003	date	O	Previously the Hogshead.	**75**	F
481	Soldiers Return		2	Kingsholm Road	1850	1851	X	Temporary name for Fortune of War. See also Beehive.	139	C/D
482	South Gate			South Ward	1722	1736	Unk			
483	Southgate Vaults	17	36	Southgate Street	1901	1901	N	Building now part of Robert Raikes's House. Premises also in Longsmith Street.	75	A
484	Southgate Vaults			Ladybellegate Street	1871	1901	D	Possibly previously the Sailor's Home. Also at 17 Southgate Street.	(75)	
485	Spa Hotel Tap			Norfolk Street	1847	1867		Probably changed name to Norfolk Arms.		G
486	Spoofers Bar		61	Eastgate Street	1998	2005	N	Opened as Spoofers Bar 1 October 1998. Previously the Old Bank. Name changed to Zebra Bar, now Water Poet.	128	F
487	Spread Eagle (Hotel)			Market Parade	1680	1972	D	Changed to Black Spread Eagle 1682–1736 and reverted.	**40**	A
488	Spread Eagle Tap			Market Parade	1865	1865	D	Presumably part of Spread Eagle.		A
489	Square & Compass Inn	82	168	Westgate Street	1871	1964	D	Demolished for improvements and new ring road in Westgate Street.	**136**	B
490	Squirrel			West Ward	1682	1682	Unk			
491	Squirrel Inn	111		Southgate Street	1830	1831	D	Demolished in 1831 and rebuilt as the Albion Hotel. New Squirrel opened on opposite side of Southgate Street at no. 79.	**88**	G
492	Squirrel Inn	79		Southgate Street	1847	1907	D	Opposite side of Southgate Street to original Squirrel at 111.	**88**	G
493	St Aldate House			King Street	1850	1851	D	Probably name changed to King's Head Inn.		A
494	St George			Southgate Street	1455	1509	D		(11) **33** (57)	G
495	Staffordshire Knot	9	22	Oxford Street	1855	1855	X	Name changed to Victoria Inn.		D/E
496	Stag			Blackfriars	1850	1850	D			A
497	Stag's Head	57		Alvin Street	1893	1920	D		(142)	D
498	Stag's Head			Unknown	18C	18C	Unk	No further information.		
499	Star			Ryecroft Street	1872	1874	Unk			
500	Star & Garter			North Ward	18C	18C	Unk	No further information.		
501	Star Inn	19		Alvin Street	1836	1919	D	Star Brewery in 1851.		D
502	Star Inn		2	Conduit Street	1861	1974	B			I
503	Star Inn/ Tavern			The Quay	1680	1908	D		(134)	B
504	Station Hotel			Bruton Way	2001	date	O	Previously the Wellington Hotel.	(16) (68) **126**	A
505	Stockyards			St Oswald's Road	1984	1984	N	Built on site of Bell & Gavel and name reverted.	98	C
506	Suffolk Arms	72	72	Suffolk Street	1847	1959	D	Closed 4 April 1959.	(142)	D
507	Suffolk Inn			Suffolk Street	1850s	1850s	D		(142)	D
508	Sun			High Street/Barton Terrace	1869	1869	Unk	Near Laburnum Brewery – possible alternative name?		
509	Sun			Westgate Street	1680	1686	Unk			

Ref	Pub Name	Old No.	New No.	Street	From	To	Status	Comments	Page	Map
510	Sun Dial			Southgate Street	1830	1830	D	Probably the same as the Dial.		A
511	Sundial			St Mary's Square	1807	1811	D	Temporary change from Dial. Also in *Pigot's Directory* of 1830.	135	B
512	Sun Tavern			Eastgate Street	1680	1744	Unk			
513	Swan			Northgate Street	1509	1753	D	Possibly became the White Swan.	**33**	A
514	Swan			South Ward	18C	18C	Unk	No further information.		A
515	Swan			Westgate Street	1807	1836	D	Probably name changed to White Swan.	136	B
516	Swan & Falcon		16	Longsmith Street	1722	1965	D	Closed 22 May 1965. Multi-storey now on site.		A
517	Swansea House			St Aldate Street	1859	1872	D			
518	Swinging Plaice			Eastgate Shopping Centre	1969	1974	Unk	The Forum, Eastgate Shopping Centre.		A
519	Sword	22		Westgate Street	1680	1736	N	Name Changed to Union.	58	A
520	Sydney Arms			Alvin Street	1865	1871	D			
521	Tabard		53	Northgate Street	1924	early 1990s	N	Amalgamated with King's Arms in late 1980s. Name changed to Cleopatra's, Kings, Gate and now Varsity.	(49) **127**	A
522	Tabard			Westgate Street (Lower)	early 17C	17C	D	Name changed from Crown Inn and reverted.	30	B
523	Tailor's House		43	Westgate Street	1990	2003	N	Name changed from the Union and reverted.	58	A
524	Talbot Inn	117	67	Southgate Street	1722	1974	B	Severn Sound Radio occupied building 1978–98. Now flats.	**56**	G
525	Tall Ship	69	134	Southgate Street	1993	date	O	Previously British Flag.	**89**	G
526	Teague's Bar		48	Kingsholm Road			O	See White Hart.	141	C
527	Telegraph Inn			Market Parade	1850	1851	D	Probably the same as New Market Inn.		A
528	Ten Bells	113		Westgate Street	1806	1856	D	Next to St Nicholas Church. Name changed to Original Ten Bells.		B
529	Theatre Vaults		30	Westgate Street	1799	1958	B	Next door to Theatre Royal. Licence lapsed 26 April 1958.	**76**	A
530	Therapy		56	Westgate Street	2002	2003	N	Previously Gresham Hotel and Lamprey. Name changed to Haus, then Grill, now Westgate.	116	A
531	Three (Red) Lions			West Ward	1680	1686	Unk			
532	Three Blackbirds			West Ward	1720	1736	Unk			
533	Three Cocks			Three Cocks Lane/ St Mary Street	1680	1878	D		**57**	B
534	Three Cups			Eastgate Street	1879	1906	D	Became Three Cups Dining Rooms.		A
535	Three Cups			South Ward	1682	1686	Unk			
536	Three Horse Shoes			Commercial Road	1906	1907	Unk			
537	Three Horse Shoes			Lower Westgate Street/ the Island	1736	1900	D			B
538	Three Horse Shoes			North Ward	18C	18C	Unk	No further information.		
539	Three Kings			Quay Street	1680	1897	D			B
540	Three Mariners			Westgate Street	1686	1736	Unk			
541	Three Pidgeons			West Ward	1722	1736	Unk			
542	Three Sugar Loaves			Lower Westgate Street/ the Island	1736	1736	D			
543	Three Tuns			North Ward	1686	1686	Unk			
544	Three Tuns			Southgate Street	18C	18C	Unk	No further information.		
545	Three Tuns			West Ward	18C	18C	Unk	No further information.		
546	TnT		112	Eastgate Street	Late 1990s	date	O	Previously East End Tavern and Gate.	**111**	F
547	Travellers Rest		181A	Lower Westgate Street/ the Island	1850	1875	D	Possibly same as Three Horseshoes.		B

Ref	Pub Name	Old No.	New No.	Street	From	To	Status	Comments	Page	Map
548	Tredegar Arms	98		Northgate Street	1860	1875	X	Probably previously the Maiden Head. Name may have changed to Railway Guard and reverted (1867–72). Name changed to No.1 Vaults then Adega.	94	A
549	Trevor Arms		72	Vauxhall Road	1872	1969	B	Now a house.		I
550	Trumpet			Westgate Street	1680	1736	Unk			
551	Trumpet Inn	105		Southgate Street	18C	1907	D			G
552	Tut 'n' Shive		86	Northgate Street	1994	1996	N	Previously Northend Vaults. Name changed to Ebeneezer Riley's Northend Vaults. Reverted to Northend Vaults, now the Vaults.	120	A
553	Uncle Tom's Cabin			Wellington Street	1867	1889	D	Name changed to Hampden Inn.		F
554	Underground			Marylone	late 1980s	late 1980s	N	Opened in cellar of Greyfriars.	(63)	A
555	Unicorn			East Ward	1722	1722	Unk			
556	Unicorn			North Ward	1682	1722	Unk			
557	Unicorns Head			North Ward	1682	1736	Unk			
558	Union	22	43	Westgate Street	1847	date	O	Previously the Sword. Dobell & Mott Wine & Spirit Vaults 1849 to 1920. See also the Tailor's House.	**57**	A
559	Union Jack		1	Quay Street	1806	1822	D	Name changed to the Globe Inn.		B
560	Upper George	138	50	Westgate Street	1680	1869	B	Originally just the George, but confused as two in West Ward – see also Lower George. See also Cathedral Tavern.	(28) **60**	A
561	Varsity		53	Northgate Street	2008	date	O	Previously the Tabard, Cleopatra's, Kings and Gate.	**127**	A
562	Vaults		86	Northgate Street	2009	date	O	Name shortened from Northend Vaults.	**120**	A
563	Vauxhall Inn	64	174	Barton Street	1832	2008	B	Closed 1 May 2008.	**152**	I
564	Victoria	98		Northgate Street	1890	1890	X	Possible name change from Adega and reverted.	94	A
565	Victoria House	28	136	Barton Street	1847	1990	N	Name changed to Molly Malone's then One Eyed Jacks	**153**	I
566	Victoria Inn	9	22	Oxford Street	1855	2009	C	Previously the Staffordshire Knot. Closed April 2009.		D/E
567	Victory			Westgate Street	1850	1879	D			B
568	Victory Hotel		167	High Street	1859	date	O		(149) **154**	I
569	Water Poet		61	Eastgate Street	2007	date	O	Opened as Water Poet 29 October 2007. Previously Old Bank, Spoofers Bar and Zebra Bar.	(73) **128**	F
570	Waterfront			Merchants Road	1993	1998	C	Pillar Warehouse. Previously the City Barge. Closed July 1998.	81	G
571	Weavers Arms			East Ward	1722	1736	Unk			
572	Wellington Arms			Barton Street	1820	1830	D			F
573	Wellington Arms		24	Wellington Street	1876	2008	C	Closed 1 November 2008.		F
574	Wellington Hotel			Bruton Way/George Street	1856	2001	N	Name changed to Station Hotel. See also New Wellington Hotel.	126	A
575	Welsh Harp			West Ward	1722	1806	Unk			
576	Welsh Harp Inn		36	London Road	1722	2007	X	Name changed to No. 36.	**61**	E
577	Westgate		56	Westgate Street	2008	date	O	Previously the Gresham Hotel, Lamprey, Therapy, Haus and Grill.	116	A
578	Wheatsheaf			Lower Westgate Street/ the Island	1722	1825	D			
579	Wheatsheaf Inn	94	109	Southgate Street	1847	1935	D	Demolished 2006. Flats now on site.		G
580	Wheelwrights			St Oswald's Road	1962	1985	D	Name changed to Baker Street Tavern.		C
581	Wherry			Quay Street	1736	1736	D			B
582	White Bear			South Ward	18C	18C	Unk	No further information.		
583	White Bear			West Ward	1736	1736	Unk	May have been South Ward.		
584	White Eagle			North Ward	1686	1686	D	Possibly another variation of the Spread Eagle.	(40)	A

Ref	Pub Name	Old No.	New No.	Street	From	To	Status	Comments	Page	Map
585	White Hart Inn	10	14	Bell Lane	1869	1966	D	Closed 18 September 1966. Demolished for building of Eastgate Shopping Centre.	**130**	A
586	White Hart Inn		48	Kingsholm Road	1830	date	O	Also known as Teague's Bar.	**141**	C
587	White Hart Inn			Southgate Street	1711	1836	D		**42**	A
588	White Horse			Barton Street	18C	18C	Unk	No further information.		
589	White Horse			South Ward	1836	1836	Unk			
590	White Horse			West Ward	1682	1682	Unk			
591	White Lamp Inn	45	87	Westgate Street	1892	1970	B	On site of part of original Crown Inn. Now student accommodation.	(32)	B
592	White Lettice			West Ward	1682	1686	Unk			
593	White Lion			Southgate Street	1680	1736	Unk	Near the Wheat Market.		
594	White Lion	38	38	Alvin Street	1836	1967	D	Closed 22 January 1967.	(143)	D
595	White Lion			Barton Street/Park Road	1861	1861	D	Probably named changed to Running Horse.		F
596	White Lion			St Mary's Square	1850	1859	D			B
597	White Pelican			North Ward	1686	1686	N	Previously one of two Pelicans. Possibly temporary rename of the Pelican, but see also the Grey Pelican.	51	B/C
598	White Spread Eagle			North Ward	1722	1722	D	Alternative name for Spread Eagle.	40	A
599	White Swan			Northgate Street	1756	1801	D	Possibly previously the Swan. Old Bank on the site by 1811.	33	A
600	White Swan	94	148	Westgate Street	1847	1972	D	Probably previously the Swan. Next to Duke of Norfolk's House.	(135) **136**	B
601	Whitesmiths Arms	109	81	Southgate Street	1871	date	O		**90**	G
602	Windmill		83	Eastgate Street	1987	2009	B	Previously Brunel's Wine Bar. Now Fever nightclub.	**131**	F
603	Windmill Inn			Millbrook Street	1854	1984	D	Closed 1984. Demolished in building of Metz Way.	**155**	I
604	Wine Vaults			Catherine Wheel Lane	18C	18C	D	Now Berkeley Street.		
605	Woodman			Barton Street	1850	1870	D			F
606	Woolpack			West Ward	1680	1836	Unk			
607	Woolsack			North Ward	18C	18C	Unk	No further information.		
608	Worcester Arms		38	Park Street	1861	1974	D			C
609	Worcester House			Worcester Street	1861	1861	D			C
610	Worlds End			Barton Street	1658	1658	D			
611	Ye Olde India House							See Olde India House.		
612	Yeoman		70	Southgate Street	1973	1985	B	Name changed from Black Swan, then reverted.	101	A/G
613	York House Inn		76	London Road	1842	2008	C	Closed 1 January 2008.	(112)	E
614	Zebra Bar			Eastgate Street	2005	2007	N	Opened as Zebra Bar in June 2005. Previously the Old Bank and Spoofers Bar. Name changed to the Water Poet.	128	F
615	Zest Bar		101	Eastgate Street	2001	date	O	Previously Crown & Thistle. See also Butlers.	**107**	F

Bibliography

Ball, Alan W., *Gloucester Illustrated: The City's Heritage in Prints & Drawings*, Halsgrove, Tiverton, 2001

Britton, John, *Picturesque Antiquities of the English Cities*, 1836

Bullock, Donald, *The Legend that was Clapham*, The Wheatley Press, Gloucester, 2002

Campaign For Real Ale, *Real Ale in Gloucestershire*, 1984, 1993, 1996

Campion, Peter, *England's Glory: The Moreland Story*, Tempus Publishing, Stroud, 2005

Cinderey, Lyn, *Paranormal Gloucester*, Amberley Publishing, Stroud, 2009

Clarke, John, *The Architectural History of Gloucester from the Earliest Period to the Close of the Eighteenth Century*, T.R. Davies, Northgate Street, Gloucester

Dodd, Arthur, and Moss, Philip, *Gloucester Alehouses: a light-hearted look at the inns and taverns of 18th century Gloucester*, author, Gloucester, 1985

Fletcher, Chris, *Ottakar's Local History Series: Gloucestershire*, Ottakar's Plc in association with Tempus, Stroud, 2001

Fosbrooke, The Revd Thomas Dudley, *An Original History of the City of Gloucester*, London, 1819

Fry, Eileen, & Harvey, Rosemary, *Haunted Gloucester*, Tempus Publishing, Stroud, 2004

Heighway, Carolyn, *Gloucester: A History and Guide*, Alan Sutton, Gloucester, 1985

Herbert, N.M. (ed), *A History of the County of Gloucester, Vol. 4, 'The City of Gloucester'*, Oxford University Press, Oxford, 1988

Jennings, Paul, *The Local: A History of the English Pub*, Tempus Publishing Ltd, Stroud, 2007

Jurica, John, *Gloucester: A Pictorial History*, Phillimore & Co., Chichester, 1994

Kirby, Darrel, *The Story of Gloucester*, Sutton Publishing, Stroud, 2007

Marchant, Ian, *The Longest Crawl*, Bloomsbury, London, 2006

Rudder, Samuel, *New History of Gloucestershire*, Cirencester, 1779

Starkey, David, *Elizabeth: The Struggle for the Throne*, HarperCollins, New York, 2001

Stevenson, W.H. (ed), *The Rental of all the houses in Gloucester A.D. 1455*, Gloucester, 1890

Stevenson, W.H. (ed), *A calendar of the Records of the Corporation of Gloucester*, Gloucester, 1893

Trade and Industry Committee, Session 2004–05, Second Report (House of Commons, 2004)

Voyce, Jill. *Pocket Images: The City of Gloucester*, Nonsuch Publishing, Stroud, 1995

Woolford, Reginald, and Drake, Barbara, *Gloucester in Old Picture Postcards*, European Library, The Netherlands, 1995

Wordsworth Editions Limited, *The Dictionary of Pub Names*, Wordsworth Editions Ltd, Ware, 2006

Websites

British History Online – A History of the County of Gloucester: Volume 4 – The City of Gloucester: http://www.british-history.ac.uk/source.aspx?pubid=281

CAMRA Real Ale in Gloucestershire: http://www.cauchy.demon.co.uk/raig/guide/GLOUCEST.HTM

Gloucestershire Pubs – Pubs & Breweries in Gloucestershire Past & Present: http://www.gloucestershirecamra.org.uk/pubs/glospubs/new/

Facebook group: Gloucester Pubs

Gloucestershire forums: www.visit-gloucestershire.co.uk/boards

If you are interested in keeping up with my ongoing ramblings on the subject of Gloucester, pubs and life in general you can:
visit my website at www.darrelkirby.com
read my blog at http://darrelkirby.wordpress.com
follow me on Twitter at https://twitter.com/darrelkirby

Picture Credits

Unless otherwise stated, the pictures in this book were either taken by me or came from my own collection of pictures and postcards with no obvious point of contact for copyright. Other photographs were produced with the kind permission of the following:

Bristol & Gloucester Archaeological Society: p. 44 (D7916 p. 42)
Campaign for Real Ale (CAMRA): p. 93
Gloucestershire Archives: p. 12 (GBR/J/5/1) (GBR/B/1/1),15,
    21 (SRPrints/GL40.22b), 23 (SRPrints/GL8.1a), 24 (GPS 154/467),
    36, 41 (SRPrints/GL50.1), 48 (SR555/45690.334),
    49 (B413/13431), 53 (D3398/2/2/44), 73 (GBR/L/6/28/9),
    76 (SR46/37156.60), 78 (GPS 154/93), 80 (SR555/45690.308),
    114 (B413/13431), 118 (SR6Postcards/GL80.284) (B413/13431 p. 6–7),
    120 (SR6Postcards/GL50.76), 127 (D7942/487), 130 (D7942/423),
    137 (GBR/L2/1/1/18), 142 (MA117), 152 (SR555/45690.325),
    156 (SR555/45690.319)
    Reproduced with permission of *Gloucester Citizen*: p. 32 (SR46/GL80.90GS),
    41 (SRPrints/GL50.40b), 51 (SRPrints/GL50.24), 74, 134 (SR46/24291.10),
    135 (SR46/24291.43), 136 (SR46/24291.3GS), 154 (SRPrints/GL50.30)
    Reproduced with permission of Heart FM: p. 57 (NZ15.4)
    Taken by Gwladys Davies: p. 107 (DP12/48535.97)
    Taken by Sidney Pitcher: p. 30 (SR46/37156.4), 44 (SR38/29157.20),
    116 (SR25/31607.23), 133 (SR25/31607.29)
Gloucestershire Archives & Gloucester City Council: p. 100 (GBR/L/6/23/B7933),
    113 (DC27/98)
Gloucester City Museums: p. 54, 133
    Taken by the author and reproduced with permission of Gloucester City Museums:
    p. 21, 44, 96, 101, 125
National Monuments Record (NMR): p. 130 (SRPrints/GL50.19a)
Martin Parsons: p. 103
Reflections of Clapham Group/Bernard Polson: p. 50, 132, 138, 143
Geoff Sandles: p. 98, 112, 140, 148
South West Regional Development Agency (SWRDA): p. 19
Reg Woolford: p. 28, 58, 61, 121

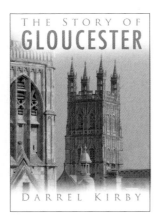

The Story of Gloucester

DARREL KIRBY

ISBN 978-0-7509-4465-6

Part history, part guidebook, this book uncovers the city's heritage from Roman times to the present day. With over eighty sites in the city explored, from Roman gates to the Kingsholm stadium, the historic docks to the cathedral, this book is a must-have for locals and visitors alike. Much of the historical record of Gloucester is still visible – you just need to know where to look!

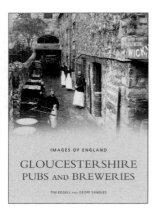

Gloucestershire Pubs and Breweries

TIM EDGELL AND GEOFF SANDLES

ISBN 978-0-7524-3524-8

Illustrated with over 200 old photographs, postcards and advertisements, this absorbing collection offers the reader an insight into the life and history of Gloucestershire's pubs and breweries. With fascinating images of important names such as Cheltenham Original Brewery, Cainscross Brewery, Nailsworth Brewery and the Stroud Brewery Company as well as many pubs and landlords, this book is an ideal companion for anyone interested in the county's brewing industry.

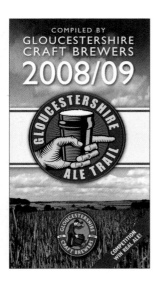

Gloucestershire Ale Trail

GLOUCESTERSHIRE CRAFT BREWERS

ISBN 978-0-7524-4783-4

With a history of brewing in the county combined with general and historical information on the pubs themselves, this illustrated book offers the chance to sample and enjoy the best Gloucestershire has to offer. Compiled by the Gloucestershire Craft Brewers, an association of eight microbreweries, this guide illustrates how important quality local beers are to consumers and pubs alike, and highlights the best places to find them.